Overture
AND
Finale

Overture
AND
Finale

Rodgers & Hammerstein
and the Creation of Their
Two Greatest Hits

MAX WILK

BACK STAGE BOOKS
An imprint of
Watson-Guptill Publications/New York

To Richard Rodgers
and Oscar Hammerstein II,
who made this book possible

Editor for Back Stage Books: Dale Ramsey
Book design: Bob Fillie, Graphiti Design Inc.
Production manager: Hector Campbell

Published in 1999 by Back Stage Books, an imprint of Watson-Guptill Publications,
a division of BPI Communications, Inc., 1515 Broadway, New York, NY 10036-8986

Library of Congress Cataloging-in-Publication Data for this title can be
obtained by writing to the Library of Congress, Washington, D.C. 20540

ISBN 0-8230-8820-0

Manufactured in the United States of America

1 2 3 4 5 6 7 8 9/04 03 02 01 00 99

Acknowledgments

No one can create an authentic work of history without the assistance of those whose reliable input is based on fact. And if the author is truly fortunate, it is when he has access to the first-hand recollections of those who were there. I would like to bring out a large cast to take proper bows for their kind help—in no particular order of billing.

I express my deep gratitude to Agnes de Mille, who graciously shared her recollections of her work on *Oklahoma!* with me. Alfred Drake, Celeste Holm, Kate Friedlich, Bambi Linn, Paul and Vivian Shiers, George Church, Marc Platt, and Hayes Gordon from far-off Australia were all lavish with their oral histories, with valuable keepsakes, private diaries, precious photos, and clippings.

Jay Blackton's insights about the musical score of *Oklahoma!* are vivid and should be an endowment for future generations. Further thanks to George Irving, John Fearnley, and Joan Roberts for their anecdotes. Elaine Steinbeck has almost total recall about backstage events during the show's production, for which she receives fervent thanks.

Miles White's generosity with his memories and his expertise as to the costuming and decor of *Oklahoma!* provided this history with necessary facts. His personal files were a treasure trove.

Helene Hanff was lavish with her wry memories of working in the Theatre Guild press department, circa 1943. Mary Hunter Wolfe helped me with incisive recollections about playwright Lynn Riggs, as did Miranda Levy. Edmund Hartmann had marvelous insight into Oscar Hammerstein's character. William Hammerstein offered encouragement and helped point me towards others who could supply more necessary history. Abe Samuel, of Allentown, Pennsylvania, and Al Remsen, continually unearthed other show business ephemera, and they have my thanks.

I am indeed grateful for having been gifted with the assistance of Mrs. Anna Crouse, whose remarkable memory has served to bring the production of *The Sound of Music* to vivid life. I also spent time in California with three stalwarts involved in the film version: Ernest Lehman, who did such a magnificent job of turning the Lindsay and Crouse libretto into a first-rate screenplay, and who generously shared his history with me; Robert Wise, who so skillfully produced and directed that screenplay into a classic motion picture; and last, but far from least, my dear friend Saul Chaplin, songwriter, producer, Renaissance man of music. Saul has, alas, passed on since he spent an afternoon sharing his hilarious memories of the production of *The Sound of Music* with me.

Ave, atque vale, old friend.

I must add a low bow to Theodore Bikel, who was so lavish with his personal memories of the two hears he spent playing Captain Von Trapp opposite Mary Martin. And as for that great lady, she generously left behind her memories, and I am indeed grateful to her son Larry Hagman for permitting me to restore Ms. Martin's autobiographical comments about *The Sound of Music* to an entirely new generation of audiences.

Lauri Peters, the original Liesl, also rates a bow of thanks for her backstage memories. Susan H. Shulman took time out from preparing the 1998 Broadway revival to give me her insights on how she conceived it.

Ted Chapin and Bert Fink at the Rodgers & Hammerstein Organization have been a constant source of assistance, for which I am very appreciative. I also thank Mike Dvorchak, Robin Walton, and Bruce Pomahac, of the same office, for their kind help. Robert Resnikoff and the managerial staff at the Shubert Theatre, in New Haven, have also been remarkably generous, especially with rare photographs. Frank Goodman, the original press agent of *The Sound of Music* in 1959, provided all sorts of inside anecdotes of events that took place decades ago.

Patricia Willis and her staff at the Beinecke Library at Yale, where the Theatre Guild archives are stored for posterity, have been constantly helpful with their knowledge and time. Katherine Metz at the Museum of the City of New York was also generous, as was Robert Taylor at the Performing Arts Library of Lincoln Center. And special thanks to John Cronin of the *Boston Herald* library, who spent several days unearthing Elliott Norton's review of *The Sound of Music* in the *Boston Sunday Advertiser* of Sunday, October 18, 1959, and supplied it to me.

For transcribing what must have seemed endless hours of oral history for me with loving care and patience, thanks to Lois Porro of Westport.

My wife, Barbara, has listened to anecdotes, complaints, and so on, and retained her equanimity throughout, for which she earns, as always, a special citation.

Dale Ramsey, the editor of Back Stage Books, has been an enthusiastic champion of this book, and so has the reliable and endlessly helpful Ruth Nathan, who is far more than a literary agent. My thanks to them both.

MAX WILK
Westport, Connecticut
October 1998

Contents

Overture

OKLAHOMA!

ST. JAMES THEATRE

The Gamblers

Just another Thursday-night opening.

That's what the "Elm City" audience assumed. Those paying customers filed into New Haven's Shubert Theatre that blustery winter night in 1943, the second year of World War II. The usual cross section of New England burghers, solid citizens, Yale faculty members, plus a sprinkling of affluent haberdashers and salespeople from the local Chapel Street tailoring emporia. A few Yale undergraduates who hadn't yet been drafted by the Army, or who were finishing up accelerated courses before shipping off with the Navy. And, of course, the regular "wrecking crew" piling in from New York: those theatrical agents, ticket brokers, movie company executives and scouts—the denizens of the Brill Building, or "21" or the Cub Room, at the Stork, here to check out the Theatre Guild's latest offering, a musical called *Away We Go!*

What did anyone know about this new show? Only that it had been written by Richard Rodgers and Oscar Hammerstein II, that it was directed by Rouben Mamoulian, from Hollywood, and that it starred absolutely nobody's name above the title.

So far, what did that tell you? Not much, but it didn't matter—Shubert regulars were dedicated gamblers from way back. For years, they had been betting their ticket money in a game of theatrical roulette to get the first look— a weekly temptation offered them by optimistic producers who proffered their latest attractions fresh from the Manhattan rehearsal halls. Interspersed with touring companies who had exhumed such chestnuts as *The Student Prince* and *Blossom Time,* with magicians known as Sim-Sala-Bim, or Gilbert and Sullivan operettas, a stream of new shows would use New Haven, Connecticut, as a launch pad. The company had three days to hang and set up the scenery, rehearse the music, and run through technical and full dress rehearsal. Thursday night, ready or not, curtain up—a harrowing schedule which only the toughest could survive. Then, muscles flexed, the show staggered on its hopeful trek to Boston, Philadelphia, and (possibly) Broadway.

Shubert openings customarily provided as much drama on one side of the proscenium as the other. Pushing through the crowded lobby around eight, one might easily spot the nervous playwright, well fortified by several double whiskies from Kaysey's Restaurant, across Church Street, smiling wanly at his fond wife and relatives. That chap over there certainly was the director; gaunt, eyes reddened by lack of sleep, followed by his faithful assistants, each holding at the ready clipboards, pocket flashes, and a supply of aspirin and Tums. Here came a group of well-dressed civilians, obviously backers, greeting each other heartily and preparing to cheer on their investment, no matter what.

Behind the last row of orchestra seats, in that space customarily reserved for the standees who paid a dollar to peer through velvet drapes, one found oneself surrounded by a convention of nervous pacers, the show staff, headed by the producer, sometimes sober but often not. As the evening wore on, one could hear from the rear of the house muttered curses at missed cues onstage, or anguished groans over malfunctioning scenery being mishandled by local stagehands. It was all a familiar game to the New Haven theatregoers, and in a perverse sort of way they relished the opening night madness. To be here tonight as witnesses made them midwives at the birth of what might be a major hit show, did it not? For years to come one could say, "Hey, I was there."

This particular Thursday offered a new musical, and if there was anything that tickled Shubert audiences it was a good razzmatazz song-and-dance show. Over the last few decades they had been treated to some of the very best: Cole Porter's *Leave It to Me!* with Sophie Tucker belting out "Most gentlemen don't like love, they just want to kick it around!" and then a piquant Mary Martin doing her cheerful striptease to "My Heart Belongs to Daddy." Witty Rodgers and Hart musicals such as *Too Many Girls*, or *The Boys from Syracuse*. Bert Lahr and Ethel Merman in *DuBarry Was a Lady*, and "the Merm" and Jimmy Durante in Schwartz and Dietz's *Stars in Your Eyes*—when the Shubert rocked with laughter as Jimmy tossed pieces of his grand piano into the orchestra pit, yelling "Don't raise da bridge, boys, lower da river!"

There were other nights when the curtain rose, the music struck up a jolly beat, and what ensued was pure disaster. A turkey. A lead balloon. A stinkeroo from the first notes of the overture. Openings in which the Shubert stage ran red with the blood of failed jokes, unreprised duets, creaky and witless libretti, and a gang of flop-sweated performers fighting gamely, desperately, to make it to the final curtain. On such nights the audience would sit it out respectfully, optimists to the end (when it blessedly came). Then they'd stagger their way out into the New Haven night, past the numb and silent producer and his coterie, the backers shaking their heads, stunned, and the weary production crew bracing itself for an all-night council of war in some suite at the Taft. And as the Shubert faithful left, they might be muttering softly to each other: Who knew? Perhaps they might be able to fix this one. Stranger things had happened, right here in New Haven, right? They had been witnesses to miracles. "Hey, I was there."

On this March night, the Shubert optimists were out in full force. If there were no marquee names up there, well, here was the newly formed partnership of Richard Rodgers and Oscar Hammerstein. Everybody could hum something by Rodgers, all those bright happy hits he and Lorenz Hart had crafted, like *I Married an Angel*, or *Babes in Arms*, which featured the lovely ballads "My Funny Valentine" and "Where or When." But tonight it was Rodgers without Hart. How come? And how long had it been since Oscar Hammerstein had had something memorable on a stage? *Show Boat*, with Jerome Kern, sure—but nothing really successful lately. *Very Warm for May*, another show he'd done with Kern, was a nice show, lovely music and lyrics, but it certainly hadn't stayed around (it was produced by the same Max Gordon who was standing there in the lobby, the short man staring gloomily through his spectacles at the customers as they entered). Hammerstein had also come through the Shubert in 1941 with an operetta he'd done with Sigmund Romberg, a piece called *Sunny River*—good, but not really good enough. It had gone on to New York and folded very quickly.

Tonight's show was the product of the Theatre Guild, and New Haven audiences had always respected that group; for years the name had been synonymous with quality. Since the 1920s, the Guild had brought plays by Eugene O'Neill, Ferenc Molnar, and Bernard Shaw, and stars such as the Lunts and Helen Hayes—class acts. On the other hand, when was the last time anyone could remember Lawrence Langner, Theresa Helburn, and Armina Marshall, all three of whom were welcoming their friends and associates in the lobby, ever showing up before with a musical? It wasn't their style, was it? Matter of fact, if one wished to be captious, it had been a very long time between hits for the Guild. Rumor had it they were in deep trouble. For once, the rumor was correct.

Now what about the director, this man Mamoulian, supposed to be a big Hollywood talent? He'd directed *Porgy and Bess*, that wonderful Gershwin opera, back in the thirties, but could he still cut it on the stage? Plenty of those big-time Hollywood types had tried it, and regularly landed flat on their cans.

8:31. Magic time. From the orchestra pit came the sound of clarinets practicing trills, the echoes of tuning fiddles, the rumtumtum of the drummer's snares. And now, that electric moment when the conductor tapped softly on the podium with his baton, and raised his arms. The houselights were down, the footlights up—time for the overture.

The audience waited, expectant for a bright, well-orchestrated piece, a new ballad, then perhaps one of Richard Rodgers' lovely waltzes, building to a finale.

Not this night. What they heard was a brief run-through of several songs, almost perfunctory, a medley that ended almost as quickly as it had begun. (In fact, it had been patched together by the arranger, Robert Russell Bennett, a scant few hours ago.) And then the curtain rose.

To total silence. Astonishing, completely unexpected, deafening.

There, on the Shubert stage, was a drop revealing a view. A Southwestern mesa? A prairie? Beyond, a mountain range, with a vista of rolling hills. Bright yellow, wondrous sunlight flooded the set and warmed the proscenium.

Still, silence.

Strange. Not a single dancing girl in sight. Okay, then, if we were supposed to be out West, where were the dancing cowboys twirling their ropes, doing a fast tap routine with their usual tricks while singing about the good life out on the range? Nope. Not a single boy dancer.

The only sign of life on that Shubert stage seemed to be some old lady sitting there, wearing her poke bonnet; in her hand was a stick; she was pumping away . . . at a butter churn? Silently. She wasn't even singing.

What sort of way was this to open a musical?

From the orchestra, more silence. No rich choirs of fiddles, no brass figures, no chords of any kind. Just golden silence and that old lady with her churn, pumping away.

The Shubert regulars were, to say the least, perplexed. Was this a musical? Where the hell was the music?

Then, offstage, there could be heard the sound of a pleasant male voice. He seemed to be singing some sort of ballad.

A ballad? No, no! You didn't open a musical with a ballad, you started with a song that was upbeat, jazzy, that told us this was a wonderful old world, especially when you had a nifty girl on your arm, and if you didn't have a penny in your pocket, what did it matter so long as she was by your side— that's how you opened a musical! The voice sang:

> There's a bright golden haze on the meadow,
> There's a bright golden haze on the meadow.
> The corn is as high as a elephant's eye,
> And it looks like it's climbin' clear up to the sky.

"As high as a elephant's eye?" Would Larry Hart have ever written anything like that?

Then the young man came strolling onstage; nice-looking chap, dressed in simple cowboy clothes, nothing fancy, but he sang like a leading man so he had to be one. In the program it said he was Curly, and as Curly, Alfred Drake was now singing:

> Oh, what a beautiful mornin',
> Oh, what a beautiful day.
> I got a beautiful feelin'
> Everything's goin' my way.

And the old lady, a character named Aunt Eller, played by Betty Garde, looked up and smiled at Curly and went on churning her butter while he kept on singing.

Some peculiar kind of an opening number. It's a safe bet that nobody in the audience of Shubert veterans that night in March 1943 had ever seen anything like it—or what would follow that lovely opening song.

Max Gordon sure as hell hadn't. He sat there in his down-front aisle seat staring, with far more than ordinary interest, at what was transpiring up there on the stage. Everyone in the small world of the Broadway theatre knew that Gordon, who'd seen many years in and out of the red, was a born worrier. How about the story of the night he'd brought Robert Sherwood's *Abe Lincoln*

Max Gordon as captured in a glum moment during a rehearsal. Famous for his pragmatic wisdom, acquired after many years in the rough and tumble of show business, when asked, "What makes a good title?" he would snap, "The title of a hit!"

in Illinois to Washington, and there had been a special performance for President and Mrs. Roosevelt, followed by an after-theatre White House reception? When FDR had congratulated the producer on the remarkable production and lavished praise on Raymond Massey's performance in the title role, Gordon's response had been, "Yeah, Mr. President, but will it make a quarter?"

Gordon had far more than casual concern about the future of *Away We Go!* He'd invested hard cash in it, his own dollars, and also those of Harry Cohn, the Hollywood dynast at Columbia Pictures, whose favorite comment about his business practices was, "I don't get ulcers, I give them!" Cohn had become impressed with the producer's track record—including, along with *Abe Lincoln in Illinois*, such smash hits as *Junior Miss*, *My Sister Eileen*, and Clare Boothe's *The Women*—and had an arrangement with Gordon to represent Columbia on Broadway. Max Gordon represented *class*, and Cohn thirsted for some so he could compete with Louis B. Mayer and Darryl F. Zanuck. Gordon's advice would assist Cohn in investing in forthcoming shows and getting the jump on the competition from MGM or Warner Bros. when the bidding started on some promising Broadway show.

Months earlier, Gordon had suggested *Away We Go!*, as something that might interest Columbia. It sounded classy enough to Cohn, a noisy rough-and-tumble type who'd begun his career many years earlier as a song-plugger in New York saloons and who had never lost his taste for popular music. But when he presented the project to his New York board, it turned him down.

"You think this turkey has a chance?" he had asked Gordon.

Gordon, never given to hyperbole, had said that he thought so. "But I'm not making any guarantees, Harry," he'd added. "Okay," said Cohn, ever the gambler. "Then I put my own money in—not the stockholders'. That way, nobody can bitch if it's a flop, and if it's a hit, I'm a hero. Now, are you going in with me, Max?"

Gordon, as much of a gambler as his new boss (he'd already lost one fortune in the 1929 stock market crash), replied, "Sure, why not?"

Tonight, at the Shubert, in his official capacity as Harry Cohn's eyes and ears—as well as his own—Gordon sat staring and listening. So did the rest of the gamblers. As the first act of Rodgers and Hammerstein's curious show continued, Curly took his intended, Laurey, for a ride in "The Surrey with the Fringe on Top." The backers patiently sat and waited, anticipating some excitement on the stage. They finally got some, forty-odd minutes into the show, when there came a rousing number called "Kansas City," sung and danced by a lad named Lee Dixon.

Later on, a pleasant gal named Celeste Holm, playing Ado Annie, launched into a crowd-pleaser called "I Cain't Say No"; there were some laughs at her wide-eyed delivery of Hammerstein's witty lyrics. But so far the Shubert hadn't exactly exploded with excitement.

Then came a song for Laurey and the other girls called "Many a New Day," and a lilting ballad for her and Curly, "People Will Say We're in Love." Certainly this score was first-class Rodgers and well-crafted Hammerstein, but where was the smash hit? It certainly didn't come at the end of Act One—but then something quite remarkable happened: The young Laurey, now danced by a ballerina, embarked on a dream ballet by Agnes de Mille, in which she tried to make up her mind whether or not she was in love with Curly. Remarkable. New and totally different.

Then the curtain fell. Applause, but nothing earthshaking. You couldn't blame those Shubert gamblers for being somewhat confused; they'd never seen a show remotely like this. Forty minutes had passed before there'd been an ensemble of girls, and even then not one of them had revealed so much as one shapely calf. As far as those ballerinas were concerned, well, they could toe-dance, but who ever figured a musical about homesteaders in Oklahoma was the proper setting for some high-class ballet?

Max Gordon made his way up the aisle and out through the lobby doors. His face was impassive, revealing none of what he truly felt, which was sheer, unadulterated panic. People lighting cigarettes were passing him. Some of the "wrecking crew" were carrying their overcoats, an ominous sign; it meant they were headed for the early train back to New York. One of them was producer Mike Todd on his way out, silently turning thumbs down.

"So, whaddaya think?" asked one acquaintance.

Gordon shrugged. "Too early to tell. How do you like it?"

"Interesting," said another. "Needs work," said a third.

"What doesn't?" asked the producer.

Nobody was prepared to commit. Except for one, who said, "I think it's amazing—never saw anything like it!"

"You really think so?" asked Gordon.

"I loved it!"

"Enough to buy a piece of it?"

"Yeah. Yeah, I could!" came the response.

Gordon beckoned him closer and lowered his voice. "Would you be willing to buy, say, twenty-five hundred dollars worth?" he suggested.

"From whom?" asked the lobby acquaintance.

The producer pulled out a pocket pad and a pencil. "Show me a check and you've bought yourself a piece," he said. Then he held out his hand. A second's hesitation, and then a handshake closed the deal.

Another passerby had been listening, a diminutive Broadway type named Al Greenstone, whose special niche in show business was in the printing of glossy theatrical souvenir books that he sold in lobbies before and after performances. "Hey, Max, can I get in on this?" he asked.

"As long as your check cashes," said Gordon. "You like the show, how much do you want?"

"I'll take another twenty-five hundred dollars," said Greenstone. Gordon scribbled out another slip, and by the time the lobby lights were flashing on and off, signaling the beginning of Act Two, he had divested himself of a good-sized piece of the investment he had made in the show. As he walked to his seat, ready to sit through the rest of this peculiar—well, could you truly call it a musical?—this hybrid stew by Dick Rodgers and Oscar Hammerstein, he nodded sympathetically to them. He knew exactly what they were going through—oh, how well he knew! Hadn't he been in the same exact spot, here in the Shubert lobby, with his own productions?

Columnist Walter Winchell's faithful and famous secretary, Rose, who'd been sent by her boss to New Haven to scout this new Theatre Guild musical, did not return for the second act. Instead she dropped by the Taft Hotel and sent a wire before taking the 10 P.M. train back to New York. Her wire, which Winchell ran in his column the following day, read: NO LEGS NO JOKES NO CHANCE.

The second act of *Away We Go!* gave the audience a rouser, "The Farmer and the Cowman," and a lovely Rodgers ballad, "Boys and Girls Like You and Me." Ado Annie and her boyfriend Will Parker did a joyful duet, "All Er Nothin'," and then came a spirited number in praise of the new state of Oklahoma, sung by a quartet and danced, in a solo spot, by George Church. Curly and Jud got into a fight over Laurey; it ended with Jud falling on his knife and Curly accused of murder. Strange . . . but it all ended happily, as Curly was exonerated. He and Laurey embraced. Music up, and curtain. More polite applause.

The New Haven gamblers were already reaching for hats, coats, and mufflers and heading for the exits. Max Gordon came up the aisle, listening to the comments around him. Some of the crowd had enjoyed their evening. Not spectacularly, mind you. The general consensus was that the show could use plenty of work. Some brave souls were saying they loved it; others merely shrugged. Then there was that favorite New Haven reaction: "Nice . . . but who knows?"

As he hurried through the frigid winter night looking for a cab to take him to the station, Max Gordon must have felt better. He'd managed to lighten his investment in this strange mishmash of a show, which would shortly go up to the Colonial in Boston, then down to the St. James on West 44th Street, probably have a couple of weeks' run, and then quietly expire.

Too bad about Dick and Oscar, two very talented guys. They'd worked hard, done their usual capable job. But somewhere along the line the whole thing hadn't come together, it had collapsed like a failed soufflé. Those girls in their long dresses, those arty ballets—no high-kicking, nothing but that little love story. It was all too . . . different. If the Theatre Guild was counting on this piece to bail them out, well, too bad.

So who can fault him for having impulsively sold off those pieces of *Away We Go!* at intermission to such fortunate people as Al Greenstone, who would for years to come cash fat weekly checks because he'd taken a wild $2,500 flyer to buy a piece of the show that would become *Oklahoma!*?

Luckily, Max Gordon hadn't sold off all his investment, and Harry Cohn's, too. Within a few short weeks the show would have its new title, a revamped second act, and a rousing next-to-closing second-act number and would become a landmark American musical comedy. And make a liar out of Winchell's Rose.

The Beginning

C urtain time, 8:27 P.M., on a pleasant summer's evening in 1940, in Westport, Connecticut. Outside the rambling, remodeled faded-red barn that was now the Westport Country Playhouse, an apprentice began to ring the bell. Reluctantly, continuing to chat and gossip, the gathering of relaxed summertime theatregoers down in the garden started to climb the creaking wooden stairs to the lobby doors. Outside, posters heralded tonight's play: a revival of *Green Grow the Lilacs*, by Lynn Riggs, starring Betty Field and Winston O'Keefe, with Mildred Natwick. "Directed by John Ford" proclaimed the bold type; but in fact that eminent film craftsman had not appeared for rehearsals, nor would he even make it to Westport. But the show had gone on, in traditional summer stock fashion (whatever happens, we get the curtain up by Monday night!), with producer John Haggott filling in for Ford.

Up the steps, in the crowd, came Theresa Helburn, a diminutive middle-aged woman with startling, cerulean-blue hair. Terry and her husband summered in Westport a few miles from the Wilton home of her Guild partners,

Lawrence Langner, a balding, portly gent who'd combined a theatre career and a thriving practice as a patent lawyer, and Langner's wife, Armina Marshall, tall and striking, who hailed from far-off Oklahoma. They composed the "troika" that controlled the Theatre Guild, a powerful, prestigious American theatrical management team that, for the past two decades or so, had thrived in New York and on the road across America. Langner and his wife also owned the Westport Playhouse, where annual summer seasons brought upscale revivals to Fairfield County and where the Guild could also, at reduced production cost, try out new and promising plays.

The Theatre Guild specialized in distinguished work studded with stars; it was synonymous with Shaw, O'Neill, the Lunts, Gershwin, Helen Hayes—in short, the best. That had been the general view of the Theatre Guild for years. But behind Guild office doors, Terry, Lawrence, Armina, and their accounting department knew how bad things actually were. There had been an oversupply of flops lately, well-mounted shows that hadn't gone well either artistically or, more important, financially. Business was bad; subscribers were unhappy. How much longer could they sustain themselves? But it's an old show busi-

Armina Marshall, her husband Lawrence Langner, and Theresa Helburn, the Theatre Guild triumvirate. (Courtesy of Beinecke Library)

ness tradition that no matter how much red ink is flowing through your balance sheets, you smile and exude optimism to the civilians you meet in the lobby. The next hit, to paraphrase Dickens's Wilkins Micawber, is bound to turn up. It might even be tomorrow. Who knows?

The house lights went down, the footlights came up, and the curtain parted. There, on the stage sat an old farm woman in a poke bonnet: Aunt Eller, bathed in bright Oklahoma sunlight, methodically working at her butter churn.

Helburn knew this play well. Nine years back, in 1931, thirty-two-year-old Lynn Riggs had brought it to the Guild. She'd liked it then; she and Langner had hoped it would succeed. They'd taken a chance with this young Oklahoma playwright who seemed to have a true poetic gift, but back in the depths of the Depression audiences hadn't been too receptive to his charming love story of a young cowboy and a feisty ranch girl. After 64 performances the show had closed; now it was getting its second chance.

She watched as Curly began to romance young Laurey, the high-spirited, independent Oklahoma lass. The Westport audience was having a good time, but then, summer audiences were notoriously easy to please. The young assistant stage manager, twenty-six-year-old Elaine Anderson Scott, a Texan who later married John Steinbeck, would remember that evening's events vividly a half-century later:

> Johnny Haggott had found Gene Kelly, who was working around the neighborhood doing a summer musical called *Two Weeks with Pay* down at the Ridgeway Theatre in White Plains, to come up and stage some square dances for us. You see, in Riggs's play there's that big party scene, and it's full of country music and dancing. So Gene put it on for us; this was just before he went to New York to become such a big hit in Rodgers and Hart's *Pal Joey*. Since John Ford hadn't showed up, Haggott directed, and it was a smashing evening. I was backstage, but naturally, being a Texan, I had to dance in the square dances!

Helburn was enjoying tonight's revival, and her producer's antennae, always tuned in to the ticket buyers around her, told her that Riggs's play was satisfying her neighbors. Who knows when the idea began to flicker in her subconscious? Just the vaguest sort of notion, perhaps, but one that wouldn't go away. As the actors went through the complications of their love story, which Riggs had so artfully set to turn-of-the-century American folk music, Helburn's mind must have begun to fill with possibilities.

"After the show, Terry came backstage to see everybody," remembered Elaine. "No matter what anybody tells you today, I was there when it happened, and I remember, it was strictly her idea. She said to us all, 'This would make a good musical!'"

Everyone agreed. It was seductive to think of the show being transformed into a musical. Sometimes the best antidote to such ideas is to lie down until they go away, or to let them drop back into the subconscious. But on this night in 1940, Terry Helburn had come up with a "what if" that was solid. It would be two years before the project would actually start. Even after that it would be a truly Sisyphean journey before her idea bore any fruit. No one, not even such hardened theatrical veterans as the three partners in the Guild, could ever have imagined how long and pot-holed the road ahead would be.

Before she was done, all the wise boys around town would refer to her project as Helburn's Folly. And she herself somewhat ruefully wrote: "I don't remember when I became convinced that *Green Grow the Lilacs* was what I had been looking for. What I do remember is trying to make other people share my conviction. When you're trying to raise a lot of money, people reminded me, you ought to offer them a sure-fire success, not a play that hasn't done so well in the past. Musicals, they said in disgust, don't have murders in the second act."

All through the post–World War I years of the New York stage, no single production group had had as much effect on public taste or done so much to raise the level of American theatre as the Guild. Into a show business famous for cheap melodramas, star vehicles, tear-jerking love stories, crook plays, and star-and-garter burlesques, the Guild introduced a theatre based on literacy, talent, and intellect. It had been founded in 1918 by Langner, Helburn, actress Helen Westley, director Philip Moeller, designer Lee Simonson, and banker Maurice Wertheim. The young group went through an intense period of birth-pangs. "For the record," remembered Helburn, "we were all people with strong convictions, creative impulses, and considerable personal ambition, and we were noisily articulate about these things. What Lawrence and I and a handful of others had in mind was an art theatre, in its best sense. But we wanted to take the curse off the word 'artistic' and provide something real and beautiful, not merely the trappings of culture and the pseudo-cleverness and the exotic unreality that are attached to the word 'artistic.'"

The Guild's first play, *The Bonds of Interest,* by Jacinto Benavente, was produced in the Garrick Theatre on 35th Street. It cost $1,100 to open. "Five hundred dollars from Lawrence," said Helburn, "and the rest of the group chipping in one hundred dollars apiece." They were fortunate to have as their landlord financier Otto H. Kahn, a true patron of the arts. "When you make the rent," he told them, "you pay the rent. When you don't make it, you need not pay it."

With the first production the Guild did not make the rent. But they had signed up a few faithful subscribers. Their second venture was *John Ferguson,* by the British playwright St. John Ervine, whose well-made plays would be staples for theatregoers on both sides of the Atlantic during the next three decades. "By that time," said Helburn, "there was the lump sum of nineteen dollars in the treasury. But it got done. The play put the Guild on its feet and started it on its career. The only other capital we had was enthusiasm for our idea and faith in the public."

The Ervine play, a stark tragedy, was an immediate hit. Subscribers began to sign up, the box office was busy, and from 1920 on, Guild productions in New York and on tour would stimulate American theatregoers and develop their tastes for avant-garde drama with Shakespeare, Strindberg, Tolstoy, Andreyev, and others. From the beginning the emphasis was on content, not stars. Helen Westley made the group's position clear: "The popular play presents the actor," she said. "The actor of the art theatre presents the play." The Guild proceeded to develop a permanent acting company, capable of performing anything.

Beginning with *Heartbreak House*, the Guild became the American producers of Bernard Shaw, who was disliked in England because of his antiwar stand. In America, on Broadway, he was restored to a position as a major satiric playwright. Soon Langner, Helburn, et al., ventured to do Shaw's interminable *Back to Methuselah*, losing $20,000 instead of the $30,000 they'd expected to (which prompted Shaw to suggest they'd actually made $10,000). For this act of faith Shaw gave them the rights to *Saint Joan* and all his ensuing works.

Ferenc Molnar, the Hungarian playwright, gave them his witty comedy *The Guardsman*. Alfred Lunt and Lynn Fontanne played the leads; the play had flopped once before, but now, in 1924, it launched the young couple's career with a brilliant success. During the 1920s the Guild produced the plays of Sidney Howard, who won a Pulitzer Prize for *They Knew What They Wanted*; S. N. Behrman, who raised social satire to an art form; Elmer Rice; and Eugene O'Neill. These were golden years.

By 1925 the Guild was financially secure enough to build its own theatre, on West 52nd Street, just west of Broadway (now called the Virginia). Between April of 1926 and October of 1928, the Guild presented no fewer than fourteen plays. By now Helburn had come to share the post of executive director with Langner, who was often absent, dealing with his legal practice. In a *New Yorker* profile, Helburn was described as "the power behind the throne. She is the terror of actors, the bane of playwrights, and the thorn of agents, managers, and kindred mortals."

In 1929 the golden years of New York legitimate theatre began to fade. The first blow was the invention of the talking picture, which ran three and four times a day in vast movie palaces; there, for far less than Broadway's box-office prices, thousands applauded such famous former stage actors as John Barrymore, Edward G. Robinson, and Paul Muni. More damaging would be the loss of many playwrights, who would go West by the trainload to become highly paid "dialoguers" for the various studios. Then came that black October day when the stock market crashed, and overnight the affluent Harding–Coolidge–Hoover years ended.

Still waving the banner of theatrical excellence, the Guild managed to remain solvent through the Depression years, but it became more of a struggle. Gone were the Lunts; they'd become managers themselves and toured across America as their own bosses. A new producing venture, the Playwrights Company, siphoned away Guild stalwarts. It was formed by playwrights Maxwell Anderson, Sidney Howard, S. N. Behrman, Elmer Rice, and Robert E. Sherwood, all of whom had previously brought their plays to Helburn and Langner, but who now desired autonomy and a larger share of the profits. The Guild did retain O'Neill and produced his *Strange Interlude, Mourning Becomes Electra, Desire Under the Elms,* and *Ah, Wilderness!* And there was the remarkable Heyward–Gershwin opera, *Porgy and Bess.* Critical kudos poured in, but financially the Guild was unsteady, and by 1939 it was $60,000 in debt.

Then Katharine Hepburn, who had been dubbed "box-office poison" by movie exhibitors, came back to Manhattan with a new Philip Barry script in hand, the charming and sophisticated *Philadelphia Story.* With Langner and Helburn as her partners ("the Guild, disrupted in management and tottering on its feet," Terry Helburn later described it), Hepburn's gamble became a hit. The Guild was saved, albeit temporarily, by the Hollywood belle.

In 1940 the Guild produced Robert Sherwood's *There Shall Be No Night,* starring their old standbys Lunt and Fontanne, and while it was a major success it was only one hit amid a batch of other ventures that quietly expired.

So, on that summer night at the Playhouse in Westport, Terry Helburn was well aware that she and her partners were on a dizzying financial tightrope. Where would the next successful idea come from to rescue them?

"I don't remember who exactly thought of this, but somebody said, 'Let's get Dick Rodgers over here,'" recalled Elaine Steinbeck. "After all, Dorothy and Dick were right nearby, up the road in Fairfield. He was called, and he came down, sat through *Green Grow the Lilacs,* and I was also there afterwards, at the discussion with Terry and Lawrence. Dick said, 'Yes, it's a good idea.'"

In her memoirs, Helburn summed up her intuitive response to *Green Grow the Lilacs:* "For years," she said, "I had been groping my way toward a new type of play with music, not musical comedy, not operetta in the old sense, but a form in which the dramatic action, music, and possibly ballet could be welded together into a compounded whole, each helping to tell the story in its own way. This was an idea which was finally crystallized years later, in *Oklahoma!*"

Now she had found herself a project, one that was still 90 percent fantasy and 10 percent fact. But she had the definite interest of Rodgers, a major musical talent, and it was no problem to secure an option on the rights to Riggs's play. Two firm assets, or perhaps it would be more realistic to gauge them at one and a half. Rodgers may have been bankable to potential Broadway investors, but Riggs's Oklahoma love story was far from the hottest property in town.

Even after Helburn called Riggs's agent at Samuel French with the notion of adapting *Green Grow the Lilacs* into a Broadway musical, Riggs's career remained evidence of Robert Anderson's dry summary: "You can make a killing in the theatre, but you can't make a living." Helburn's option money was welcome indeed. Riggs, as usual, was working on another play, and whatever dollars came from the Guild would go to keeping him at his typewriter.

Years later, when *Oklahoma!* was established as a mammoth success, Ev Simms, one of Riggs's neighbors on Shelter Island, New York, where the playwright had settled in the 1950s, remembered him ripping open an envelope to remove a check one day at his mailbox. The money represented Riggs's share of the sale of the motion picture rights to *Oklahoma!* "My God!" cried Riggs. "I'm rich! This is seventy-five thousand dollars! It's more money than I've ever had in one piece all my life!"

In today's theatre, we have few regional playwrights; over the years we have become homogenized, and original dramatic voices with a local accent are few and far between. But even back in the thirties, Lynn Riggs was a rarity. Born in 1899 in Indian territory that would become part of the state of Oklahoma, in 1907, he grew up on the same open prairie that was the background, the essence, the wellspring of his writings.

His father had been a cowboy who turned to farming. Young Lynn worked on the family farm but soon developed an attraction to the theatre that would continue all his life. When he left Oklahoma for the first time, it was on a train carrying cattle to the Chicago stockyards. There he made an abrupt career reversal; he found a job singing in a local movie theatre. He moved on to New York, where his career was mainly a succession of dead-end jobs that supported him but led nowhere. He returned to his native Oklahoma and began to write, first poetry, then drama.

His plays met with predictable rejections. His first production, a love tragedy called *Big Lake*, had no success but did draw some attention to his talent. In 1930 he achieved his first professional production, under the aegis of the distinguished New York producer–director Arthur Hopkins. The play, *Roadside*, flopped, but it earned Riggs a Guggenheim Fellowship. He used that welcome endowment to underwrite a trip to Paris, and there he wrote *Green Grow the Lilacs*.

With the sturdy homesteaders of turn-of-the-century Oklahoma, Riggs was writing about his own kind, celebrating his homeland and the people he knew intimately. When his script reached Terry Helburn, she became one of its staunchest supporters. This was precisely the sort of play the Guild needed: It had a fresh setting, peopled by robust characters, and there were folk songs and dancing, a touching love story, and a dramatic climax in the second act when Jeeter (Jud's original name in *Green Grow the Lilacs*) Fry was stabbed. It was far more than entertainment; it was truth. The Guild bought Riggs's play.

Cheryl Crawford, the Guild's casting director—later a major Broadway producer with the Group Theatre—found the right actors for the 1931 production; the two leads were played by Franchot Tone and June Walker. Aunt Eller, shrewd and salty-tongued, was played by Helen Westley. For the supporting cast Crawford hired several genuine cowboys who happened to be in

New York for the Madison Square Garden Rodeo; their presence added to this folk play an authenticity rarely found on Broadway.

Audiences enjoyed Riggs's love story and responded warmly to the folk ballads and cowboy laments interspersed through it, but *Green Grow the Lilacs* did not exactly set New York on fire. Perhaps the 1931 audiences were more involved in their own day-to-day financial survival than they were with the problems of Curly's pursuit of Laurey in another, simpler time. Or perhaps a Western was more suited to the screen, where cowboys roamed the range in search of justice. Whatever the reason, after its allotted sixty-four performances for the Guild's subscription audiences the play closed and went on tour. It finally ended up between the covers of Burns Mantle's *Ten Best Plays* of 1931, and in the Samuel French catalog of plays available for stock and amateur groups, and there it remained until Terry Helburn called to discuss her plans for a musical version.

When the play was first printed, Riggs supplied some perceptive notes for future producers and directors. "My play might well have been retitled *An Old Song*," he wrote.

> My intent was to recapture in a kind of nostalgic glow . . . the great range of mood which characterized the old folk songs and ballads I used to hear in my Oklahoma childhood, their quaintness, their sadness, their robustness, their simplicity, their hearty or bawdy humors, their sentimentalities, their melodrama, their touching sweetness. . . . I considered it wise to throw away the conventions of ordinary theatricality—a complex plot, swift action, etc., and to try to exhibit luminosity in the simplest of stories, a wide area of mood and feeling. After the people are known, I let them go ahead, acting out their simple tale, which might have been the substance of an ancient song.

Later these notes would be vital to the eventual conception, so simple and effective, of Hammerstein's libretto and the style of the Rodgers and Hammerstein score. Not only did his adaptors start from Riggs's original concept, they strengthened it.

After *Lilacs* closed, Riggs migrated west to Santa Fe, where the standard of living was so modest that he could afford to write more plays. By the time Helburn had begun her campaign to turn the play into a musical, he'd finished another play, *The Cream in the Well*, which opened in New York in 1941 to respectable notices but added no black ink to Riggs's assets. Even though he could take confidence in the knowledge that Helburn had sufficient drive to bring her fantasy to eventual commercial life, he was also a realist. If it happened, it might earn him a decent royalty; after all, his new contract with the Guild called for 1 percent of whatever weekly gross the musical took in. But being a man who'd had considerable experience on Broadway, Riggs was wise not counting on anything—not until it happened.

But before there was Rodgers and Hammerstein there was Rodgers and Hart, and there Terry Helburn encountered her first roadblock. She'd discussed *Green Grow the Lilacs* as a project for Richard Rodgers and Lorenz Hart, and Rodgers had been enthusiastic. With such talents as these two, the future for her project seemed rosy indeed. A natural, right?

Wrong. While Rodgers was willing, he could not commit to his partner's participation. Worse, it didn't seem as if their collaboration could last much longer. And so Helburn's dream, born that 1940 summer night in Westport, had to be put on hold until Rodgers settled his future with Hart.

Rodgers & Hart & Hammerstein

Rodgers without Hart was as difficult to imagine as, say, Sears without Roebuck, or Rolls without Royce. For the past two decades, ever since *The Garrick Gaieties*, they'd been a team. They were *the* team, who had turned out a stream of love lyrics, brilliant comedy songs, gorgeous waltzes, and charming ballads. Irving Berlin himself had encapsulated their qualities years before:

> *Tuneful and tasteful,*
> *Schmaltzy and smart.*
> *Music by Rodgers,*
> *Lyrics by Hart.*

Praise from Caesar indeed.

LARRY HART

During the late twenties, when Broadway was treated to as many as thirty-odd musical shows a season, there were years when Rodgers and Hart accounted for as many as three—with sparkling musical-comedy gems in each one. One Rodgers and Hart legend touched on the question, "Where do you guys get your ideas for your songs?" The young songwriters were in Paris, riding in a taxi with two young women in 1926. Their cab skittered into a truck, and one of the women blurted out, "Oh, my heart stood still!" From the floor of the cab, where the collision had thrown him, his hat jammed over his eyes, Larry Hart is supposed to have responded instantly, "Hey, there's a good title for a song!"

Even in those earliest years, Rodgers had difficulty in getting his partner to work. His own pattern was fixed; he got up early, sharpened his pencils, and went to work. By that time, Larry Hart may have been asleep for only two hours, having finally ended an all-night party at his apartment. This wasn't so easy. It meant throwing out a crowd: half of Paul Whiteman's band, an act from the Cotton Club, the bartender from Louie Bergin's midtown bar, and a dozen chorus girls from his latest show.

How does one paint a portrait in mere prose of the mercurial, witty Hart, that cigar-smoking diminutive genius whose generosity was as legendary as his bubbling wit? ("I never saw Larry let anybody else, even a complete stranger, pick up a check," remembered George Church, who danced in *On Your Toes*.) Hart's profligacy extended not only to his wallet but also to his brilliance. Hart's hair-trigger wit functioned in rapid spurts. Mere alcohol could do nothing to dull it. Lyrics poured forth in torrents as if from an uncapped gusher.

Rodgers actually met Hammerstein before he met Hart. He recalled years later, in the *Dramatists Guild Quarterly*: "I was twelve and he was nineteen when my older brother Mortimer, a fraternity brother of Oscar's, took me backstage after a performance of a Columbia Varsity Show. Oscar played the comic lead in the production, and meeting this worldly college junior was pretty heady stuff for a stagestruck kid." He met Hart four years later:

> I was still in high school at the time, but I had already begun writing songs for amateur shows and I was determined even then to make composing my life's work. Although I had written words to some of my songs, I was anxious to team up with a full-fledged lyricist. A mutual friend, Philip Leavitt . . . introduced us one Saturday afternoon at Larry's house.
>
> Larry came to the door of the brownstone, wearing house slippers, a pair of tuxedo trousers, and some kind of a shirt. It was a Sunday, so he needed a shave, but then Larry always needed a shave, except on state occasions. Larry was twenty-three. To me he was the old man of the mountain, and I was a naive child. But I wasn't so naive that I didn't know I was in the presence of talent. What Larry had to say about lyrics and the making of lyrics and the relationship of lyrics to the theatre was exciting and tremendously stimulating. In one afternoon I acquired a career, a partner, a best friend.

At the time, Hart was gainfully but gloomily employed translating German plays and librettos for the all-powerful Shuberts. Rodgers and Hart shortly thereafter formed a partnership with another Columbia alumnus, Herbert Fields (son of the great Lew Fields of the legendary comedy team Weber and Fields). For a long time very little came of their efforts. Even with Fields supplying clever librettos it was—as it always was and ever shall be—tough for aspiring writers to break down doors. Dorothy Fields, Herbert's younger sister, herself a great lyricist ("I Can't Give You Anything but Love, Baby," "On the Sunny Side of the Street," "Big Spender," to name but a sampling of her catalogue), remembered the frustration well—she was later to encounter it herself: "They had bright, fresh, wonderful ideas, but no one gave them an ear," she said. "Fields, Rodgers, and Hart peddled their wares to diverse producers, who fixed a baleful eye on brother Herbie and said, 'If you guys are as good as you think you are, how come your father . . . isn't interested in producing your show?'" Fields pére did interpolate one of their earliest songs, "Any Old Place with You," into a 1919 show of his called *A Lonely Romeo;* Hart's lyric contained the marvelous couplet, "I'll go to hell for ya,/Or Philadelphia."

But in general it was a long, trying period. Fields went looking for jobs as a librettist. Rodgers and Hart then went to see Max Dreyfus, a major force in popular music who was then with the publishing firm of T. B. Harms. Dreyfus agreed they had talent but felt they were too young for the business. He advised that they go somewhere and study. Hart returned to his job with the Shuberts. Rodgers enrolled at the Institute of Musical Art to study classical music under Dr. Frank Damrosch. At the end of a year there, he was selected to write the Institute's annual show; obviously his talents for popular, rather than classical, music were evident to his instructors.

But he and Hart continued working; they wrote no fewer than twenty amateur shows over the next two years, including benefits for girls' schools, churches, and synagogues. It was work, certainly, but a dead end, and worst of all it brought in little if any money. One of Rodgers' family friends, a businessman in the garment district, had been lending the young composer small sums of money. By the time Rodgers owed him a hundred dollars, he decided the onus of such a debt was overwhelming and decided to throw in the towel. He would take a job and earn a regular living. His friend led him across the hall to a Mr. Marcin, who was in the children's underwear business and was looking for a young man he could train to succeed him upon his retirement. He offered young Rodgers $50 a week to start immediately. Rodgers asked for a day or so to think it over.

That evening, at home, he was called by Benjamin Kaye, the lawyer for the Theatre Guild, who offered Rodgers the task of writing *The Garrick Gaieties.* Rodgers suggested his partner Hart, who had recently spent most of his money trying to produce two shows that had been spectacular failures. Luckily for the American musical theatre, the Guild agreed to employ them both, and the next day Rodgers passed up a possible career in childrens' underwear.

After their success at the Garrick Theatre, the young team were recognized. Reunited with Herbie Fields, they went to work for their early patron Lew Fields, for whom they wrote a show called *Dearest Enemy,* in 1925. Along with the song "Manhattan," they now had another hit, "Here in My Arms." Then, in rapid succession, came the Fields productions of *The Girl Friend,* which contained "The Blue Room" and the title number, and a second edition of *Garrick Gaieties,* which contained the lilting "Mountain Greenery."

To call the ensuing decades of the twenties and thirties the golden age of songwriting (certainly one cannot make a like claim for the libretti supplied by assorted gagwriters to fit the stars who twinkled in those shows) is no understatement. One has merely to run down the list of practitioners of the period: George and Ira Gershwin; Irving Berlin; Cole Porter; Jerome Kern;

Sigmund Romberg; P. G. Wodehouse, B. G. DeSylva; Lew Brown; Ray Henderson; Bert Kalmar; Harry Ruby; Harold Arlen; E. Y. Harburg; Vernon Duke; Harry Warren; Richard Whiting . . . on and on goes the roster of major talents. Truly, Times Square and its environs were host to a movable, eight-performances-a-week musical feast.

Rodgers and Hart quickly moved to the forefront during those melodious years. "The great thing about Larry," remarked Rodgers years later, "was that he was always growing, creatively if not physically. He was fascinated by the various techniques of rhyming, such as polysyllabic rhymes, interior rhymes, masculine and feminine rhymes, and the trick of rhyming one word with only part of another."

Innovation was Hart's mainstay, and he and Rodgers demonstrated it successfully over the years of their partnership. Formulae were meant to be broken. In a 1926 hit, *Peggy-Ann*, they abandoned the opening chorus in favor of fifteen minutes of spoken dialogue before the first song was sung. *Chee Chee*, in 1928, tried to meld songs and book into a single entity. It didn't succeed commercially, but it inspired the team to break other rules. *Time* magazine summed up their attitude in 1938: "As Rodgers and Hart see it, what was killing musicomedy was its sameness, its tameness, its eternal rhyming of 'June' with 'moon.' They decided it was not enough to be just good at the job; they had to be constantly different also. The one possible formula was *Don't have a formula*; the one rule for success, *Don't follow it up*."

They had written no less than eleven hit shows before they ventured to Hollywood, in the early thirties, to work at Paramount for director Rouben Mamoulian on *Love Me Tonight*, starring Maurice Chevalier and Jeanette MacDonald. Their score contained such brilliant work as "Isn't It Romantic?" "Lover," and the title song. Once back on home turf, in November of 1935, they started on Billy Rose's mammoth new spectacle for the Hippodrome Theatre, *Jumbo*. That score contained "The Most Beautiful Girl in the World," "Little Girl Blue," and "My Romance." All through the runs of their next shows, *On Your Toes, Babes in Arms*, and the political satire *I'd Rather Be Right*, ticket buyers lined up at the box office, cheerfully plunked down their cash, and, when the show was over, ran out of the theatre, humming, to buy Rodgers and Hart sheet music and/or the recordings.

But beneath the lines Hart dashed off for Rodgers' melodies, beneath the charming lyrics, the sharp-edged wit, the laughter his couplets induced, there was another, darker and tortured Larry Hart. His depressions, fueled by a self-hatred that had seeped into his soul, deepened. Once he said to Ted Fetter, another very talented lyricist (he wrote "Taking a Chance on Love" with John Latouche): "I can't believe I make so much money. It's completely disproportionate for the work I do to earn it." He might have been able to come to terms with that lack of self-worth, but another, far more deeply rooted angst gnawed at Hart, his sexual appetite. Unlike his partner Rodgers, who was happily married to the lovely Dorothy and lived an ordered life with his children, Hart was a homosexual. In the twenties and thirties, good Jewish boys from middle-class families who'd been educated at Columbia were supposed to live a middle-class married life. Homosexuality was still "the love that dares not speak its name," as in Oscar Wilde's time. In England its practice was still punishable by law, in America it was a powerful taboo. During the Jazz Age sexual license extended primarily to heterosexuals.

He was short, he wasn't very attractive, and inside the dark closet of his soul Hart must have wept. Every so often his scribbling pencil would reveal the pain he constantly lived with. "Spring is here," he asked, "Why doesn't my heart go dancing?" And he finished that lament by saying "Maybe it's because nobody needs me."

In 1940, the year following *Pal Joey*, while Terry Helburn waited for Rodgers to persuade Hart to join him on *Green Grow the Lilacs*, the two discussed the possibility of turning Edna Ferber's *Saratoga Trunk* into a musical. In July of 1941, Rodgers had gotten in touch with Hammerstein, their old Columbia chum, about writing the libretto. But as often happens on Broadway, too many disparate elements were involved, and the project eventually was negotiated out of existence.

Shortly afterwards, Rodgers did something hitherto unheard of in his partnership with Hart. He took on a project without him, so frustrated was he at his partner's erratic work habits, and became George Abbott's silent producing partner in a new musical, *Best Foot Forward*, with a score by the extremely talented Hugh Martin and Ralph Blane. After that show opened in Philadelphia, Rodgers drove out to visit Hammerstein at his Doylestown, Pennsylvania, farmhouse. There he explained to Hammerstein the predicament he now found himself in; he had taken on the Abbott project without any credit on the marquee or in the program, simply because he was afraid that if Hart found out he was working without him, his partner might go completely to pieces.

But he and Hart also had committed to do the score of a proposed musical to be based on Ludwig Bemelmans' *Hotel Splendide*, for which screenwriter Donald Ogden Stewart was writing the book, and he had become convinced that his troubled partner would be unable to do his share of the work. Would Oscar consider collaborating with them? That way, at least there was a guarantee of the project being finished. Hammerstein thought it over, then demurred. No, he could not, would not, be a party to such an arrangement.

"I think you should keep working with Larry just as long as he is able to keep working with you," he told Rodgers. "It would kill him if you walked away while he was still able to function. But," he added, "if the time ever comes when he cannot function, call me. I'll be there." With that assurance, Rodgers returned to Philadelphia and his chores with *Best Foot Forward*, which came into New York and was highly successful. *Hotel Splendide* was eventually abandoned.

By 1942, producer Dwight Deere Wiman had brought Rodgers and Hart into the production of *By Jupiter*, a musical version of an old play, *The Warrior's Husband*, starring Ray Bolger. But Hart's efforts were by now so erratic that he had to be placed under a doctor's care. When Hart had to be hospitalized, Rodgers took the medico's advice and moved into the hospital; there he could work at a piano that had been installed in the interns' quarters when Cole Porter had been a patient. *By Jupiter* opened to enthusiastic notices and was a wartime hit.

DICK RODGERS

Hart had come to Dante's dark wood, but Rodgers would not follow. He turned to the *Green Grow the Lilacs* project in earnest. The Theatre Guild and Terry Helburn were waiting, not so patiently. It had been two years since Helburn had conceived her plan; she and Langner well understood what healthy box office grosses from a smash Rodgers and Hart show such as *By Jupiter* would bring into their depleted bank accounts. What they did not yet understand was that Rodgers could no longer work with his partner. Joshua Logan recalled:

> Few people knew I was headed for the army, so at a party given by the Theatre Guild, Theresa Helburn asked me to direct an old play . . . which was being turned into a musical for Rodgers and Hart. . . . I had to beg off because of my draft. I told Dick how sorry I was and asked that he and Larry think of me in the future.
>
> Dick said, "Josh, I don't know how to put this, but Larry doesn't want to work any more. I don't know if it's some kind of boxed-up panic, or whether it's me. . . ."
>
> "You mean, you'll work with some other lyricist?"
>
> "I'll have to, Josh. Oh, I'll do something with Larry again. Maybe the only way to scare him out of this is to find someone else. What would you think of Oscar Hammerstein?"
>
> Just hearing the name made my heart beat faster. The *Show Boat* lyrics were one of my early enthusiasms. I said, "Dick, you and Hammerstein would be unbeatable."
>
> "Can he do comedy songs? Larry was always able to get laughs. I don't know. I don't know."

According to singer Michael Feinstein, Ira Gershwin related how Rodgers, on a trip to California, had also offered him the task of writing lyrics for Riggs's play. But Gershwin had regretfully refused. It wasn't Riggs's play that bothered him; he liked it. But he simply did not feel himself right for the job. "If I had written the lyrics," he mused years later, "they'd have been part of a completely different kind of show . . . and nowhere near as important as it became." While Gershwin certainly had the benefit of hindsight for his statement, he was probably correct.

Rodgers decided to make one last try, out of affection for his old and dear friend. He told Hart of his fondness for *Green Grow the Lilacs* and sent him a copy of the script. The two men met at the Chappell Music publishing office, where Max Dreyfus, their friend and associate for all those successful years, reigned. Even years later, Rodgers' memories of that day were painful:

A haggard and pale Larry walked in. He had obviously not had a good night's sleep in weeks, and I realized I could no longer avoid talking about what was on my mind—that if necessary I'd have to be brutal to make him understand what he was doing not only to himself but to our partnership. I began by telling him I wanted to get started on the new show right away but that he was obviously in no condition to work.

Larry admitted this and said that he needed a rest and was planning to leave soon for a vacation in Mexico. He was sure it would straighten him out and he'd return feeling much better. This was nonsense; he knew it and I knew it.

"Larry," I said, "the only reason you're going to Mexico is to drink. When you come back, you'll be in worse shape than ever."

Larry looked as if I'd stabbed him. This was the first time in all the years we'd been together that I had ever spoken to him this way.

"We've got to work something out for the good of both of us," I continued. "I want you to have yourself admitted to a sanitarium, and I'll have myself admitted along with you. We'll be there together and we'll work together. The only way you're ever going to lick this thing is to get off the street."

Larry, who had been avoiding my eyes, looked at the floor and said, "I know, Dick, I'm sorry. But I want to go to Mexico. I have to."

I felt the blood rushing to my head. "This show means a lot to me," I told him. "If you walk out on me now, I'm going to do it with someone else."

"Anyone in mind?"

"Yes, Oscar Hammerstein."

Even the realization that I wasn't bluffing, that I actually had someone else waiting to take over, couldn't shake him. Still looking at the floor, all that Larry said was "Well, you couldn't pick a better man." Then for the first time he looked me in the eye. "You know, Dick," he said, "I've never understood why you've put up with me all these years. It's been crazy. The best thing for you to do is to forget about me."

There wasn't much more either of us could say. Larry could no more fight his compulsive drinking than I could have thrown aside my family and career. He got up to leave, and when he reached the door he turned around and said, "There's just one thing. I really don't think *Green Grow the Lilacs* can be turned into a good musical. I think you're making a mistake."

With that he was gone, and so was our partnership.

I walked out of the boardroom to tell Max Dreyfus, who was waiting in his office, what had happened. But I never got there. I simply broke down and cried.

Larry did go to Mexico. When he returned a month later, he had to be carried off the train on a stretcher.

By that time, Rodgers had gotten in touch with Hammerstein. In July, four days after Hammerstein had finished the libretto and lyrics for a modern-day version of Bizet's *Carmen*, which he called *Carmen Jones*, Rodgers called. The two arranged lunch at the Barberry Room, and Rodgers came to the point even before the food was ordered. Letters, telegrams, and phone calls to Larry in Mexico had brought no response. The time had come when he had to be replaced. "The Guild wants me to do a musical based on one of their early plays," Rodgers told Hammerstein. "Terry Helburn approached me about doing it, and I think she's right. I wonder if we could get together? Why don't you read it and see how you like it?"

"What's the play?" asked Hammerstein.

"*Green Grow the Lilacs*," said Rodgers.

"I don't have to read it," said Hammerstein. "I know it, and I'm crazy about it. I'd love to do it with you."

OSCAR HAMMERSTEIN

The fortyish, burly gentleman who was shortly to go to work with Dick Rodgers as his new collaborator was a radically different personality from Larry Hart. Hart was mercurial, Hammerstein stable—and thoughtful, generous, and disciplined. He worked every day at the tall desk in his study, standing while writing. If Hart was the hare, Hammerstein was the tortoise. But Hammerstein had developed the sort of determination described in the lyrics of a song by his friend Dorothy Fields: He coped with failure by picking himself up, dusting himself off, and starting all over again. From his flops he accumulated scar tissue.

It began very early. Hammerstein wrote his first produced play in 1919, when he was twenty-four, *The Light*, which was tried out in New Haven. "After the first act, Dad knew he had a flop," recalled Oscar's son William. "In fact, later he always referred to it as 'The Light That Failed.' Well, he left the Shubert Theatre during the first intermission and went for a walk around the Yale campus. He wasn't just going out for a depressed ramble; what he was doing was thinking what he would write for his next play."

That inner resilience would stand him well his entire life. As would his keen social consciousness: Rodgers said of him years later, "He was a joiner, a leader, a man willing to do battle for whatever causes he believed in. He was not naive. He knew full well that man is not all good and that nature is not all good; yet it was his sincere belief that someone had to keep reminding people of the vast amount of good things there are in the world."

His kindnesses to others in the business were legendary. He never forgot the old show-business adage, "Help people on the way up; you never know whom you'll meet on the way down." Edmund Hartmann, who became a successful writer–producer in Hollywood, came to New York seeking his start in the theatre in the gloom of 1932. A mutual friend sent the unknown young Hartmann to consult with Hammerstein, who'd already made a considerable career with Kern, Romberg, and Harbach. "I went over to the theatre where he was in the midst of rehearsals for *Music in the Air,* a new show he'd written with Jerome Kern," remembered Hartmann. "Here I was, a total nobody, with an armful of material, hoping to get a break somewhere. Who needed to bother with me? But Oscar took time out from his hectic rehearsal, we went to the back of the theatre, he sat down with me, he read my stuff, and spent almost an entire hour telling me which of my things was commercial, which was funny, and why, and which wasn't. It was so helpful and generous—I've never forgotten it—a big-time guy, the author of *Show Boat,* sitting down to consult with a bewildered kid!"

Hammerstein was a pragmatic teacher, not only a critic, willing to share what he'd learned. In the rough-and-tumble of show business, he was a rarity.

He was also a perfectionist. "Even when songs were completed, they might not satisfy him," recalled his son William. "Take that final couplet of 'All the Things You Are,' from *Very Warm for May,* which he wrote with Kern; a song which everyone else considers near-perfect. Not Oscar. That next to last line—'To know that moment divine'—he wanted to change that word divine. It always bothered him." The song was written in 1939, and as late as 1949, in his book *Lyrics,* Hammerstein is complaining still: "Nothing served as well as that unwanted *divine.* I never could find a way out."

Hammerstein had grown up in a theatrical family. His grandfather, Oscar Hammerstein, was a major impresario of the 1890s and early 1900s. In 1906 he built the Manhattan Opera House on West 34th Street, in an effort to give the Metropolitan a run for its money. Someone asked Hammerstein if there was any money in grand opera. "Yes," replied the impresario. "*My* money is in it." Under his management the greatest singers of the day, such as Mary Garden and John McCormack, appeared on his stage.

His grandson Oscar entered Columbia University in 1916. His family wanted him to become a lawyer, and for one year he dutifully studied law, but he gave it up soon after he began appearing in the Columbia varsity shows. In the 1917 show, *Home, James!* Oscar did a dance in a leopard-skin costume. He had also written most of the lyrics, and when the show was a success, the young Columbia student, hopelessly infected with the family disease, left law behind. He went downtown and persuaded his uncle Arthur to put him to work as an assistant stage manager; similar jobs followed. While he worked backstage he kept on writing lyrics and concocting possible storylines for musical shows. Soon enough, in 1920, his uncle put him to work on two shows, *Always You* and *Tickle Me*.

Later Hammerstein recalled, "I was born into the theatrical world with two gold spoons in my mouth. One was my uncle Arthur, who took me into his producing organization and gave me wise guidance. It was he who supplied the second gold spoon, Otto Harbach. Harbach, at my uncle's persuasion, accepted me as a collaborator. His generosity in dividing credits and royalties with me was the least of his favors. Much more important were the things he taught me about writing for the theatre." He and Harbach began writing in 1922, and their first show was *Wildflower*. To the music supplied by Herbert Stothart and Vincent Youmans they produced two hits, "Bambalina" and the title song. In 1924 came *Rose-Marie*, with a score by Rudolf Friml.

Years later Hammerstein wrote, "Like most young writers, I had an eagerness to get words down on paper. Harbach taught me to think a long time before actually writing. He taught me never to stop work on anything if you can think of one small improvement to make." Harbach's credits are formidable indeed, including *No, No, Nanette, Whoopee, Sunny, The Desert Song, The Cat and the Fiddle,* and *Roberta*. "It is almost unbelievable," mused Hammerstein, "that a man with this record of achievement received so little recognition."

In the busy Broadway musical theatre of the twenties, Hammerstein became one of the most sought-after lyricists, and soon he began to collaborate with Sigmund Romberg, a prolific composer whose music was so easily appreciated that Broadway wits liked to quip, "His is the kind of music you hum as you go into the theatre."

"Romberg got me into the habit of working hard," Hammerstein said. "In our first collaboration, *The Desert Song,* I used to visit him. I remember bringing up a finished lyric to him one day. He played it over and then he said, 'It fits.' Then he turned to me and asked, 'What else have you got?' I said that I didn't have anything more, but I would go away and set another melody. He persuaded me to stay right there and write it while he was working on something else. He put me in another room with a pad and pencil. Afraid to come out empty-handed, I finished another refrain that afternoon. I have written many plays and pictures with Rommy, and his highest praise has always been the same 'It fits.' Disappointed at first with such limited approval, I learned later that what he meant was not merely that the words fitted the notes, but that they matched the spirit of his music, and that he thought they were fine."

It would be in collaboration with Jerome Kern that Hammerstein would reach the high-water mark of his early success. In 1927, when he was only thirty-two, he did the adaptation of Edna Ferber's novel *Show Boat* and wrote the lyrics to such indestructible classics as "Can't Help Lovin' Dat Man," "Make Believe," "Why Do I Love You?" and the powerful "Ol' Man River."

Prior to Florenz Ziegfeld's production of *Show Boat*, Broadway musicals were mostly assembly-line concoctions, arranged to show off a star comedian's talents or a leading lady's charms. Hammerstein summed up the state of the librettist's art years later: "The composer and the lyric-writer concentrated mainly on a few major efforts, a big dance number, a love ballad, a light comedy duet, and one or two songs for the comedians. In the latter, while the author would write the best jokes he could, the composer would write music which was not out of his top drawer—he did not want to waste a good melody on a comedy song. The librettist was kind of a stable boy. If the race was lost, he was blamed for giving the horse the wrong feed. For many years I read theatrical criticism and comment which contained the statement 'The book of a musical doesn't matter'; and yet, in the case of most failures it was pointed out that the book was so bad that it could not be survived."

Show Boat heralded a new era, in which the musical's book and lyrics would be treated by knowing producers with more respect. The musical theatre began to mature. The Gershwins provided scores to satirical books by wits such as George S. Kaufman and Morrie Ryskind. Howard Lindsay and Russel Crouse collaborated with Cole Porter, as did Moss Hart; Howard Dietz and Arthur Schwartz, E. Y. Harburg, Harold Arlen, and Vernon Duke worked on sophisticated revues, and eventually a major operatic work, *Porgy and Bess*, found its place on a Broadway stage. *Show Boat* had led the way.

Producer–director Harold Prince, who staged a major revival of *Show Boat* in the 1990s, lavishly praised Hammerstein's contribution to musical theatre. "His book is solidly constructed, like the very best play," he said. "If you analyze it, you find he still retains elements of past clichés—for instance, the two subsidiary comedy characters, male and female, who were played by Eva Puck and Sammy White out of vaudeville. They sang and danced and provided comedy relief—straight out of old musical comedies. But around them Hammerstein assembled this highly dramatic story which dealt with bigotry, race prejudice, tragedy—all sorts of elements nobody in those days had ever dared to touch."

In the early thirties, Hammerstein joined other dramatists who had migrated West, where the studios were rolling out all-talking, all-singing, all-dancing musicals monthly. "Everyone in those days was seduced by Hollywood," says Hammerstein's son William. During his years in Hollywood, Hammerstein continued writing lyrics. But it was essentially a dry period. The money didn't satisfy him. "He worried about what was happening to him. With all his capacity for enjoying life, it simply wasn't sufficient," William Hammerstein said. "Perhaps he wouldn't agree with this, but I don't think Dad ever felt comfortable in movies. He understood the stage—he had a fantastic instinct for timing, for climactic construction of a play, how to deal with a live audience, how to fashion an entertainment for the people sitting in a legitimate theatre. But I don't think he ever really grasped the movie as a form."

In the late thirties Max Gordon reunited Kern and Hammerstein for *Very Warm for May*, and while its songs were brilliant, the book was tedious. Despite "All the Things You Are," now a standard, Broadway wags quickly retitled the show *Very Cold for Max*. There were a pair of flops in London and *Gentlemen Unafraid*, which played one week at the St. Louis Municipal Opera in 1938 and, despite the presence of a young Red Skelton in the cast, never got any further. Hammerstein could not get a project completed that would justify the hard work he brought to them.

At one point he considered retiring and leaving the United States. Robert Russell Bennett, the arranger who had worked with Hammerstein since *Music in the Air*, recalled, "One time in 1938, when my wife and I were living in Paris, Oscar and his wife came to see us. He had had failures for quite some time, and at this dinner he said, 'Dorothy and I are going to live in a little place here in France, and she's going to cook and take care of the household, and I'm going to write poetry.' And I told him then, 'Nothing on earth could ever make me happier than to hear that, because you have poetry in you—you have great poems in you! But if you always stay in show business, it'll never come out.' He said, 'Well, it's going to come out now. This is it.'"

This Parisian evening, bittersweet in recollection, was, of course, before Hammerstein gave us *Carmen Jones*, which amply demonstrated his enormous poetic gifts and proved that both he and Bennett were partially correct but basically wrong.

In 1941, Hammerstein and Romberg's operetta *Sunny River*. was given a summer tryout at the huge St. Louis Municipal Opera. Set in New Orleans in the early 1800s—certainly a reliable operetta background—the plot dealt with another surefire contrivance, two separated lovers. Max Gordon came to St. Louis, saw it, and arranged sufficient backing to bring the show to New York. *Sunny River* arrived in December of 1941, far from an auspicious time. Within three days after its opening, the United States was at war. The New York critics found the show dated and boring. It closed after thirty-six performances.

In a letter to Gordon, Hammerstein penned an epitaph to his past body of work. "Operetta," he said, "is a dead pigeon, and if it ever is revived, it won't be by me. . . . I have no plans, and at the moment I don't feel like making any."

But Hammerstein's resilience sustained him again, through the dreary winter following Pearl Harbor. On a visit to Kern in 1942, he broached the subject of the two men collaborating on another show, based on Lynn Riggs's *Green Grow the Lilacs*. Hammerstein explained that he was impressed with the vitality under the play's gentle surfaces and was attracted to those well-defined frontier characters. He was especially fond of Riggs's dialogue, which he considered "earthy and lyrical." But after he read the play, Kern demurred, finding Riggs's second act, with its climactic death, completely hopeless. He pointed out that the play hadn't exactly set New York afire back in 1931. Why should current audiences find it more interesting?

By spring, Hammerstein had found a new project. Years before, he'd attended a performance of Bizet's *Carmen* in the Hollywood Bowl. The opera, sung in French, was almost inaudible in that vast place, and the lyrics were lost to spectators beyond the first few rows. Yet, as Hammerstein concluded, the music alone still told the story. Searching for an American equivalent of Bizet's Spanish gypsies, he eventually decided that a close approximation to the grace, fire, and humor of the opera's characters could be found among American blacks. Thus to his fertile mind came the first notion to transpose Bizet's opera into what would become *Carmen Jones*.

Working from a translation of the original work, Hammerstein wrote his version without a contract or the slightest prospect of one. Standing at the waist-high sloped desk he always used, he spent his days working, totally on his own—a remarkable venture for a man who'd worked on hundreds of published songs, forty produced shows. But doing it was typical of his attitude toward work. The project was worth the effort; if nobody was around to take a chance on it or on him, he would go it alone. Later, Oscar admitted that he had enjoyed this work more than any he had ever done.

Adapting Bizet with a new set of lyrics brought forth that essential gift in Hammerstein which Bennett was so certain existed—his poetry. Later, when *Carmen Jones* was produced by Billy Rose, composer Virgil Thompson described Hammerstein's work as "ingenious, neat, and wholly triumphant." The Broadway critics would be equally lavish in their praise.

In the spring of 1942, Hammerstein's future seemed cloudy. Even though faithful Max Gordon had taken an option on *Carmen Jones*, any plan to go into rehearsals had to be put on hold until Gordon's bankroll could be replenished. In California, Arthur Freed and the MGM executives were discussing another contract with Hammerstein, one which would take him back to Culver City. Now that there was a war on, film musicals were sure-fire winners. But Broadway was Hammerstein's turf.

And then Rodgers called.

When Rodgers and Hammerstein finished their lunch at the Barberry Room, the musical version of *Green Grow the Lilacs* was a definite project. So delighted was Terry Helburn that Hammerstein would sign on with Rodgers that she promptly announced it to her staff and to the press. And two years after that summer night in Westport, Helburn's Folly was finally on track.

The Writing

I n the spring of 1942, Rodgers and Hammerstein sat down beneath a tree at Rodgers' pleasant Fairfield, Connecticut, home, where the two began to exchange their ideas for turning *Green Grow the Lilacs* into a musical. A production that might, or might not, make it to Broadway under the auspices of the Theatre Guild.

"At the beginning of 1942," Helburn remembered, "we had about forty thousand dollars in the bank. Lawrence was dividing his time between Washington and New York, immersed in work at the National Inventors Council, which he'd initiated." Later, Langner took a six-week vacation from his work in Washington to help Helburn raise money. "At that historic and uncertain period," continued Helburn, "serious interest in the theatre seemed like fiddling while Rome burned. Because of the tremendous demands on capital, it was almost impossible to wheedle or beg any money for the stage from investors. As we only had that forty thousand, I was also in the new position of finding investors who would put up the estimated ninety to one hundred thousand to produce the show. . . ." and to provide the Guild with a reserve against losses.

Up in Fairfield, and down in Doylestown, a great American partnership was being melded, one whose impact on musical theatre would be revolutionary. "It didn't seem great at the time, however," Helburn commented. "At least to the people whom I bombarded with pleas to invest. Hammerstein, they told me sourly, had had two successive flops since his big hit with *Show Boat*.

"Dick and Oscar, knowing the financial situation of the Guild," she recounted, "went to work without even asking for an advance." Years later, Helburn assessed their partnership's virtues: "These two men have proved to be the most outstanding partners in their field, not merely financially, not even because of the magnificent work that has grown out of their collaboration. What has impressed me the most is the way in which two totally different personalities can complement one another so perfectly. Perhaps the only other comparable team was Gilbert and Sullivan . . . but that partnership was marred by personal hostility and bitterness."

Examined from a distance of fifty years, *Oklahoma!* seems a deceptively seamless piece of theatrical craftsmanship, simple and unsophisticated, but it is far more than that: It is a brilliantly imaginative, integrated work, one which broke many of the established rules of its time. There is an old adage that in order to break the rules one must first learn them. Both Hammerstein and Rodgers had paid their dues over the years while working with others. Together they applied everything they'd already learned to create a musical show that changed the form forever.

Years later, Stephen Sondheim perceptively commented on the magic worked by Rodgers and Hammerstein when they wrote their first score, weaving together libretto with music and lyrics and always welding it all to the characters. "You can transpose songs from *Lady Be Good* to *Funny Face*," said Sondheim, "but you can't move songs from *Oklahoma!* to *Carousel*." Everything they wrote that summer was of a piece, with the one exception of "Boys and Girls Like You and Me," a beautiful ballad which would be cut on the road because the director and the choreographer could not find a way to stage it. Translation: It had no relationship to any of the characters in the show.

Rodgers and Hammerstein had no idea that summer that this new musical they were working on would radically alter the form. But fortunately, each of them would later recount how their day-to-day labors would bear such remarkable fruit—Hammerstein, in his *Lyrics*, and Rodgers, in his *Musical Stages*.

HAMMERSTEIN: The first serious problem that faced us involved a conflict of dramaturgy with showmanship. As we planned our version, the story we had to tell in the first part of the first act did not call for the use of a female ensemble. The traditions of musical comedy, however, demand that not too long after the rise of the curtain the audience should be treated to one of musical comedy's most attractive assets—the sight of pretty girls in pretty clothes moving about the stage, the sound of their vital young voices supporting the principals in their songs. Dick and I for several days sought ways and means of logically introducing a group of girls into the early action of the play. The boys were no problem. Here was a farm in Oklahoma with ranches nearby. Farmers and cowboys belonged there, but girls in groups? No. Strawberry festivals? Quilting parties? Corny devices! After trying everything we could think of and rejecting each other's ideas as fast as they were submitted, after passing through phases during which we would stare silently at each other unable to think of anything at all, we came finally to an extraordinary decision. We agreed to start our story in the real and natural way in which it seemed to want to be told!

RODGERS: By opening the show with the woman alone onstage and the cowboy beginning his song offstage, we did more than set a mood; we were, in effect, warning the audience "Watch out! This is a different kind of musical." Everything in the production was made to conform to the simple open-air spirit of the story; this was essential and certainly a rarity in the musical theatre.

HAMMERSTEIN: This decision meant that the first act would be half over before a female chorus would make its entrance. We realized that such a course was experimental, amounting almost to the breach of implied contract with a musical comedy audience. I cannot say truthfully that we were worried by the risk.

Now, having met our difficulty by simply refusing to recognize its existence, we were ready to go ahead with the actual writing.

RODGERS: For twenty-five years the only way I could get Larry to do anything was virtually to lock him in a room and stay with him until the job was finished. Oscar's working habits were entirely the opposite. I remember that when I first started to talk to him about our method of collaboration, he seemed surprised at my question.

"I'll write the words, and you'll write the music" was all he said.

"In that order?" I asked.

"If that's all right with you. I prefer it that way. You won't hear from me until I have a finished lyric."

And for ninety percent of the time, that's the way we worked together.

HAMMERSTEIN: Searching for a subject for Curly to sing about, I recalled how deeply I had been impressed by Lynn Riggs's description at the start of his play:

> It is a radiant summer morning several years ago, the kind of morning which, enveloping the shapes of earth—men, cattle in the meadow, blades of the young corn, streams—makes them exist now for the first time, their images giving off a visible golden emanation that is partly true and partly a trick of the imagination, focusing to keep alive a loveliness that may pass away.

On first reading these words I had thought what a pity it was to waste them on stage directions. Only readers could enjoy them. Yet, if they did, how quickly they would slip into the mood of the story. Remembering this reaction, I reread the description and determined to put it into song. "Oh, What a Beautiful Mornin'" opens the play and creates an atmosphere of relaxation and peace and tenderness. It introduces the lighthearted young man who is the center of the story. My indebtedness to Mr. Riggs's description is obvious. The cattle and the corn and the golden haze on the meadow are all there. I added some observations of my own, based on my experience with beautiful mornings, and I brought the words down to the more primitive poetic level of Curly's character. He is, after all, just a cowboy and not a playwright.

RODGERS: Though Oscar was not a musician, he did possess a superb sense of form. He knew everything about the architecture of a song—its foundation, structure, embellishments—and because we always had thorough discussions on the exact kind of music that was needed, this method of collaboration helped us enormously in creating songs that not only were right for the characters who sang them but also possessed a union of words and music that made them sound natural.

HAMMERSTEIN: "The corn is as high as a elephant's eye"—I first wrote "cow pony's eye." Then I walked over to my neighbor's cornfield and found that although it was only the end of August, the corn had grown much higher than that. "Cow pony" was more indigenous to the western background, but I had reservations about it even before I gauged the height of the corn. It reads better than it sounds. Sing "cow pony" to yourself and try to imagine hearing it for the first time in a song. It would be hard for the ear to catch.

"All the cattle are standing like statues." This picture had come into my brain several years before I wrote the song, and it had stayed there, quietly waiting to be used. When I came to the second verse of "Oh, What a Beautiful Mornin'," I remembered it. I remembered sitting on a porch in Pennsylvania one summer's day, watching a herd of cows standing on a hillside about half a mile away. It was very hot and there was no motion in the world. I suddenly found myself doing what I had never done before and have never done since. I was thinking up lines for a poem to describe what I saw. It was not to be used in a play, not to be set to music. I got this far with it:

> The breeze steps aside
> To let the day pass.
> The cows on the hill
> Are as still as the grass.

I never wrote the lines on paper, nor did I ever do any work to polish them, nor did I extend the poem any further. Perhaps I was called to the phone, or perhaps I was infected with the laziness of an inactive landscape. But those cows on the hill "as still as the grass" were crystallized in my memory by the words I had quite idly and casually composed, and up they came several years later to inspire me when I needed them. . . .

It takes me a week, and sometimes three weeks, to write the words of a song. After I give them to [Dick], it takes him an hour or two and his work is over. He responds remarkably to words, and when he likes them, they immediately suggest tunes to him.

RODGERS: I was a little sick with joy because it was so lovely and so right. When you're given words like that you get something to say musically. You'd really have to be made of cement not to spark to that. . . . When the lyrics are right, it's easier to write a tune than to bend over and tie your shoe laces. Notes come more spontaneously than words. . . .

I remember that shortly before beginning the score Oscar sent me an impressively thick book of songs of the American Southwest which he thought might be of help; I opened the book, played through the music of one song, closed the book, and never looked at it again. If my melodies were going to be authentic, they'd have to be authentic on my own terms. . . . This is the way I have always worked, no matter what the setting of the story.

HAMMERSTEIN: The problem of a duet for the lovers in Oklahoma! seemed insurmountable. While it is obvious almost from the rise of the curtain that

Curly and Laurey are in love with each other, there is also a violent antagonism between them, caused mainly by Laurey's youthful shyness, which she disguises by pretending not to care for Curly. This does not go down very well with him, and he fights back. Since this mood was to dominate their scenes down into the second act, it seemed impossible for us to write a song that said "I love you" and remain consistent with the attitude they had adopted toward each other.

RODGERS: Oscar hit on the notion of having the young lovers warn each other against showing any signs of affection so that people won't realize they're in love. (Larry and I had already written a different song of this kind in "This Can't Be Love," and later Oscar and I would try another variation on the theme with "If I Loved You.")

This song also demonstrates another familiar problem, especially for lyric writers. There are, after all, only so many rhymes for the word "love," and when Oscar decided to call the duet "People Will Say We're in Love," he was determined to avoid using any of the more obvious ones. After spending days thinking about this one rhyme, he called me up exultantly to announce that he'd solved the problem. His solution: The girl ends the refrain by admonishing the boy:

> *Don't start collecting things,*
> *Give me my rose and my glove:*
> *Sweetheart, they're suspecting things—*
> *People will say we're in love.*

The next song would be "The Surrey with the Fringe on Top," also derived from Riggs's play. In the scene as written, Curly lures Laurey into going to the box social with him and describes the carriage in which they'll travel: "A bran' new surrey with fringe on the top four inches long—and yeller! And two white horses a-raring and faunching to go! You'd shore ride like a queen . . . and this here rig has got four fine side-curtains, case of a rain. And isinglass winders to look out of! And a red and green lamp set on the dashboard, winkin' like a lightnin' bug!"

RODGERS: Oscar's lyric suggested both a clip-clop rhythm and a melody in which the straight, flat country road could be musically conveyed through a repetition of the straight, flat sound of the D note, followed by a sharp upward flick as fowl scurry to avoid being hit by the moving wheels.

Hammerstein went to Doylestown, leaving Rodgers in Fairfield to spend that evening working on the beginning verse and the end. But he had no middle part, so he sat not so patiently waiting for his new partner to provide one. The following day Hammerstein arrived with lyrics that included a middle verse that gave Rodgers the exact meter.

The wheels are yeller, the upholstery's brown,
The dashboard's genuine leather.
With isinglass curtains you can roll right down,
In case there's a change in the weather.

That was all Rodgers needed to complete the song melodically forthwith.

RODGERS: Oscar was so moved by this song that just listening to it made him cry. He once explained that he never cried at sadness in the theatre, only at naive happiness, and the idea of two boneheaded young people looking forward to nothing more than a ride in a surrey struck an emotional chord that affected him deeply.

HAMMERSTEIN: Jud Fry worried us. A sulky farmhand, a "bullet-colored growly man," a collector of dirty pictures, he frightened Laurey by walking in the shadow of a tree beneath her window every night. He was heavy fare for a musical play. Yet his elimination was not to be considered because the drama he provided was the element that prevented this light lyric idyll from being so lyric and so idyllic that a modern theater audience might have been made sleepy, if not nauseous, by it. It was quite obvious that Jud was the bass fiddle that gave body to the orchestration of the story. The question was how to make him acceptable, not too much a deep-dyed villain, a scenery-chewer, an unmotivated purveyor of arbitrary evil. We didn't want to resort to the boring device of having two other characters discuss him and give the audience a psychological analysis. Even if this were dramatically desirable, there are no characters in this story who are bright enough or well-educated enough to do this. So we solved the problem with two songs, "Pore Jud" and "Lonely Room." They are both sung in the smokehouse set, the dingy hole where Jud lives with no companions but a mouse who nibbles on a broom and a gallery of "Police Gazette" pictures on the wall—a most uncompromising background from a musical standpoint.

In "Pore Jud," Curly, after suggesting to him how easy it would be for Jud to hang himself by a lasso from a rafter, goes on to describe what his funeral would be like. Unwelcome as the idea seems at first, Jud finds some features not unattractive to speculate on—the excitement he would cause by the gesture of suicide, the people who would come from miles around to weep and moan, especially the "womern" what had "tuk a shine" to Jud when he was alive. Jud is incredulous about these, but Curly points out that they "never come right out and show you how they feel, less'n you die first," and Jud allows that there's something in that theory. He becomes then, for a while, not just wicked, but a comic figure flattered by the attentions he might receive if he were dead. He becomes also a pathetic figure, pathetically lonely for attentions he has never received while alive. The audience begins to feel some sympathy for him, some understanding of him as a man.

In the second song, "Lonely Room," he paints a savage picture of his solitary life, his hatred of Curly, and his mad desire for Laurey. This is a self-analysis, but it is emotional and not cerebral. No dialogue could do this dramatic job as vividly and quickly as does the song. When Lynn Riggs attended a rehearsal of *Oklahoma!* for the first time, I asked him if he approved of this number. He said, "I certainly do. It will scare hell out of the audience." That is exactly what it was designed to do.

RODGERS: Oscar and I made a few changes in the basic plot and the characters. We added the part of Will Parker, Ado Annie's girlfriend, and we made her a more physically attractive girl. For the ending, we tied the strands together a bit more neatly than in the play by having Curly being found innocent of murdering Jud Fry, rather than being given his freedom for one night to spend with his bride.

Long after the fact, a friend asked Rodgers how long he had taken to compose the entire score. "Do you mean 'flying time' or 'elapsed time'?" asked Rodgers. When pressed for a definition, he explained: "Counting everything—overture, ballet music, all the songs, the most I could make it come to was about five hours—'flying time.' But the total 'elapsed time' covered months of discussion and planning."

At the Theatre Guild, plans were being laid to find financial backing. Though casting for the new production hadn't officially begun, an actor named Alfred Drake was called by the Guild—could he come in to discuss being part of the backers' auditions?

DRAKE: It was Dick Rodgers who suggested me. He knew me all the way back to *Babes in Arms*, in which I was one of the kid singers. I'd worked for the Guild the year before in *Yesterday's Magic*, and they were sure I could act. I'd missed out on Rodgers and Hart's *By Jupiter* because the Guild had no understudy for me in *Yesterday's Magic* and I couldn't leave it. The Guild had told me it was going to continue, so I stayed in that play instead of going with *Jupiter*. Then Paul Muni left *Magic*, after six weeks, and we closed—and there I was, waiting for the phone to ring.

Oscar didn't know me, so he asked if I'd come up and read for him. I went up and I read the part of Curly, with Oscar reading the other parts; he read very well. . . . I'd read about a page, and he stopped me and said, "Let me tell you what this is going to be." And he began to tell me about what he intended to do with the speech in which Curly describes the surrey to Laurey—he was going to make that into a song. He was charming, as always, and very enthusiastic. When he finished, I was as enthusiastic as he was; I was looking forward to it.

Then, a little while later, Rodgers asked me to meet him at Steinway Hall, in one of the studios. He wanted to play me some of the music and lyrics because they were going to do auditions for backers and I'd been asked to sing at them. So this was the first time I'd heard the score, and I was mad about it. It wasn't all written at this point, but I was terribly excited by what I'd heard. . . . But this is the strangest thing. If you knew Richard Rodgers, it's hard to think of him as being insecure. "Well, tell me," he asked, "do you really *mean* it?" "Yes, of course, I mean it!" I told him. "It's wonderful!"

"Well, you know," he said, thoughtfully, "this is the first time I've written with anybody excepting Larry. . . ."

Then he gave me copies of the sheet music—the very first lead sheets, and I went home and learned them. That private audition for me was pretty exciting; not only was the score beautiful, but he played so beautifully. When Richard played for me "Oh, What a Beautiful Mornin'," and I told him how much I loved it, it was so charming—he said, "Alfred, I must warn you, this is really only to set the scene. Don't expect much applause at the end of this number—it's *not* an applause-getter."

Broadway, Backers, and 1942

At the Theatre Guild offices, an aspiring playwright named Helene Hanff, who would later achieve success with her book *84 Charing Cross Road*, had managed to land a job. Hanff recalled years later in her memoir *Underfoot in Show Business*:

> "Joe Heidt needs an assistant," Terry Helburn said to me. "He's our press agent. Run up and tell him I said you need the job and you're very bright." So we found a typewriter for me, and I was assistant to the Theatre Guild press agent. The first show I assisted on was *Hope for a Harvest* by Sophie Treadwell, which flopped so badly that the stars, Fredric March and his wife, Florence Eldridge, took an ad in the papers the next day depicting a trapeze artist missing connections with his flying partner in mid-air, with a caption underneath that read, "Oops, sorry!"

By now the Guild was teetering on the brink. Hanff described the mood after yet another Guild failure, that of a play called *The Russian People*, in 1942:

> Looming up, according to the brochure we had sent out to Guild subscribers in nineteen subscription cities, was a new American Folk Opera. Like *Porgy and Bess*, we assured everybody. It was to be based on a flop the Guild had produced in the 1930s, and in true operatic tradition it was to have not only a murder committed onstage but a bona fide ballet.
>
> Considering our track record on even the most standard fare, this proposed epic had given everybody the jimjams. But it was budgeted at $100,000, and the rumors that reached us on the bleak December morn-

ing after *The Russian People* opened put an end to our worries about a $100,000 folk opera. The rumor was that after sixteen flops the Guild was bankrupt. By noon the next day word had spread from floor to floor that Terry and Lawrence were selling the Guild Theatre and building to pay their debts. When the sale was completed, the Theatre Guild would go out of existence.

People from the other departments wandered morosely into our office all day, to indulge in the usual morning-after castigation of the management. Our top floor was ideal for this, since it was the one place where Terry and Lawrence could be counted on not to set foot, especially in December.

On this particular day, the tone was especially bitter. Not just because December is a very cold month to be thrown out of work in, but because for all their talk, nobody who worked there was terribly anxious to see the Theatre Guild close down. Most of them could remember the great days: the Lunts, and the Shaw openings, and the five-hour O'Neill drama which one doorman was said to have referred to innocently throughout its run as "Strange Intercourse."

Joe and I made up the ads in a thick gloom. . . . Then Joe went down to get Lawrence's OK on the ads, and I went down to get Terry's. She was in her office, in an armchair, having tea. Her fluffy white hair was rinsed a deep cerulean blue that season, and her toy-bulldog face was as cheerful as ever.

"Well, dear," she said, "we seem to be having a run of bad luck!". . . glancing at the bad reviews now and then to check a quote against the ad and murmuring, "I don't know what the boys want!"

As I reached the door she said, patting her hair casually, "I notice Lawrence was first on the program, dear. That's twice in a row, isn't it?"

If the program for one show read "Produced by Lawrence Langner and Theresa Helburn," the program for the next show had to read "Produced by Theresa Helburn and Lawrence Langner."

I said I was sure Mr. Langner hadn't been first twice in a row, because Joe was always careful to rotate and always had me check the last program before he made up the new one.

"All right," she said agreeably. "Just remind him; I'm first on the new show."

My gloom evaporated. *The Russian People* hadn't been the one-flop-too-many after all. We were going to do another one.

We read about it the next day in one of the gossip columns. Joe came in with the afternoon papers and said resignedly: "Terry scooped her own press department again."

She was always scooping us. . . . It now turned out that between acts of *The Russian People* she had told a columnist—in strictest confidence—

that the composer and librettist had finished the new Theatre Guild operetta and that it was to be called *Away We Go!*

Down the hall, Jack, the auditor, floating on a sea of unpaid bills, screamed at anybody who went past, "What the hell do they think they'll produce a musical with? What are they using for money?" And the question was indeed pertinent.

Helburn herself confirmed Jack the auditor's outcry. "I don't think I've ever worked harder than I did on trying to wrest and beguile that hundred thousand dollars from reluctant and frankly skeptical investors," she said with feeling. She'd certainly picked a dreadful time to try to raise money. The summer and fall of 1942 were far and away the darkest times of World War II. Americans, still smarting from the astonishing defeat at Pearl Harbor, gritted their teeth at the loss of the Bataan peninsula, with the ensuing dreadful Death March of General Wainwright's troops. People were learning to do without. Consumer goods were set aside until the war was over (who knew when?). So a new car was a fond dream, and even if you had wheels, where could you go on severely rationed gas? Cigarettes, Scotch whisky, new tires, sirloins and porterhouses, nylons—all were suddenly unavailable, except on the black market. Of course, for years Manhattan theatregoers had known how to get two good seats to Broadway's latest hit. You slipped the cash into the scalper's open hand and presto, you were down front, in third row center.

In Manhattan's theatre district, and everywhere else in town, there was a nightly brownout to save energy. Restaurant signs, theatre marquees, and those old reliable Times Square advertising displays were dimmed or totally put out. And Sardi's Restaurant, on West 44th Street, served cottage cheese instead of scarce butter; since old Mr. Sardi vehemently refused to deal in the black market, his patrons did without meat. Ergo, one plowed through piles of spaghetti with tomato sauce and endless servings of canneloni stuffed with cheese and left Sardi's feeling virtuous, if a bit gassy. But the crowds kept coming to the theatres. They'd had their shoes repaired (or half-soled) to save leather, gone without sugar, cut down on cigarettes, given to the USO and knitted sweaters and socks for the boys overseas, bought War Savings Stamps, and done without practically everything.

Except amusement. That was a necessity. These would be boom times for movie houses, and for the West Coast studios that were cranking out films. More ticket buyers than ever jammed the picture palaces (which in some towns across the land were staying open twenty-four hours, featuring 4 A.M. double-feature bills called "swing-shift matinees"). Escapist entertainment kept the orchestra seats in New York's legitimate theatres filled nightly with tired businessmen and their customers, fresh-faced soldiers and sailors in town for a hurried two- or three-day pass, and home-front citizens taking a few hours off, all of them seeking a couple of hours of release.

Audiences needed hope—served up with bright lights, laughter, and foot-tapping songs—the same prescription that had sold tickets to our grandparents in World War I. It's a mess over there, but we'll come out of it winners, you bet we will! That was what show business could assure us.

When the Theatre Guild came knocking on doors and making phone calls, searching for potential backers for this new Rodgers and Hammerstein musical version of Riggs's play, the response was negative. Not passively negative, but aggressively so. For openers, this Guild venture had no stars. Helburn made a valiant try to do something tangible about that. Despite Rodgers and Hammerstein's initial disapproval, she suggested box-office names. Since her debut in *Leave It to Me*, the brightest young leading lady in town was sparkling Mary Martin. Unfortunately, she was already booked for a new musical called *Dancing in the Streets*, a venture that would make it to Boston, where it would close, ironically enough, while *Oklahoma!* was running there at the Colonial.

Shirley Temple for Laurey? Miss Temple's parents did not feel the part was right for their daughter. Deanna Durbin was suggested, but Universal's president, Nate Blumberg, refused to release his star to appear in a chancy Broadway show. For the part of Ali Hakim, the peddler, Helburn thought of Groucho Marx. When Marx turned her down, Helburn began to waver. Rodgers and Hammerstein were certain they were right: No "stars"; let their work stand or fall on its own merit.

When Helburn conceded to them, she was back to square one—where and how to raise the necessary funds to get this show produced. "Lawrence and I put our heads together, did some figuring. We decided to put in $25,000 of the Guild's own capital. That left us $15,000 for 'emergencies.' A private pool of regular backers [among them Lee Shubert and the American Theatre Society] came in with an additional $15,000. So we started with $40,000, knowing we must double it to raise the curtain."

Going out to unknown investors was a new experience for the Guild. Helburn began a series of auditions. Hammerstein read aloud from the book and did Aunt Eller. Alfred Drake sang Curly, and a pert young leading lady, Joan Roberts, who'd recently been in Hammerstein's last failure, *Sunny River*, sang Laurey. The duo-piano accompanists were Rodgers and his faithful rehearsal pianist, Margot Hopkins. (Helburn chafed at the $25 extra rental for the second piano, but reluctantly agreed.)

The tiny troupe began a tour of what Rodgers later referred to as "the penthouse circuit." Upper-echelon Park Avenue audiences sat and listened, drinks in hand, while the script was read and the two young singers performed the lovely score. The reactions were polite. But night after night the Guild came away empty. "It's ironic," said Helburn later, "to think of the difficulty we had in promoting thousands for a show which was to gross millions." But to such society audiences, nothing about this new show was attractive. "I remember the flat, empty feeling I had when a woman for whom we put on this performance, our hostess at a particularly splendid apartment, all white-and-gold and filled with chic people, all her friends, said, in a chilly voice, 'I don't like plays about farmhands.'" Helburn wrote in her autobiography.

"Then came those Broadway regulars, 'angels,'" she continued. "Their response was universal. 'Helburn's Folly' began to be known on Broadway as the Guild's 'No-play.'" One of those old Broadway hands was Howard S. Cullman, a dapper, successful businessman who thrived on investing in plays and musicals produced by his many theatrical pals. A good friend of Rodgers, he'd invested over many years in Rodgers and Hart musicals, with excellent returns. When Helburn approached him, he read the script and sent her a polite demurral. Years later, Cullman asked for his letter back. He framed it and hung it on his office wall, to remind himself of his fallibility. Ten years after the fact he ruefully remarked, "That letter must have cost me $970,000."

MGM had the screen rights to *Green Grow the Lilacs*, and Helburn hurried over to see J. Robert Rubin, head of the East Coast office. Rubin offered to forward Hammerstein's libretto to his boss, L. B. Mayer, to ascertain whether MGM would consider investing in the show. It was a fairly straightforward proposal: Helburn suggested MGM put up $69,000 in return for 50 percent of the musical's eventual profit and an additional $75,000 if it wished to acquire the screen rights. (MGM owned the rights only to Riggs's play, which it had purchased from RKO, which had bought them in 1931.) Should the show succeed, MGM would recoup its original investment, and if it were to fail, the studio would have lost a mere $69,000, which, for the Culver City studio at least, was petty cash.

Back came an abrupt Mayer turndown. MGM, it seemed, was "not interested in backing Western musicals."

But Helburn did not quit. As Rodgers fondly remarked to her, "Your name is Terry, but it should be Terrier." Since MGM wasn't investing, and owned the underlying rights to the play, it looked doubtful that the Guild could interest any other prospective backers, whose lawyers would (rightly enough) point out that should the show succeed the backers would have no future share in any film rights. So she returned to MGM with another proposal concerning the eventual film rights to the new Hammerstein libretto. And this time out, Hammerstein pulled a few strings. He'd been negotiating a contract with MGM to function as Arthur Freed's associate producer at the studio (insurance lest this current venture flop). Freed was a Hammerstein fan, as was L. B. Mayer. Hammerstein pleaded Helburn's case: The Guild desperately need an option from MGM on the film rights in order to lure backers. Could Mayer see his way clear to granting the Guild such an option? If the show flopped, it would cost MGM nothing.

The request seemed fair enough, so MGM granted the Guild an option to exercise the purchase of the film rights to Riggs's original play for $40,000 within thirty days after the opening of the Guild's new musical play version of said show. The MGM people reasoned that this show wouldn't get on, and if it did it couldn't be a hit—hadn't L. B. Mayer already passed on it? Which meant that Hammerstein would eventually have to show up for work at Freed's MGM unit after it flopped. So why not do Oscar this favor? Some day he'd be called on to pay it back. Meanwhile it cost MGM nothing.

Helburn and the Guild got their option on the film rights. (It would be exercised within twenty-four hours after the successful opening of the show in March by a triumphant Helburn and her creative associates.)

Meanwhile, raising the nonexistent backing continued, with nightly auditions.

"All those auditions that we held never raised a penny," commented Alfred Drake years later. "And believe me, we did quite a few."

"I turned to rival producers," said Helburn. "They usually bought a slice of each other's productions. They looked over the book. 'Too clean,' they declared. 'It hasn't a chance.' When you're raising money, people reminded me, you ought to offer them a sure-fire success, not a play that hasn't done so well in the past. Musicals, they told me with disgust, don't have murders in the second act."

But she never wavered. "I became almost demented in my attempts to get investors," she said. "For the first time since the Guild had really got into its stride, years ago, we had no business manager. Warren Munsell, our staff of strength, had been called into the army. For one dark period Dick Rodgers expected to get a commission in the air force, and Oscar wondered if perhaps he'd be wiser to call it quits and go out to MGM in California."

Harry Cohn had been invited to the Park Avenue audition in that white-and-gold apartment. But the gruff, outspoken boss of Columbia Pictures ("He was a great friend, and a great enemy," one Hollywood wit remarked) hadn't shown up; he'd been busy. Remarkably enough, at a restaurant the following night, Langner and Helburn were seated adjacent to Cohn, who was dining with Columbia executive Nate Spingold and one of his stars, Grace Moore.

"Harry was somewhat apologetic," said Helburn. "He came over to our table, put his arm around me. 'You know, folks,' he said, 'I'm not really interested in the theatre; I'm a picture man. If I go in, then I must take less of the play but more of the picture rights for Columbia.'

" 'If you're really serious,' we said, 'there'll be a special audition for you.' It was arranged for the following Saturday afternoon at Steinway Hall.

Cohn had begun his career years back as a "song-plugger" along with songwriter Harry Ruby, going from cafe to saloon, vaudeville house to beer garden, demonstrating the latest wares of music publishers to prospective buyers and performers. He'd never lost his affinity for songwriters. The prospect of having Richard Rodgers and Oscar Hammerstein demonstrate their newest work for him, and for him alone, must have gratified Cohn's ego mightily.

On Saturday afternoon Hammerstein read, Drake and Roberts sang, and

Rodgers and Hopkins played to a small but powerful audience. "As we came to the end of Act One," remembered Helburn, "I said, 'At this point, the ballet takes over.'

"Cohn grimaced. 'Ballet? In a musical show? One of these?' He stood on his toes, hands flipped over his head in an airy circle, and all but pirouetted.

"My storytelling couldn't compete, so I stopped. Harry listened to the music for a while; then he jumped up impetuously.

"'I like it!' he'd decided. 'Dick's songs. Oscar's book. The whole idea! If you'll all come out to the studio and make the picture, I'll put up all the money!'

"It was a typical offer, but one we all felt was impossible to accept. Finally, the offer was withdrawn, and Cohn suggested Columbia merely invest."

It seemed a *fait accompli*. But remarkably, Columbia's board of directors would not go along with their boss's enthusiasm. Once again, despite the reaction from Cohn and his New York associate, producer Max Gordon, the Guild was back to square one. That is, until Cohn agreed to invest, at Gordon's urging, $15,000 of his own money—provided that Gordon would join him for an additional sum.

Other monies trickled in. Helburn continued nagging, arguing, persuading. Playwright S. N. Behrman, who'd had many successes with the Guild, was approached (or perhaps a better word would be "sandbagged") by the diminutive Terry. When she finished twisting his arm and reminding him of the Guild's loyalty to him, he conceded and wrote his check for $5,000. At the time he thought he was lending Helburn the money. Happily for Behrman, he was a limited partner, and his $5,000 would net him thousands of dollars return over the years, as well as a reputation for theatrical astuteness. Behrman later, somewhat wryly, pointed out, "I now have a reputation as the most discriminating of investors."

As the backing arrived slowly and none too lavishly, Helburn was faced with another calculation. The Guild might be able to put the show into production in that dreary fall of 1942, but could they proceed without the full capitalization of $100,000? No matter how she and Langner skimped on production costs, pinching pennies here and there, they still faced an out-of-town tryout. In New Haven and Boston they would play the show to audiences that might or might not buy tickets under a starless marquee, even if the reviews were good. Many a previous show had foundered on such reefs and sunk out-of-town without a trace. One of the last of the Rodgers and Hart collaborations, *By Jupiter*, starring Ray Bolger, an established "draw," had lost $17,000 on its tryout the previous year. Producer Dwight Deere Wiman had brought it to New York where it succeeded and recouped those losses eventually. But Wiman had money in the bank. The Guild had little reserves. The cost of this show hadn't been raised. Could it withstand any future disasters?

"In reserve," said Helburn, "we had the slender fund of $15,000. Lawrence said to me one day, 'This is how it is. If we lose five thousand dollars a week

March 5, 1943.

Scenery:	Designing		3100.	
	Building		6300.	
	Extras: Traveler	- 823.		
	Drapes	- 650.		
	Extra Set	- 590.	2288.	
	Extra Border	- 225.		
	Painting		4500.	
	Labor		400.	16,588.
Props:	Purchase		1500.	
	Labor		425.	1,925.
Electrics:	Purchase		700.	
	Labor		850.	1,550.
Cartage				650.
Costumes:	Design		2000.	
	Purchase		15000.	
	Shoes		1760.	
	Labor		130.	18,890.
Rehearsal:	Stage Labor		2500.	
	Musicians		3000.	
	Producing Dir.		3500.	
	Dance Director		1500.	
	Cast Salaries		5500.	
	Theatre Rental		1000.	
	Piano Rental		125.	17,125.
Press:	Agent's salary		350.	
	Newspaper		500.	
	Signs, printing		750.	
	Photos		700.	
	Press, other		150.	2,450.
Auditions			725.	
Scripts			150.	
Insurance			50.	
Author's Expenses			800.	
Director's "			400.	
Board's "			500.	
Orchestration			5,000.	
Transportation			350.	
Social Security			300.	
Office Expense			1,250.	
Audit			60.	9,585.
			SUB-TOTAL	$68,763.
Bonds:	15,200.			
Loss Provision:	15,000.			30,200.
				$98,963.

Here, in a historic document, we may note the cost figures for the Guild's production of *Away We Go!* which seem ridiculously low from the perspective of today, when Broadway musicals are budgeted at around $6 million.

during the three weeks we're out of town, and we use our own money now as an investment to cover that, then the Guild treasury can be wiped out.' So, to my later regret, we went out and raised additional funds, as a safeguard." Had the Guild used its own capital, the eventual profits derived from that $15,000 would have accrued not to those lucky backers whom they finally persuaded to invest but to the Guild itself!

It would take Helburn more time to dragoon the rest of the $100,000. For the record, the entire capitalization of what would eventually be *Oklahoma!* came from a small list of twenty-eight hardy investors. And while she pursued them, Helburn had many more problems confronting her. Foremost was the vital question: Who should direct this show, not *if* it went into production— no one could deter her from achieving that—but *when?*

Putting It Together

T he search for a director had begun as early as June 1942, when Rodgers got in touch with Joshua Logan; both were fresh from their success with *By Jupiter.* Logan would have been delighted to work with Rodgers, especially now that it would give him a chance to join forces with Hammerstein, but that would have to wait until after the war. Logan had also gotten a call from Uncle Sam.

Helburn then suggested Bretaigne Windust, a director who'd done *Arsenic and Old Lace, Life with Father, Idiot's Delight,* and *Amphitryon 38,* a string of solid legitimate hits. But his background as far as musicals went was limited to a rag-tag exhibit called *Strip for Action.* By mutual agreement with her partners Helburn moved on, and she decided to try for the brilliant Elia Kazan, who had just directed the highly successful production of Thornton Wilder's *The Skin of Our Teeth.* On November 21 she sent him a wire at the Plymouth Theatre suggesting he pick up a copy of Hammerstein's script at the Guild Theatre box office. "Please keep confidential," cautioned her message.

"I reread *Green Grow* carefully," said Kazan's return wire, "and I just don't click with it. I'm afraid I'd do a very mediocre job and neither of us would benefit. I'd feel so proud and honored to do a show for you, but this had better not be it. Best always, Gadget."

Then, in December, Rouben Mamoulian came to town.

The Guild's association with that talented director had begun years back when Mamoulian won the critics' ovations for staging DuBose Heyward's play *Porgy,* in 1927. In the following years the Armenian-born Mamoulian had done considerable work for the Guild, staging Eugene O'Neill's *Marco Millions,* Karel Capek's *R.U.R.,* and Turgenev's *A Month in the Country.* In 1929 he'd made the crossover from the Broadway theatre to film, at the Paramount Astoria studios, where talking pictures were being produced with New York theatre talents. He went to Hollywood and made a remarkable version of *Dr. Jekyll and Mr. Hyde*, with Fredric March and Miriam Hopkins. Then, in 1932, he directed *Love Me Tonight*, starring Maurice Chevalier and Jeanette MacDonald singing the Rodgers and Hart score. Mamoulian then made the first feature film in Technicolor, *Becky Sharp*, again with Miriam Hopkins.

He returned to the Guild and Broadway in 1936, when he staged the now-classic Heyward–Gershwin opera *Porgy and Bess*. But these were the 1930s, and the theatre was unable to lure talent away from high-salaried Hollywood assignments that had long-term studio contracts attached to them. Mamoulian went back West to do more films.

Helburn sent a script to Mamoulian's Gotham Hotel suite in December 1942. Mamoulian had been occupied making *The Mark of Zorro* and *Blood and Sand* for Twentieth Century-Fox. The script struck a responsive chord in him: "When I laid the story down," he told Helburn, "I knew I was on my way back to Broadway and the theatre."

Compared with his customary Hollywood salary, the terms Mamoulian agreed to with Helburn and Langner were minuscule. His fee would be $3,000, to be paid at $500 per week for five weeks and $250 for the two weeks after opening out of town—plus a weekly royalty of 1 percent of the weekly box-office gross after the show opened in New York. Certainly Mamoulian had gambled before, but never would he end up with such a jackpot as that 1 percent of the show's gross eventually provided him, week after week, year after year.

Now that Helburn finally had her director to stage the show when and if the rehearsals began, she needed a choreographer. When one was finally hired, it would be the Guild that was gambling. Earlier that fall, Langner had written to Rodgers:

Sept. 30, 1942

Dear Dickie:

Agnes de Mille, who is an old friend of mine, asked me if I would speak to you about the possibility of her working on the dancing for *Green Grow the Lilacs*. She has done some very good comedy ballets as well as aesthetic ones. She is doing a Wild West Rodeo Ballet at the opening of the Metropolitan Ballet season, and you really should go and see this because it shows her ability to handle Western material.

Please give this your usual kind consideration.

Sincerely,

Lawrence Langner

"Dickie" and his partner Hammerstein accompanied Helburn to the opening night of de Mille's ballet *Rodeo*, which she had choreographed to the music of Aaron Copland, on October 16, 1942. "This was not a great performance," de Mille said later. "We gave better, later. Neither was it a great ballet. . . . But it was the first of its kind, and the moment was quick with birth." The approving audience granted the young de Mille, her choreography, and her dancers twenty-two curtain calls.

The next day she received a telegram from Theresa Helburn: "We think your work is enchanting. Come talk to us Monday."

Agnes de Mille's colorful dances for *Oklahoma!* echoed her spirited 1942 ballet *Rodeo*, which firmly established her as an outstanding dancer and choreographer. (Courtesy of Beinecke Library)

Hammerstein had known of de Mille's work for many years. He had attended her first recital in 1930, in California, and in de Mille's own recollection, "stood by the side of his handsome wife and gazed with benevolence and kindly enthusiasm." Hammerstein had been certain that this young daughter of film producer William de Mille had talent. His only reservation was the question of how she might channel it.

Rodgers wasn't certain she could make the crossover from ballet to the Broadway stage. He understood well what was involved; he had been one of the first Broadway composers to tackle ballet. In *On Your Toes* he'd created the first act "Princesse Zenobia" ballet, a sly take-off of Rimsky-Korsakovian opulence, and he'd followed it with the climactic "Slaughter on Tenth Avenue," in which Ray Bolger, Tamara Geva, and George Church danced to George Balanchine's choreography. But that show had been a musical in which the ballets were part of the story of a hoofer from a vaudeville family trying to make it in ballet.

In the Guild's new show, the choreography would reveal character and further the story. There was no precedent for this; it was all new. Could this young woman carry out such a major task? Rodgers was worried, and de Mille understood the problem. "He recognized clearly the crucial difference between the two media," she remarked later.

Langner and Helburn both felt certain that de Mille would provide an excitingly fresh element to the show, but the final decision was slow in coming. "Even after the success of *Rodeo* I just barely succeeded in getting the show," de Mille wrote in her memoirs. "Indeed, I heard nothing official until I met Oscar Hammerstein, by chance, in a New York drugstore, and knocked a plate off the counter in my haste to speak to him. Dick had qualms, he said. I continued pressing until Dick capitulated."

When de Mille's deal was negotiated she would receive $1,500 for six weeks' work and thereafter $50 a week for ten weeks after the production cost of the show was paid off. Hardly munificent, but it was de Mille's big chance. The terms agreed upon, she went on her scheduled Ballet Russe de Monte Carlo tour. Before she left, Rodgers played her his score so she would be familiar with the work she had to do. "When I heard it the first time," she remembered, "I was just open-mouthed, and I said to him, 'Why, that's like Schubert, some of that.'

"On my tour went a blank copybook labeled 'Lilacs,' with pages entitled 'Ballet—Many a New Day,' 'Cowman and the Farmer,' 'Kansas City,' 'Jud's Postcards,' and as I sat happily in hotel bedrooms, I made my notes." She toured California and returned to New York ready to work.

"I went for my first interview very firm and determined," she remembered. "Hammerstein seemed understanding, but as I had found out, one could never tell. First, I informed him, I must insist that there be no one in the chorus I didn't approve. 'Oh, pshaw!' he murmured. He was sorry to hear I was going to take that attitude—there was his regular girl, and Lawrence Langner had two, and Dick Rodgers always counted on some. For one beat I took him literally, there being no trace of anything except earnestness on his face, and then I relaxed on that score for the rest of my life."

But Hammerstein would soon enough discover that de Mille was ready to lock horns on more basic problems. She'd been doing her homework on their script and already had big questions for him and Rodgers. She didn't agree with Hammerstein's first-act closer. "The ballet that was outlined by Hammerstein was to be a circus," she said. "And I was the one who said it didn't make any sense. Oscar said, 'You've got to have a light ballet to end our Act One with, you can't send them out into the lobby with gloom.' I said, 'Why not? Just depress the hell out of them.' And I did my spiel, and they listened. Now this was so because they were very gifted men. But I absolutely threw out that circus ballet." De Mille's brilliant solution would be another ballet, "Laurey Makes Up Her Mind."

Between steady badgering and arm-twisting of potential investors—for the final backing was not yet all in place—Helburn went on assembling a creative cadre for the show. "The locale of the show, the Oklahoma Territory at the turn of the century, was an ugly period for clothes," she observed. "The choice of a costume designer was of vital importance for this reason. At the Guild we'd been impressed by the brilliant color and flair two young men had provided, for Alfred Lunt and Lynn Fontanne, in our previous production of S. N. Behrman's *The Pirate*. One was Miles White, who'd designed the lavish costumes. I told him I was worried about the 'period.' Those high, tight little collars on our chorus youngsters? The white shirtwaists, long skirts hiding pretty legs? The hats in those days seemed so unwieldy. Would the effect of all those birds' wings, ruffles, and flounces be comic? We certainly didn't want the costumes to have a dated charm, but instead be lovely to remember."

The show must have been a challenge for young White, who'd come to New York from California and spent his first years in the theatre doing costumes for traditional musicals like *Best Foot Forward* and the newest edition of *Ziegfeld Follies*, both light-years away from turn-of-the-century Oklahoma. But he went to his studio and returned with designs for this off-the-beaten-track venture. "Laurey's wedding gown . . . "exulted Helburn, "Ado Annie's gay pink flounces . . . the checkerboard suit of Ali Hakim, the peddler . . . all those warm blends of color and grace which would cause such gasps of delighted comment when the ballet swept onstage."

Miles White's inspiration? "I borrowed a 1904–5 Montgomery Ward catalogue from Dazian's—that was the fabric house where Emil Friedlander supplied us with all the various materials. When I went through those pages I found out exactly how the people dressed in that period, both men and women—it was all there, even the hats. And I knew that even if they didn't buy them, or couldn't afford those outfits in the catalogue, people in Oklahoma would copy them," said White.

The scenery was designed by the other young man from *The Pirate*, Lemuel Ayers, who would go on to become the coproducer of Cole Porter's 1948 smash musical *Kiss Me Kate*. Ayers's challenge was to evoke the broad Oklahoma plains but to keep it simple, not only aesthetically but also—and most important, considering the present state of the Guild's bank account—financially.

Against sweeping vistas Ayers placed a few minimal stage props—a chair, a table, here a butter churn, there a piece of fencing. "He caught at once the clear blue blaze of sky we wanted," said Helburn. "The hot yellow sunshine of Oklahoma, the shades of wheat and tall corn." Ayers's designs had the simplicity of genre painting, but on a stage they became most evocative.

"What we also needed, as supervisor of the overall production, was a top stage manager," said Helburn. She recalled:

> Someone thoroughly skilled in the routine of stage details. Dick Rodgers got hold of Jerry Whyte, who'd been so efficient on several of Rodgers and Hart's previous musicals, most recently *Pal Joey* and *By Jupiter*. A big, tough "sergeant-major" type of man, Whyte knew his Broadway. Over at the Guild, we hadn't met him before. "Go around and drop in on the Guild directors," Dick told him. "Stop in and ask for Terry Helburn."
>
> I found out later how Mr. Whyte first expected he'd be meeting some burly Irish type named "Terry." I am probably the shortest living producer in town. Five feet one in my nylons. Billy Rose tops me by an inch or two. My office desk is large; that day, it was piled high. Behind scripts and contracts I had my nose well down in a cup of tea. Big Jerry Whyte peered down at me; he was looking for somebody named Terry. Could I help him? I could. "How about stage managing this show for us?" I asked.
>
> "Us?" he asked.
>
> "Me, and Lawrence Langner, here at the Guild," I explained.

Jerry quickly got the message. Out came his large hand with a firm tingle of good will attached.

Elaine Steinbeck, who'd been present two years before when the whole project sparked into life, was already on the Guild's staff, and now she would work with Jerry Whyte.

Robert Russell Bennett would do the orchestrations for Rodgers' music. To conduct, Rodgers wanted young Johnny Green. A successful songwriter in his own right ("Body and Soul," "Out of Nowhere," and many others), Green had conducted *By Jupiter*, and that venture had so pleased Rodgers that he proposed to Green that he assume that task for the Guild.

Lemuel Ayers's now aged set-design drawings, with their details of rural life at the turn of the century. For the old smokehouse, home to the menacing Jud Fry, Ayers provided an especially dismal environment. (Courtesy of the Museum of the City of New York)

"I had already signed," Green remembered, "and I was particularly happy about that because Dick had teamed up with Oscar, whom I adored. But Arthur Freed of MGM insisted, 'You've got to come to Metro!'"

Hammerstein had another young man in mind, a talented newcomer who'd been at the St. Louis Municipal Opera for six years working on summer seasons of musicals. His name was Jacob Schwartzdorf, and he had conducted Hammerstein's *Sunny River*. But Schwartzdorf, who would shortly change his name to Blackton, wasn't sure he wished to commit to the project. "In my pocket I had a contract for a seventh summer in St. Louis, a firm commitment," he said. "I was also coaching at the Juilliard School. To me, the gamble of being on Broadway was a little more than I was willing to accept." Blackton's ambition was to become an opera conductor. This new venture did not seem all that promising. Did he want to give up a permanent summer season for something which could flop and leave him stranded?

The first meeting of the cast, at which Rodgers and Hammerstein would demonstrate their score, was imminent. Blackton was invited. "I reluctantly came," he said.

> I wanted to be there, but I didn't want them to feel in any way that I'd committed myself. I'd spoken to Dick and told him my problem; he appreciated it, he understood. Oscar was a little firmer in trying to push me into making up my mind. . . .
>
> They started off with the first song, which was 'Oh, What a Beautiful Mornin'.' When the song was over, I was filled with emotion at the beauty and the simplicity of this work, which had such a wonderful lyric! It sparkled, as the morning sun sparkles! I was overcome with it. I leaned over, and I very boldly whispered in Rodgers' ear, in the most affectionate manner . . . I just blurted out . . . *"You son of a bitch!"*

Casting

When it came time to assemble a cast for the musical version of *Green Grow the Lilacs*, there arose a new set of problems. Each of the creative minds on Helburn's crew had entirely different sets of images in mind for the performers who'd populate the show. "Auditioning was no bed of roses," remembered Helburn, who quickly discovered she'd opened a Pandora's box of complex priorities. "Oscar wanted people who could speak his lines. Dick wanted people who could sing. . . . So we held auditions for a long time, hearing everyone we could."

In rugged circumstances. Vivian Smith, who would shortly become one of de Mille's most reliable ballerinas, shuddered at the memory: "Oh, those auditions at the Guild Theatre! I remember Dick and Oscar were sitting out front, all bundled up in their overcoats, in that cold barn. Remember, the Guild was about to sell the theatre, and they were so short of money, nobody could afford to turn on the heat!"

Day after day they sat, watching and listening. "Our intent was to discover actors who could sing," said Helburn. "The leading parts must be played by actors with dramatic talent, plus the unusual combination of an attractive singing voice. That's how we ended up with a cast of people most of whom were fresh to musical comedy."

Alfred Drake had been cast for Curly, and Joan Roberts, who had joined him in all those fund-raising auditions that so far hadn't raised many funds, would be Laurey. As the auditions continued, other talents joined the cast list.

Lee Dixon, a jovial young song-and-dance man who'd had a modest success in Warner Bros. musicals in Hollywood, was the ideal choice for Will Parker, who'd pursue Ado Annie and marvel at the virtues of up-to-date Kansas City. Betty Garde, a leading New York radio actress for many years, seemed right for Aunt Eller and was promptly signed. (Alas, after rehearsals began her part became subject to constant cutting. Trouper that she was, Miss Garde swallowed her disappointment and pride and stayed with the show.) Joseph Buloff, a star with considerable experience at the Yiddish Art Theatre, had the correct comic sense to play Ali Hakim, the peddler, and Howard Da Silva, who had shuttled between Broadway's Group Theatre and Hollywood for the past decade, was the choice to play the dark and menacing Jud Fry.

The real controversy began when it came to the dance ensemble. The young dancers de Mille brought in for auditions were far different from what the producers expected. "Agnes," said Helburn, "wanted people who could dance." Whether or not the dancers fit the acceptable Broadway dancing-girl mold was of no interest to the choreographer. "Why, I kept asking, can't we have girls who can dance and also have pretty legs? It seemed reasonable to me. It seemed unreasonable to Agnes."

"I knew these girls," de Mille recalled later. "I'd studied with them and we'd had classes together. I'd seen them grow up from brats to mature sixteen-year-olds, and they were extravagantly gorgeous. Bambi Linn, Diana Adams, and Joanie McCracken. These were personalities, and they were soloists, and they had big, strong techniques. But when Bambi came to a rehearsal, with braces on her teeth, and she looked like hell, she had a fur hat on that made her look like a rabbit in a tea cozy, I'd never seen such goings on." (Neither, it is safe to say, had Messrs. Rodgers, Hammerstein, and Mamoulian.) An amateur in the world of show business Bambi may have been, but not when dancing. "I'd say to Bambi, 'Jump!' and she'd spring like Baryshnikov," said de Mille. "She had the jump of a deer—it was simply amazing."

Arguments ensued, the show business veterans insisting on some representation of sheer beauty in the ensemble, whether such women were dancers or not. "Just for appearance's sake," says de Mille, "we took in two chorus girls.

At auditions for chorus and ensemble, Rodgers is in a watchful mood.

They seemed terrified at the vigorous company they found themselves suddenly in, and sat or stood, locked close together from pure loneliness."

For the lead in her ballet "Laurey Makes up Her Mind," which would close Act One, de Mille cast her good friend, the beautiful Katharine (Katya) Sergava, of the Ballet Theatre. "And then I brought in Diana Adams," she said, "who had extraordinary techniques; I mean, she could do anything you asked for."

Adams was a demure beauty. "She could be the typical showgirl type that Rodgers was used to," commented Bambi Linn. She pleased Hammerstein as well. ("She's like everybody's little sister," he'd remarked fondly.) But Linn and McCracken were different: "We were little girls with piano legs," Linn said. "And Rodgers took one look at us, and he said to Agnes, 'Uh-uh. No.' Agnes started bargaining. She said, 'Well, let me have one of those, and you can have two of yours.' That's how she bargained. I remember that so well; my life was on the line, so how could I forget it? And Agnes was furious that she had to bargain that way."

Originally, de Mille had thought of Linn to be her Laurey in that first-act closing ballet. But eventually, when Sergava was cast, Linn 's characterization had to be changed; she would be a very young girl in the same scene. "So whenever I appeared in the ballets," Linn recalled, "my skirts were shorter, I had pigtails, and that's why you noticed me. Not that I had that much to do—I stood out because I was the little girl."

Another of de Mille's choices was Kate Friedlich, a longtime friend of the choreographer who'd been dancing professionally for many years. The two had met in Des Moines, where Friedlich lived. "I was also asked by Agnes if I'd put in some rehearsal time before the actual rehearsals began," Friedlich said. "Sometimes a choreographer will work with a few dancers for several weeks, in order to get a running start on the choreography."

When it came to a discussion of Friedlich's salary, the young dancer was far removed from the starry-eyed amateur who'd begun in Des Moines. "I knew the Guild was notoriously chintzy, so I asked the stage manager of the show I'd just been in, *Star and Garter,* how to go about getting a decent salary. He was a lovely man named Frank Hall; he told me, 'Take your current salary and almost double it. The Guild will cut you down, and they will be pleased with themselves. You'll be earning more than you are now, and you'll be happy.'"

Hall's strategy, albeit elementary, worked. "I ended up making more than most of the dancers!" chortled Friedlich. "Of course," she added, a bit ruefully, "later on, after I'd been injured on opening night in New York and I was out of the show, I asked if I could see the matinee from out front. I'd never seen the show as a spectator. They agreed, and got me an orchestra seat. Six weeks later, when I finally came back into the cast, I found the Guild had docked me $6 for my matinee ticket!"

The grueling audition process continued.

"I wanted talent and personality, Rodgers wanted faces," de Mille reiterated, "but he was inclined to stand by me on many occasions. His idea and my idea of a face, I found, had frequently to do with the character in it."

The ultimate decision brought on an explosion, resulting not from arrogance and ego—as is usually the case in such creative arguments—but from de Mille's own frustration. Years later Celeste Holm would remember that scene with exactitude:

Agnes had them all lined up, and she brought Mr. Mamoulian down—he always had that cigar with him—and he said, "Agnes, they're certainly not pretty. They're useless to me". . . .

She said, "You'll see. They're not chorus girls, they're dancers."

"Well," he said, "That little girl, though, with the braces on her teeth, and the tiny head, and those big legs. . . ."

Agnes picked up her purse and threw it against the back wall of the theatre, and she said, "If she goes, I go! I quit the show!"

The detonator of the explosion, Bambi Linn, stood by, nervously watching.

De Mille never forgot Mamoulian's reaction. "He shrugged, and then said,

'Just keep them out of my way.' Later on," she added, "Dick Rodgers looked at my ballet dancers and remarked, 'I don't know—they're sort of endearing.'"

Marc Platt had been dancing with the Ballet Russe for almost six years, under the name of Marc Platoff. (In those days American ballet dancers needed a Russian cachet to be taken seriously by audiences.) He recalled:

> I was a soloist. I'd done a lot of good work for them and I was well known in the dance ballet. I was making $325 a month; I wanted $400. They refused. George Balanchine came to do a couple of ballets with the company, and I asked, "George, can you get me into a musical comedy where I can earn some real money? It won't happen here." George said, "Let me think. I vill call you."
>
> A week later he called me up and said, "Here, you vant vork in a Broadway show? Get here quick, right away. I have show for you." So I went over with a girl named Luba Rostova, and we did a comedy ballet for George. The show was *My Dear Public*. Total bomb. From there I went into something called *The Lady Comes Across*, with the British star Jessie Matthews. Closed in less than a week. Now I was out of work, didn't have any money, had to get a job. Third show, *Beat the Band*. Also a flop. Now I was really in trouble.
>
> Danny Kaye was playing in *Let's Face It*, and I went backstage to see one of the dancers; as I was coming downstairs, I met Dick Rodgers coming up. I knew him from the ballet *Ghost Town* he'd written for the Ballet Russe. So I said, "Dick, do you have anything coming up? I'm here in New York, and I want to work."
>
> "Do you know Agnes de Mille?" he asked. Well, I certainly did. "Why don't you call my office, get her number, and get in touch with her?" said Dick.
>
> Next morning, I did it. Called Agnes. We met, we talked, I had a job!

Rodgers had worked with many other dancers in past seasons. Among them was George Church, a strapping chap who'd danced the "Slaughter on Tenth Avenue" ballet in *On Your Toes*. "I'd already heard how Marc Platt had just been hired to double for Curly in the dream ballet. . . . I also knew they had to find a ballet dancer to double for Jud Fry—for that part they'd already hired Howard Da Silva, who was six feet tall and weighed over two hundred."

Armed with such information, Church called Rodgers, and was asked to dinner at Sardi's for a friendly chat:

> During dinner, Dick explained how Jud, in the ballet, would be called on to choke Curly, and then he said, "Now, who do we know that's six feet tall, weighs two hundred, and is a ballet dancer?"
>
> I laughed. I knew what Dick was getting at, but I waited.
>
> Dick said, "Agnes de Mille saw you dancing the Big Boss in "Slaugh-

ter on Tenth Avenue" in *On Your Toes*. She says there's no one else alive who can do Jud. I say there isn't, the Theatre Guild agrees there isn't, and Mamoulian says there isn't. What do you say?"

I sat there in silence, thinking this over. This show looked like a sure loser. No stars. Based on a flop play. Dick had just lost his longtime partner, Larry Hart, and the Guild hadn't raised all their backing. And compared to what I'd been making, I knew the salary they'd pay would be small. "We need you, George," Dick continued. He waited for me. "Okay, Dick," I said. "If I can have a two-week cancellation clause in my contract, I'll do it." What I'd figured out was that if the show, and my part in it, turned out badly in the out-of-town tryout, I could give my notice and not be embarrassed on Broadway. (It was, as it turned out, shrewd enough reasoning on Church's part, especially since changes were made in Boston that eliminated Church's second-act solo.) Dick went right to the phone and called the Guild, and told them they could make out a contract for me.

Simultaneous with the casting auditions were endless backer auditions. The indefatigable Helburn was everywhere, consulting, conferring, and moving her crew forward. Hammerstein would later describe her as "a very small sheepdog, always pushing you relentlessly to some pasture that she felt would be good for you"—as on one particular night when she, Alfred Drake, and Joan Roberts accompanied Rodgers and Hammerstein uptown to a fund-raiser at the home of Jules Glaenzer, head of Cartier.

On the way, Helburn murmured to Hammerstein, "I wish you and Dick would write a song about the earth." Somewhat surprised by this suggestion, which had dropped so abruptly into their conversation, Hammerstein asked her what she meant.

"Oh, I don't know," said Helburn. "Just a song about the earth—the land. . . ."

Hammerstein was somewhat nonplussed by Helburn's vague suggestion, intuitive though it certainly was. But, according to his biographer Hugh Fordin, two days later Hammerstein found himself writing a lyric he'd never intended to write, describing a "brand new state" that would provide "barley, carrots and pertaters, pasture for the cattle." He wrote of wind sweeping down the plain, and how sweet the waving wheat smelled when the wind followed the rain. It was a song about a young couple expressing happiness that they belonged to the land. Helburn had seeded what would become one of the show's hit songs, and an American anthem.

The new song became part of the second act, as a next-to-closing number. De Mille choreographed it with a small ensemble of Oklahomans singing the song blithely, and in the middle of the number George Church, wearing boots, did a character tap dance which he choreographed for himself. "George and I were both hired as soloists," recalled Marc Platt. "But later on, when we started rehearsals, Mamoulian began to put us into every scene in the show, because he wanted everybody to act as his chorus. We resented that; we were soloists. So every time they called the entire ensemble onstage we would go back and hide behind some flats, or back of the house, or behind the curtains. And finally the stage managers became disgusted. They said, 'Forget it, they're gone.' And we were never bothered again."

"We were wrong, of course, and Mamoulian was absolutely right," said Church. "The play was the thing, and when they took out those specialty numbers, one of which was mine and the other of which was danced by Eric Victor up in Boston, the show went much, much better."

And what was Victor's long-gone solo spot? Paul Shiers, another mainstay of de Mille's original ensemble and a reliable performer who was often called on to substitute for others, especially Lee Dixon, remembered the number, which Victor did with Linn: "He did a tap step, not a conventional one, and Bambi caught on to the sound he was making. It was that sound which fascinated her, so she followed him around as if he were the Pied Piper. Charming number; it was a show-stopper. But once we had opened in New Haven, they realized this number wasn't advancing the plot at all. Even though the audience responded to it, out it went." Eric Victor's response was immediate. He took a settlement of his contract and left the show.

One major character was as yet uncast during those frigid audition sessions at the Guild Theatre: Ado Annie, the acquiescent lady friend of Will Parker, whose flirtation with Ali Hakim would induce the second-act comedy climax. The role, which would eventually prove to be a passport to stardom, needed someone special. There had been numerous casting suggestions, but so far no one had been selected.

"Celeste Holm was a prime example of how we unearthed unexpected musical comedy talent," Helburn remarked. "She was a talented young actress who'd appeared for us in the Pennsylvania Dutch comedy *Papa Is All*. She then did a short, fragile scene in William Saroyan's *The Time of Your Life*. Now she was appearing in a new straight play called *The Damask Cheek* by John Van Druten. Then she came over to audition for us."

Elaine Steinbeck had been stage-managing at all the auditions. "The day Celeste came, I walked down to the footlights and I leaned over and said to Dick and whomever else was out there, 'I think I'm going to apologize first. I'm going to bring on somebody you all know. I can't imagine she can possibly sing, but she says she can.'" She chuckled. "I was embarrassed about bringing her out, can you imagine?

"They asked me, 'Who is it?' and I said: 'Celeste Holm.'

"'Hey,' said a voice, 'If she can sing, she'd be great for you-know-what.'

"'Ado Annie?'

"'That's it!'" Then Steinbeck returned to the waiting Holm, who recounted the audition:

She thumped me on the back and said, "Be great! It's only the best part in the show!" In my excitement, I didn't notice the three steps leading down onto the stage. I couldn't see over my music, which I was hugging to my chest like school books. I fell flat on my face, with the music skating out in front of me.

"That's pretty funny," said a voice. "Could you do it again?"

"I'd rather not," I said, fishing for my belt, which had popped with the impact.

The voice said, "I'm Richard Rodgers."

And I said, "Hello."

"And what are you going to sing?"

"'Who Is Sylvia?'" I answered.

"Oh, good," he said. "I haven't heard that this year." He let me sing all three choruses. When I finished there was a stunned silence, and then he said, rather disappointedly, "But you have a trained voice. Could you sing as if you'd never had a lesson in your life?"

"You mean I've studied for three years for that?"

"Oh, you have to know how to in order to know how not to," he said. "I want a loud, unedited sound, like a farm girl."

"I can call a hog."

"I dare you," he said.

I leaned back and let fly. "*Sooeee!*" None came.

"Okay," he said. "That's loud enough. Come on down here." I jumped down off the stage and we shook hands. "But aren't you in a hit? I don't steal actors," Dick Rodgers said. I was in a hit. I was playing in *The Damask Cheek,* and it had been voted the most literate play of the season by the critics.

"Well, it's before Christmas," I said, "and business is okay now, but I don't know how solid we'll be later."

"You'll hear from me." He smiled. And when I left the theatre I didn't mind the rain at all.

A week passed, and then Miss Holm was called back to repeat her performance, complete with hog-calling.

It was for the Theatre Guild people and Oscar Hammerstein. Meeting him was like meeting an old friend. He was big and kind and comfortable. Then I was asked to read a scene from the new show. They seemed pleased, but when I left that day there was no decision. It was all rather vague. On the corner of 48th Street and Sixth Avenue, there was a Gypsy Tea Kettle on the second floor. Wouldn't it be fun, somehow, magically, to know the future? My gypsy wore just what you'd expect; a chiffon scarf with bangles on the edge, and all those flowered skirts. When she 'read my leaves,' I tried not to show my disbelief.

"Do the initials RR mean anything to you?"

"No," I said, not thinking of Richard Rodgers. We'd barely met!

"They will," she said seriously. "I see you surrounded by dancing cowboys. And there will be a tremendous change in your life."

I thanked her for what I thought was complete nonsense and left.

Shortly afterward, Flora Robson, the star of *The Damask Cheek*, became ill, and the play promptly closed. But Celeste Holm would not be out of work for long.

When I got the call to come to the Theatre Guild, to talk contract, I didn't have an agent, so I called Edith Van Cleve at MCA. I told her about my auditions. She thought I was crazy. I was coming along nicely as a serious actress, she insisted, and what did I know about musical comedy?

Would she please negotiate a contract? I asked. Against her better judgment, she did. I was to receive $250 a week to play Ado Annie, and I was to receive fourth featured billing. But it wasn't until we actually opened in New Haven, and I'd gotten a big hand for "I Cain't Say No," that I remember Jo Healy, who was the guardian of the Theatre Guild switchboard, admitting, "Well, now I guess it's all right to tell you, but all during rehearsals they had me calling Hollywood to get someone to replace you—mostly Judy Canova and Shirley Booth."

As for young Jay Blackton, the as-yet undecided conductor, the Guild drew up a contract for his services and sent it to him. Deeply moved as he had been by the Rodgers and Hammerstein score, he still hesitated. However, as if drawn by an irresistible magnetic force, each day he would return to the Guild Theatre to sit in on the conferences and early preparations for *Green Grow the Lilacs.*

Which could no longer be the name of the musical. MGM owned the title to Lynn Riggs' play, along with the film rights. Therefore, under the terms of their new agreement with L. B. Mayer's corps of lawyers, the Guild could acquire those rights, as well as the title to same, only if and when they exercised their option *after* the show opened. A new title was in order forthwith. Ideas were tossed back and forth. Helburn, Langner, and Rodgers proffered suggestions that would lead to the final choice, *Away We Go!* Final, at least, for New Haven and Boston.

Rehearsals

They began on February 8, 1943. "That afternoon," said Celeste Holm, "on the stage of the Guild Theatre, Richard Rodgers played, and Oscar Hammerstein sort of sang the songs. That moment is particularly memorable to me. Those two men, who were to become the titans of our musical theatre, presented their work so unpretentiously. No matter how many ways the work has been sung and played since then, I'll always remember Dick and Oscar 's version for us."

George Irving, later to become a Broadway star, was a singer cast in his first show ("the lowest of the low" is how he defined his status). "When Dick came out to play for us," he recalled, "I remember noticing that there was no music on the piano at all. He played everything from memory, and not only was it a wonderful score, but his performance was very impressive."

Before rehearsals began, Lawrence Langner made a brief speech to the assembled cast. Obviously moved by the circumstances that had forced the Guild to sell its theatre, he told them, "This is the last time that Guild thespians will tread these boards."

Mamoulian was also moved. "I remember him looking at the bare back wall," said Irving, "with all those steam pipes running up from the floor, and he made a very touching speech, almost a monologue, totally extemporaneous, about how much those pipes reminded him of the interior of a cathedral . . . that they were like organ pipes. 'For me, this theatre is a holy place,' he said to us, 'and this work here in which we're involved is a noble, holy thing.' We were all very moved."

Then the work began.

According to Actors Equity rules, the Guild had five days to decide which members of the cast would be kept on permanently, after which the contracts would be formally issued. Thus, Bambi Linn, who kept a diary, could note, "[I] was told today we are in the show for sure." The following day's entry reads, "Signed my contract today. I was hoping it would be white, but it was pink. We get $45 on the road, and $40 in town, less than other shows, I'm told. . . ."

"There wasn't an inch of the theatre that wasn't being used by chorus, principals, dancers," reported Helburn. "Mamoulian, who integrated drama and song and dance, sweated at his task. Agnes drilled her dancers relentlessly. Dick sat at his keyboard, watching, listening. I bit my nails and scurried around and wondered if I had made the most fatal mistake of my life. Everyone else thought so."

During those weeks Helene Hanff was at her post in the Guild press department offices, working for Joe Heidt. "People from other floors drifted into our office with progress reports," she remembered. "This was, they informed us, the damnedest musical comedy anybody'd ever hatched for a sophisticated Broadway audience. It opened with a middle-aged farm woman sitting alone on a bare stage churning butter, and from then on it got cleaner. They did not feel a long sequence of arty dancing was likely to improve matters on the farm."

Downstairs in the drafty lobby, on rugs that had not been vacuumed in months, de Mille worked at top speed. "Since Mamoulian took the stage," she recalled, "I worked below in what had been the foyer and way above in what had been costume and rehearsal rooms."

"That deserted and badly lit box room, which was way upstairs, was filled with cartons," said Bambi Linn, "and we placed them all in one corner, and then the dust began to come up. There was no way of opening a window to let the dust out, and you didn't want to open the window because it was very chilly. So, sooner or later, we would all get sick."

"With the assistance of Marc Platt and Ray Harrison, another dancer, I kept three rehearsals going at once," said de Mille. "I was like a pitcher that had been overfilled; the dances simply spilled out of me. I had boys and girls in every spare corner of the theatre sliding, riding, tapping, ruffling skirts, kicking. We worked with enormous excitement, but always under great strain. For the first three days, Richard Rodgers never left my side. He sat with fixed surgical attention, watching everything. This made the dancers nervous, but it was I who really sweated. He did not relax until the third afternoon, when, smiling and patting me on the shoulder, he gave the first intimation that I would not be fired."

Linn depicted de Mille at work. "Agnes did tremendous homework. She does it in her mind first, then gets up and walks it. Then she'd call us together and say 'try this,' and we worked that way. Then she'd suggest a movement to us, say, 'Sweep across the floor,' so you'd sweep across the floor—each of us would try it—and she'd say, 'Okay, try this arm movement,' and she would evolve it into a movement, or something that was usable. . . ."

Jay Blackton had still not made up his mind to sign a contract to conduct the show, but whenever he was free he'd drop by the theatre to watch the rehearsals.

Every time I was there, Rodgers would urge Oscar to talk to me. He told me that later. So Oscar would ask, "Well, what about it, are you with us or not?" I was torn. I liked what I was seeing, but I was afraid to give up my steady job in St. Louis at the Municipal Opera in order to commit to this untested new show. . . . But one time, when Mamoulian declared a break and everybody left to go get coffee, Hammerstein nailed me. He took me out on the bare stage, backed me into a corner, and gave me a tongue lashing I have never forgotten. I've never seen Oscar that disturbed, before or after. Berating me! He said, "You've got to make up your mind! You're a man who's got to be on Broadway. That's where you *belong!*" He kept on urging me—*"Make up your mind!"*

That more or less did the trick. I left him with my tail between my legs. I was really desolate because I knew I had to make up my mind. And I went home, and Louise and I decided I had to do this show, whether or not I lost the St. Louis job. Believe me, it was a big step.

Dick Berger, who ran the Municipal Opera, was great. He said he'd try to hold off hiring anybody else for my job until this new show opened in New Haven. I went back to the rehearsals, and now I went downstairs to the lobby, where Agnes de Mille was working out her choreography. . . . Now that I was the musical director, I became her liaison with what was going on upstairs. It was fascinating to watch her at work. What amazed me was how she took Dick and Oscar's lyrical songs and used them as the framework, the roots, the sperm of her choreographic devices.

As the frenetic days passed, the only available heat in the soon-to-be-sold Guild Theatre was that of creativity. "It was February, and frigid," recalled Kate Friedlich. "I got a wicked cold. Missed two days of rehearsals. I came back to find that Joan McCracken had been given the part of 'the girl who falls down' in the 'Many a New Day' ballet, which de Mille had already begun to choreograph for me, and so I was steamed."

To add to the misfortunes, the youngest dancer in the show, Kenneth LeRoy, came down with German measles and had to retire temporarily from rehearsals. But, alas, not before he had infected many of his confreres. So while the rehearsals continued at a furious pace, the dancers, unaware they were now in an incubation period, went on taking direction from de Mille, who herself had developed a dreadful cough and would have to spend a valuable day at home recuperating.

Mamoulian sat upstairs in the drafty theatre, puffing incessantly on his cigars and staging scenes from Hammerstein's libretto. "He never relinquished that stage to Agnes," said Alfred Drake. "And he insisted on having everybody up there on the stage while he was rehearsing the scenes. That meant a lot of people were playing poker on the sides of the stage, and we were all most unhappy about that. It could be that he'd be rehearsing a simple scene between the two of us, but everybody else had to be there!

"I can remember the first day of really tremendous excitement," Drake went on. "It was the day Agnes brought the dancers upstairs and had them go through the ballet." Elaine Steinbeck described it:

It was on a Sunday, and Rouben said, "I think it would be nice to put a few things together today." Oscar wasn't there, he was at home in Bucks County, and Dick was with his family, here in town at a hotel. Rouben said, "Elaine, go down and see if Agnes would come and bring up a num-

ber or two and we'll run them just to try them—a little bit together."
Without an audience, without anything, with just the rehearsal piano
and her dancers on that bare cold stage, she ran some numbers for us,
and I suddenly thought, "Uh-oh!" and without asking or telling anybody,
I ran to the phone and called Dick up at his hotel where he was with
Dorothy, and I said, "Can you come?" He asked, "What's the matter?" I
just said, "Something here looks awfully good, and it looks so different
from anything, and please come!"

And Dick came, and he sat in the orchestra, and when he saw what
had been put together he grinned and said, "Oh, *that* was worth making
a Sunday trip for!"

"Rodgers is not only a great songwriter," commented de Mille, years later. "He
is one of the most astute theatre men in the world. He concerns himself
relentlessly with every detail of production. Nothing escapes his attention,
and he takes vigorous and instant action. This might be interfering if he were
not sensitive, sensible, and greatly experienced. . . . Mamoulian and the Guild
frequently said 'It can't be done.' It was always Rodgers who urged 'let's see.'"

There were more than the usual crises, some of which were due to the
problem of finances. Helburn was still hunting for more badly needed backers. "By now," she said later, "it was so bad that Dick Rodgers used to say to
me, 'There's even a Chinese gentleman in Shanghai who's turned us down!'"

"We all got increasingly nervous," recalled de Mille, "and when Terry Helburn started interrupting rehearsals to show unfinished work to prospective
backers in her frantic efforts to raise money, I blew every fuse I had. Huffing
my pocketbook at her head, I shouted and flounced and was dragged off
screaming by Marc Platt and held under a faucet of cold water until I quieted
down."

According to de Mille's journal, she accomplished an enormous amount of
work in the first two weeks of the rehearsals; she set all the dances in the
show, including "Boys and Girls Like You and Me," a ballad that would eventually be cut.

"I'm well again," she reported in the third week. "I never worked so fast in
my life. I've set forty minutes of straight dancing in less than three weeks. The
company raves. Rodgers put his head on my shoulder this afternoon and said,
'Oh, Aggie, you're such a comfort in my old age.' And Marc Platt said this
evening, 'In all soberness, I've never worked with anyone I respected more.'

"We live in the basement," she continued. "I see sunlight only twenty minutes a day. The dust from the unvacuumed Guild rugs has made us all sick, and
I put away three thermos bottles of coffee an afternoon. I look awful."

De Mille, reflecting later on the impact of her work on the final production, said: "It was that first-act ballet which changed the quality of the show.
Once Laurey realizes that she's really frightened of Jud, and why she's fright-

ened, you can see the change. Up till then it's been an innocuous gingham-aprony Sunday-school sort of a show. That first act, there was nothing in it, no threat, no suspense, no sex, no nothing. And I told this to Oscar, who said, 'No sex?'

"'No, Mr. Hammerstein,' I said. 'None.'

"'What have we done with those postcards of Jud Fry's?' And he looked at me, and then he went to the phone and called Dick. 'Dick, get over here immediately.'"

Jud Fry's French postcards, which he kept hidden in his lonely lodgings, would come to life in costumes by Miles White, who drew inspiration for their images from turn-of-the-century "cigarette cards," which were tiny pho-

Miles White's cigarette-card figures brought to life as the dance-hall beauties of Jud Fry's dream: (*left to right*) Joan McCracken, Kate Friedlich, Vivian Smith, Margit DeKova, and Barbara Barrington.

tos of the buxom belles so favored by the young "sports" who puffed on the "coffin-nails" of the day. Now they would be danced by de Mille's ballerinas.

"I put them on the stage, and that was the first big belly laugh," de Mille says. "And then, when I also introduced the dramatic motif that Laurey was scared of the violence inherent in Jud, the danger in that man, I let the act curtain come down on that, which introduced a dark, suspenseful, ominous note which the show hadn't had. And it made everything else more real."

"With those ballets," commented Helburn, "created out of so much travail and turmoil, nerve strain and confusion, Agnes came into her own as one of America's leading choreographers."

Ten days before the crew was scheduled to leave for New Haven the first run-through was held. As Celeste Holm remembered it:

> We came back after supper to find the stage newly marked off with laths to indicate walls and openings for gates or doors. The Theatre Guild people arrived. They were followed by a most unexpected group: well-dressed gentlemen and ladies, wearing hats—looking as though they had just come from "21."
>
> The strangers walked down the steps from the stage and took seats out front. They all looked at us in that odd way civilians look at performers; through a glass wall, with gentle, phony smiles.
>
> "Who are they?" I asked Terry Helburn.
>
> "Just think of them as friends," she said sweetly.
>
> How could we have known that the Guild *still* needed money for the show? When we started our first complete run-through, those "strangers" were thirty prospective backers, scattered lumpily out front. . . . The rehearsal piano began, and so did an over-controlled nightmare! As I was about to make an entrance, a whole ballet came on, and I got out of its way just in time. Cues were missed, actors tripped over the laths and forgot their lyrics, and no one out front laughed at all. I watched the civilians leave. The phony smiles were still there, frozen on. And not one of that bunch had a dime's worth of confidence in us.
>
> We rehearsed all day; and at night, from then on, there'd be more of those well-dressed people, picking their way across the stage, taking seats in the orchestra. We made them laugh on subsequent nights, but not one backer ever emerged from those groups.

As the day loomed closer on which the company was to leave for New Haven, there were the customary outbreaks of tension and temperament. "I had trouble with Joe Buloff," recalled Celeste Holm, whose character Ado Annie would be romantically involved with Buloff's Ali Hakim.

> The first day we did our scene he came on eating a banana. Well, the chorus girls thought that was the funniest thing they'd ever seen. The

next day he came on with a cane, with which he began hitting me on the ass. . . . You see, as far as I'm concerned, a scene is a covenant. I promise to be standing in the same spot every night, so you can do what you have to do, and I can do what I have to do, and then we get the play on. If you start doing something that I don't know about, out goes the show!

One day Joe stood on my foot; didn't even *know* he was standing on my foot! So I went to Mamoulian and I explained very quietly that I'd have to get this scene set, one way or the other. I said, "I'm his partner in this scene and I want to know what he's going to do!"

So Mamoulian went to Joe Buloff, and in front of the entire company he said to him, "Joe, you carry one more prop on this stage which I have not seen before and I come back and break every tooth in your head. I have seen you in show after show, always you get good notices, always you steal the show, and the show closes. You've never been in a hit in your life. This time I want you to be in a *hit!*"

I hadn't realized I was reaping a whirlwind. . . . But you know something? From then on, Joe behaved himself. He was very good, and he was in a hit! And years later, a quarter of a century after we opened, we met at a party and he said to me, "Oh, I love you so much, I love you!"

I said, "You never told me, you never let me know."

He said, "I *couldn't.*" But he was now eighty or so, and he finally could say it!

"However ruffled temperaments became, we had our lighter moments," said Helburn. "Mamoulian wanted more atmosphere of the Oklahoma farm when the curtain rose. 'How about a donkey, or a goat?' he asked. But we couldn't travel with a barnyard on the road." Langner thereupon suggested a cow, to be tethered by Aunt Eller as she churned the butter in the opening scene. The cow never made it to the stage.

Mamoulian had other ideas. "One morning, during the third week of rehearsals," remembered George Church, "Moo-Moo, that was our name for him, declared, 'What we need is spectacle—to build up the last scene of the show! Max Reinhardt was right—go out and find some agent who has some specialty acts we can audition—find us *spectacle!*'"

The next afternoon brought on the auditioners. The first to arrive in the theatre was an honest-to-goodness cowboy from Oklahoma, an authentic roper. "He spun his ropes in spectacular fashion," said Church, "and Moo-Moo jumped up, ecstatic! 'Now, we're getting somewhere!' he said, and proceeded to improvise a moment onstage in which Alfred Drake and Joan Roberts would sit together with the cowboy standing behind them. He ordered the roper to spin the rope around all three, and then suggested that Drake and Roberts, on cue, would sing 'Oklahoma.'

"The cowboy promptly began spinning his rope above his head, paying it out until he had a huge circle some fifteen feet in diameter, and then he lowered it on himself and the two performers. '*Sing!*' shouted Mamoulian. Drake and Roberts began, but that rope kept whipping around them, coming dangerously close. They were scared silly," said Church, "and they were right. Suddenly that rope scraped Alfred's face and gave him a pretty good rope burn! He grabbed the rope and threw it to the floor! Neither he nor Joan Roberts would permit themselves to be roped a second time.

"Moo-Moo shouted, 'There's no danger! I'll show you how to do it.' He sat down and the roper started again, this time with only himself and Mamoulian in the circle. 'Faster, faster!' cried Moo-Moo. The roper revved it up until you could hear the whine of his rope. Suddenly the rope came near Moo-Moo's face; it sideswiped Mamoulian's ever-present cigar. The hot ashes ended up in Moo-Moo's ear . . . and that Oklahoma roper ended up out in the Guild Theatre alley, his opportunity to become part of the Reinhardtian 'spectacle' forever terminated."

Unfazed, Mamoulian continued searching for "spectacle" right through the New Haven tryout. Could there be pigeons in the barnyard? "A flash of white wings, sweeping across that blue sky?" That suggestion took flight. At a given cue the birds could flash across Lem Ayers's blue backdrop, then fly back and perch on a fence until the curtain came down. A pigeon trainer was located, along with his troupe of birds, and plans were made for his journey to New Haven.

Everyone was worried about the future, none more so than Celeste Holm.

"I'd ask Mamoulian for some idea of how to play Ado Annie; each day I tried something a little different and each day I awaited some disagreement or corroboration, but Mr. Mamoulian would just say, 'Fine, darling,' and puff on his cigar. So it wasn't until we saw Miles White's wonderfully vivid costume sketches that I began to feel Ado Annie take shape. Big pink polka dots and all those ruffles—and a parasol!

"Next day I spoke to Agnes. I need something . . . reassurance, criticism, a response of some kind. 'You're fine,' she told me, 'but your performance is too small. It's a big stage. Oklahoma was a big, wide-open territory. Think of Ado Annie that way and everything you do will be all right.'" That advice satisfied Holm for the moment and would carry her through opening night in New Haven.

But even de Mille wasn't certain all the work she'd been doing was correct; after those endless hours of creating dances as rapidly as she could, she'd lost all perspective. "We worried and groused and fretted," she wrote. "There was only one man who rode the froth quietly and failed to turn a hair." That was the composer.

"He was standing in the shadows listening to all of us—there wasn't anything formal about this, we were just saying what we thought was wrong with the show. And he very quietly came out and said, 'Would you like me to tell you what I think is wrong with the show?' And we told him of course we would. He said, 'Nothing. I think it's simply wonderful. It's extraordinary. You have no idea how extraordinary it is.' And he listed all the things he liked. 'Now, why don't you all quiet down?' And we went home chastened and quiet."

Just before the company packed up and left that drafty theatre, there would be a run-through for an invited audience. No sets, no costumes, merely the bare stage with one work light. Mary Hunter Wolfe remembered that night. The theatre that night was far from filled. "Each of the Guild people sat far apart from the others," she said. "Terry Helburn sat in one section with her secretary, who was there to take down Terry's notes. Armina Marshall sat in another area with her secretary. Lawrence was separated from both of them, and he had two secretaries. Afterwards, when it was over, they'd get together and pool their notes into one report."

With music supplied by the rehearsal pianist, the run-through began. "Right off, from the very beginning, I found it very exciting," said Wolfe. "They'd caught the spirit and the flavor of Lynn's play so marvelously. From that moment when Alfred strolled on singing his opening song, it all went so well. It was lovely. I also remember that when Alfred and Howard Da Silva did their duet, 'Pore Jud Is Daid,' it struck me as being so funny I began to chortle out loud. The Guild people turned around to me very sternly and went 'Shhhh!'"

Dorothy Rodgers was also there that night. "Afterwards, everyone got together to discuss what they thought. Dick put me in a cab. I went home and wrote a note which I put on his pillow. It said, 'Darling, this is the best musical show I have ever seen in my life.'"

The post-run-through conference went on for some time. "I remember there was a big argument," said Wolfe. "Mamoulian was quite upset. He told Helburn and Langner, 'This first-act ballet of Agnes's is beautiful—a wonderful theatre piece—I admire her work, it's remarkable to see Laurey in her dream of her future and how she makes up her mind. But when it's over we have told the entire story of the second act! What does that leave me to do? The play is over.'

"He was correct, of course," Wolfe added. "He was telling them the truth, and there was a large controversy over this. Finally, he was told the ballet had to stay."

Who prevailed that night?

"Oh, it had to be Terry Helburn," affirmed Elaine Steinbeck. "She stood up to Mamoulian, and Agnes's work was left exactly the way it was."

But Mamoulian's appraisal was right on the mark. The second act would provide the problems out of town. And when they arose, in New Haven and Boston, could they be solved?

The troupe left on Sunday morning, March 5, 1943, for the New Haven opening. Agnes de Mille and her dancers (plus some invisible measles germs that were incubating in many of them), Rodgers and Hammerstein, the singers, Mamoulian, the actors, and the rest packed their bags and headed for Grand Central Station. Indeed, some of the troupe were already ill. "Dorothea MacFarland was the first one in our group who got sick," remembered Vivian Smith. "And then I got it, and the doctor didn't want me to leave New York. But I went anyway. That was my training. You go."

Along with the performers went the Lem Ayers scenery; all of Miles White's costumes, as yet unseen on a stage; Jay Blackton and his key musicians (the rest of the orchestra would be recruited in New Haven); Robert Russell Bennett and his copyists, some racing to finish the parts of Bennett's arrangements for the pit orchestra; Jerry Whyte and his backstage assistants; Elaine Steinbeck and John Haggott; Helburn, Langner, and his wife, Armina Marshall; office assistants; plus the latest members of the troupe, a flock of white pigeons and their trainer.

Certainly, for the Guild it was a make-or-break situation. Did the cast think they might have a hit?

"At that point," said Alfred Drake, "I don't know that anybody thought much of anything, except that it was a good show and we were very happy to be working."

New Haven

Away We Go! had been scheduled by the United Booking Office (an arm of the Shuberts, who were the Theatre Guild's partners in the show) to open at the Shubert Theatre in New Haven on March 11 and play through Saturday, the 13th. Four performances, three evenings and one matinee—known in the trade as a "split-week."

An accurate appraisal of a 1943 New Haven split-week of a new show would be "trial by fire." An obstacle course. A crucible. Behind this simple, noncommittal phrase "split-week" lay terrors for all who entered the Shubert stage door. Inside those walls there awaited a grueling, nonstop six days' worth of mounting tension, usually *sans* regular meals and/or sleep for any and all of the hapless souls consigned to open a brand-new, untried show on Thursday night at 8:30 P.M. and play four performances, ending on Saturday, with luck, by 11:30 P.M. (Anything that lasted onstage past that magic hour meant overtime for the stagehands and musicians.)

Today, merely to attempt such a three-day booking with a full-scale musical would be financially disastrous. Based on contemporary running costs, a touring show needs at least a full week in a theatre, usually with subscription audiences, in order to turn some sort of profit.

But in 1943 there was still a supply of masochists, such as those Helburn and Langner had assembled, willing to endure New Haven tryouts. For years, theatrical entrepreneurs had considered the Shubert Theatre their regular jumping-off place. Season after season they ascended the ladder to the diving board, held their noses, and Thursday evening at 8:30 P.M., ready or not, they jumped—into uncharted seas, complete with crises, glitches, temper tantrums, errors and omissions, gags that didn't get laughs, songs that didn't get applause, nervous actors going up on their lines or missing cues, scenery that did or didn't work or that fell on performers, costume changes that held up the show's action. Name a crisis, and it was guaranteed to happen during a New Haven split-week. Little wonder that anyone who ever ran that gauntlet would fervently tell you: "If you haven't died in New Haven, you've never died at all!"

Some shows emerged triumphantly from the Shubert and rode the fast track to glory. Others limped to Boston and Philadelphia, headed for major repairs. And some sank without a trace on Saturday night, never to be heard from again.

For *Away We Go!* it was six days of angst at the Shubert. On Monday, March 8, the technical staff arrived from New York. Inside the theatre stagehands and truckers worked feverishly to "load in" the freshly painted backdrops and scenery. Then the designer and his technical people set up everything for the first time. Spots and kliegs had to be hung, focused, and cued to the backstage lighting board. Not today's state-of-the-art computerized marvel, with its capability of programming hundreds of cues that function automatically throughout each performance; in the 1940s, every individual lighting cue had to be switched on or off by hand.

Amplification? Blessedly, there was none to install. Performers in those days relied on their vocal chords.

The previous week, the costumes had been seen in New York at a dress parade at Brooks Costume, but now White's creations would be distributed by the wardrobe mistress to the various dressing rooms, to be worn for the first time onstage. At 10 A.M. there would be a reading rehearsal onstage of the entire show; for the first time the cast could familiarize itself with the actual set. For the rest of the day there would be rehearsals at which frenetic last-minute changes and "fixes" would be put into the show under the eye of the director and the choreographer.

On Wednesday, the musical score, until now heard only on a rehearsal piano, had to be distributed in all its individual parts to be ready for a 10 A.M. orchestra reading by musicians who had heretofore not seen a single note. Freshly copied by a corps of expert copyists, many of whom might still be down in the basement finishing up the last pieces of the arranger's work, the score would arrive on the conductor's stand. Then in came the New Haven musicians, to be led by the conductor through the orchestra reading. At the conductor's side would be the composer, guarding his music like a mother hen, cringing at errors, missed notes, and nuances of interpretation.

The company would rehearse with the orchestra until 6 P.M., then break for supper, with attendant conferences, arguments, and urgent last-minute decisions. At 7 P.M. a weary company would reassemble in costume, ready for the dress rehearsal—followed by more explosions: Why was this outfit so garish? Who picked this color? Why didn't this damned skirt fit properly, and more important, why did the chorus girls' outfits in the big second-act number look better than the star's?

"Dress" finally began. Still glitches: missed entrances; blown cues; scenery that didn't work properly; light cues that missed by beats, leaving performers in the dark or revealed at the exact wrong time! Anger. Frustration. On and on it went, into the wee hours of the morning, and one could be certain of only one truth this ghastly night: Everything that could possibly go wrong would.

Inexorably the clock ticked on. Frazzled nerves. Thursday morning, a final lighting rehearsal to eliminate any more mistakes. Should something not be ready for tonight, too damn bad—forge ahead, damn the torpedoes! Tonight's curtain loomed above everyone's head like some implacable Damoclean sword. From noon to three or so, a full company rehearsal with orchestra.

Zombies by now, the cast dragged itself to Kaysey's across the street or to a nearby coffee shop to take in some nourishment, perhaps even 86-proof liquid restorative. Then back to the Shubert and into the dressing room to put on makeup and get into costume, cross oneself, mutter a brief prayer, run downstairs and yell "Break a leg!" to the rest of the doomed souls on this journey, and psych oneself for whatever would take place on this opening night.

A vanguard of customers was already filing into the Shubert lobby. Ready or not, there they came. Tonight was the night.

The wonderful thing about actors and actresses is that, in spite of all the disasters that had gone on in the past, they were now willing, at 8:30 on Thursday, March 11, to take the plunge.

Such was the madness of a split-week in New Haven, circa 1943. That any cast, any creative crew, any producer would venture—nay, that any backer would invest in such an incredible process without being consigned to a sanitarium (and who is to say some were not?) is hard to believe. When Larry Gelbart, who has been there often himself, quipped, "Hitler should have had to go out of town to try out a new musical," he obviously meant New Haven.

Helene Hanff, in *Underfoot in Show Business*, recalled:

Joe Heidt, the press agent, went up a few days before the opening to "beat the drum" for it. He was very worried. Not about the show. Joe admitted frankly that there was still some work to be done on it, but he believed that by the time it opened in New York it would be the greatest show since *Hamlet*. What worried him was that some drama editor or some columnist's assistant like Winchell's Rose would sneak up to New Haven and see the show before it was Ready. As of now, Joe did not feel it was Ready.

It was always a producer's worry that somebody in a newspaper's drama department would sneak out of town to a pre-Broadway tryout and write a report that would kill the show before it ever opened. But no drama department editor scared them half as much as Winchell's Rose. Walter Winchell's column appeared in cities across the country, including all the Guild's subscription cities, and was immensely influential. If Winchell's Rose—she must have had a last name but I never heard her called anything but "Winchell's Rose"—snuck out of town to see the tryout, the effect might be devastating.

Heidt's fears were right on the mark.

At the March 4 dress parade at Brooks Costume, in New York, Miles White and his assistant, Kermit Love, had tried out their costumes on cast members. Kate Friedlich recalled: "We were up at Brooks, where each costume was

In New Haven, Alfred Drake makes his first appearance in cowboy duds as Betty Garde, playing Aunt Eller, eyes him approvingly. (Photo by Eileen Darby)

being checked out. I disliked a hat assigned to me, and so did McCracken. I said so. But McCracken put hers on the floor, took aim, and jumped on it! Absolutely smashing it beyond repair. She got a hat to her liking, and I stuck with mine. You know, we learn something from this, don't we?"

Now the final dress parade took place in New Haven. It was late at night. "It was a real event," said Bambi Linn. "All the boys came out in their yellow, pink, and blue shirts, and the costume people had spent days hand embroidering circles into polka dots—these weren't printed on, mind you, but they were sewn! So out came the 'cowboys,' all polka-dotted, and they had chaps on, and boots on, they had big hats, they had gloves with fringes on, I mean, they looked like the typical Hollywood cowboys! Well, everybody looked at that, and each one of the producers starting picking away, and if I remember correctly, it was Agnes who said, 'Well, let's get rid of the polka dots!'"

One can readily imagine the ensuing scene; a determined director and a distraught designer, both defending their creative work. "Once they got rid of the polka dots and they were down to a solid color, then they told Miles White, 'Let's get rid of those chaps,' except for a couple of the cowboys who could wear them—Alfred Drake could, because he was the lead, but not everybody else—they wanted him highlighted. Then Agnes and Helburn went to work on the gloves, to get rid of those fringes, and then they changed the boots, so the boys could dance in them—they certainly couldn't dance with those high heels . . . and then the hats—well, it was 'Let's keep them all simple, all uniform!'"

"Poor Miles!" said Linn. "I thought he was going to *die*. . . . Then, they started on the girls. They had shawls and lots of flowers and things. But Agnes said, 'Okay, let's strip!' and I think Joanie McCracken ended up with *one* flower. Away went the shawls. And then they were down to basically silhouettes and color, which was beautified by being seen in front of Lem Ayers's settings. Agnes was absolutely right; each scene ended up looking like a painting."

White argued, pleaded, but to no avail. Helburn stressed simplicity; de Mille wanted authentic designs in which her people could dance.

"We saw this man moaning and groaning, he was obviously fighting for his own concepts," Friedlich recalled, "but it had to be. His costumes were delightful, with wonderful colors, but remember, they were also heavy. During most of the show we wore camisoles, great long bloomers, petticoats, bustles, high suede shoes, and sometimes gloves. Dancers have to work through all these yard goods. It makes it a whole lot harder. If you have a real wispy chiffony thing, with a leotard underneath, you're absolutely free. But I remember the fright when we had to start moving in those costumes in New Haven. It felt as if you were moving yourself and a Mack truck around!"

Many years after that disastrous session in New Haven, Miles White chuckled at the memory. "Oh, I learned my lesson on that show," he said. "The next show I did with Agnes and Terry was *Carousel*. I knew they'd be after my

Joan Roberts, Alfred Drake, and Celeste Holm. (Photo by Eileen Darby)

costumes, cutting here and trimming there, the way they had in *Oklahoma!* . . . so, I purposely put all sorts of additional stuff on my costumes . . . and sure enough, when I'd go downstairs into the basement of the theatre, backstage, I'd find them by my racks, cutting away! But this time I was ready for them!"

In the Shubert pit the New Haven musicians were ready to play the first orchestral reading of the score. Blackton remembered:

We had in all about thirty men, which was unusual. But Dick Rodgers felt we should have more strings than usual. Ten violins! Unheard of. . . . In those days New Haven was such a regular stopping-off place for musicals that there was a sort of bank of local musical talent on which we could draw, so we had about twenty-five from New Haven. They were very good, they had to be, because working on brand-new orchestrations is a very ticklish job. If there are mistakes, and let me first say that with Robert Russell Bennett doing the orchestrations there were not—but there always is *something* to correct, a printing mistake, a copyist's mistake, and while we're running through the score, the conductor has to have cat's ears in order to hear those errors and to try to correct them during those precious musical rehearsals. Which cost *money*—musicians do not come cheap—even in those 1940s!

So you want to do them and get through as quickly and as efficiently as possible. That particular day I said to the musicians as I was rehearsing, "I can't take too much time on this." And it was Dick Rodgers, sitting behind me, who leaned over and whispered into my ear, "Jacob, take all the time in the world!"

But tryouts are filled with improvisations as well. "We still hadn't had time to prepare a proper overture for Thursday night's opening," said Blackton. "So we had to use a little improvised thing that Robert Russell Bennett pasted together in time for that first performance. It was later, when we got to Boston, that we had the time to prepare a full overture. By that time it was easy. We opened with 'The Farmer and the Cowman' and we ended with 'Oklahoma'—one started it, the other ended it. It's the usual vaudeville gimmick—no matter what you do in the middle, get on and get off right."

"Things were very, very tight that week," said Linn. "I remember a second-act number with Lee Dixon and Celeste . . . that was done at the very last minute. I don't think they even had a chance to try it out. . . . They realized that song needed something, like a tag . . . and it was done 'in one'—out in front of the curtain—because backstage, behind the drop, they needed time for a change."

"Agnes had to do that very fast," said Vivian Smith. "When she did it that day she had gotten sick and was bedridden in New Haven, in her hotel room, there were three of us there, maybe four, and we were working between the foot of her bed and the hotel room wall!"

"We're working around the clock now," de Mille wrote in her diary on March 10. "Thursday we open. Dick Rodgers took my hand in his yesterday and said, 'I want to thank you for doing a distinguished job.' . . . There's hell ahead, and unless we pull the show up very quick we're sunk." On March 13 she wrote:

All Broadway shows are simply fierce during rehearsals, but this one has been insanity. . . . And only Dick Rodgers has kept me from flouncing out.

Everybody's temper went absolutely to pot. I began to become aware of Oscar Hammerstein, who had stayed up to this point almost exclusively in the book rehearsals. He sat through the endless nights, quietly giving off intelligence like a stove. He never got angry, or nasty, or excited, but when people were beating their heads on the orchestra rail he made the one common-sense suggestion that any genius might think of if he was not at the moment consuming himself. . . . Lawrence Langner expounded. Terry Helburn snapped and badgered and barked at our heels with a housekeeper's insistence on detail. Mamoulian created, in spite of the hour and other peoples' nerves. But Oscar just quietly pointed the way.

"He was always around," says Linn. "Quiet. Listening, like some sort of a gentle giant. We always felt this giving coming from him."

Just before the first dress rehearsal those second-act-closing pigeons that Mamoulian wanted for "spectacle" arrived at the theatre. George Church recalled:

Out on the stage of the Shubert, there came this old vaudevillian carrying his special cage of white birds, which cooed and fluttered. "I vill now show you how mine pigeons do vat I tell zem," he announced, with a decided Teutonic accent. He then opened the top of the birdcage and the birds obediently emerged from the opening, fluttered onto the top. Then he held up a stick, about three feet long, and he proclaimed "Zis is mine magic vand." He swung the stick in a circle above his head and the birds took off and flew in formation in a huge circle around the Shubert orchestra. It was a beautiful sight.

And then, just outside the theatre doors in the street, a truck backfired with a resounding bang! Whereupon those birds scattered in every direction and in complete panic they flew away, to disappear into the far reaches of the Shubert backstage loft, high up in the flies! The distraught trainer waved his wand, called and whistled to his birds, trying to get them back to where they could assume their proper role in the second-act finale.

No use. The pigeons were no troupers. They stayed up in the flies, cooing and grooming and steadily dropping little messages on the busy scene below. "To hell with them!" came the collective decision. "Let 'em stay there—we've got a show to do!"

"And there they remained," said Alfred Drake. "When we left for Boston they were still flying around up there in the flies."

Suddenly, it was Thursday evening, March 11. Time to do the first performance for a paying audience.

"I sat in my ruffles and polka dots cut to there—no, even lower," remembered Celeste Holm. "I put on my mouth three times because my right hand trembled. There was a knock on my door. Lawrence Langner came in. He said, 'Just remember the Chaplinesque quality of the part. The fact that she can't say no is a terrible problem to her.'

"'All the time?' I asked.

"'That's the spine of the part,' he said, and left, like Hamlet following his father's ghost.

"Terry Helburn came in. 'Up, up, up!' she twinkled. 'We're counting on you for the comedy. Lift every scene you're in.'

"'Oh, God!' I thought fervently. 'Have they been seeing the same rehearsals?'

"Then Armina Marshall came in. She kissed me and said, 'I suppose I shouldn't say this, I think you're absolutely wrong for the part, but good luck!'"

The house lights went down. The audience was in place, except the inevitable latecomers pushing their way into the rows past the impatient theatregoers already in place. The New Yorkers (Hammerstein referred to them as "grave-diggers" or "smarties") who had made the trip in order to pass judgment on this new work sat back and stared at the curtain. Jay Blackton raised his baton, and his orchestra went into the first improvised "overture."

Then, silence. The curtain rose.

"Alfred Drake's lovely, familiar sound filled the theatre," Holm recalled, "now abetted by a marvelous orchestration, and as I waited, listening, I thought to myself, 'Well, now it's up to God and the audience and me to work it out together.'"

When Ado Annie's cue came, she opened her parasol and ran onstage. "I'd never been in a musical before, so I didn't know what to do when the audience didn't stop applauding after I had finished 'I Cain't Say No.' I kept trying to continue with the dialogue, but they wouldn't let me. It was embarrassing, but it was glorious!"

De Mille stood at the rear of the theatre, in the narrow carpeted space traditionally reserved for anxious production people who needed room to pace up and down, fight back nausea, or dash out through the lobby doors into deserted areas where they could weep and groan and argue without disturbing the paying customers inside. When her dancers finished their first number, "Many a New Day," their performance again stopped the show. "Dick Rodgers, standing beside me, threw his arms around me and hugged and hugged," she remembered.

On went the first act. On this March night an event of major importance to the American musical was taking place; the audience was being treated to history. A new form was being born, one in which the integration of plot, music, lyrics, and ballet with character would triumphantly affect the creators of musical theatre for years to come.

But tonight the event was as yet unrecognized. In fact, from the Shubert stage, behind the footlights, the cast could see an audience that was often far from overwhelmed. "I'd worked for Mike Todd in *Star and Garter*," said Friedlich. "So I knew his looks without seeing every feature, and I can distinctly remember seeing him walking out during the show."

"Oh, they were all there," said de Mille. "The 'wrecking crew' from New York, that's the name Ruth Gordon gave them, up to New Haven to see this show. It certainly wasn't the show you see today, but all the good songs were there. So a lot of them left early, and most of their reactions were, 'Well, too bad. This means the end of the Theatre Guild. . . . This is their last flop.'"

After intermission, most of the others returned for the second act. They applauded the rousing "The Farmer and the Cowman," to which Marc Platt and Eric Victor performed their ebullient solo dances. They beamed at the young lovers, parading back and forth to a lovely ballad, "Boys and Girls Like You and Me," then chuckled to the lyrics of "All Er Nothin'" performed by Celeste Holm and her intended, played by Lee Dixon.

Then, in the third scene, there came a song called "Oklahoma," a paean to a "brand new state." Tonight it featured George Church, and in front of the ensemble he performed his tap solo. "I did a pirouette," he recalls, "an inside pirouette, in which you turn right, with your left leg dragging, and as it drags, you do a tap with it. A real flash solo, turning and turning . . . and it got a big hand." Successful or not, that solo number would be performed only a few times more.

Meanwhile the Hammerstein libretto came to its climactic scene. Curly and Jud had their fight. Jud was inadvertently stabbed. Curly was eventually released from custody and reunited with his new bride, Laurey. All ended happily, to a reprise of "People Will Say We're in Love," and the curtain fell.

Applause.

The audience filed out into the night.

Was this going to be a hit? Who knew? Maybe. Maybe not. Not much sense in saying "It needs work." Every show that opened at the Shubert in New Haven did. A very wise showman once remarked, "Anybody with enough dough can call himself a producer and bring a show up to open at the Shubert. But my definition of 'producer' is the guy who can take a half-baked show *out* of the Shubert, and bring it into New York a *hit!*"

Yes, there was work to be done, but not tonight. Tomorrow, after they'd had some sleep. Then the work would begin.

"My wife and I just found ourselves a place where we could have a snack and go to bed," remembered Blackton. "We didn't congregate with any of the cast. I was beat . . . and remember, I was doing this show with one foot still in the St. Louis Municipal Opera! I still wasn't sure it would last."

Right after the show the producers filed into Celeste Holm's dressing room. "Lawrence said, 'That's just what I meant!'

"Armina said, 'I'm so glad I was wrong.'

"And Terry said, 'Will you sign a run-of-the-play contract at the same salary?'

"And I said, 'No.'"

Blackton recalled: "Most of the 'experts' who'd come up from New York thought the show charming and ineffectual. But the audience had loved it. . . . Later I signed my run-of-the-play contract, which actually meant a year from June 1, and asked, and got, $100 more, or $350 a week, which seemed at the time an enormous sum."

According to Helburn, the Guild's own backers were still uncertain. "You cannot have a murder in a musical show," they said, referring to the stabbing of Jud. "The love story's weak," pointed out someone else. Said another, "Build up your jokes, give the comedian more to do."

But there were others who sensed something marvelous on the stage that night. "A young man in the audience turned to me impulsively," Helburn recalled years later. "'This show is just great!' he said. 'Can I put all the money I have into it?' He had just one hundred dollars.

"At that stage," she said, "even we didn't know what we had. But we did know that the New Haven audience had liked the show . . . for whatever that was worth."

Which at this moment wasn't enough. Far from it, in fact.

Max Gordon was not the only one dubious about the show's future. (He would send a note to Hammerstein later which said, "Did I tell you I thought you ought to try to bring the girls in sooner in Act I?") When Walter Winchell's legendary Rose, the dreaded seer, had wired to her boss NO LEGS NO JOKES NO CHANCE, Winchell, always a point man for disaster, would show that wire to a Theatre Guild backer who had previously agreed to make a substantial check out to Helburn *et al.* As a result, the backer was about to renege on his promise. Small wonder that the ensuing days would be filled with a certain amount of panic.

"I was an undergraduate at Yale in 1943," recalled Philip Barry, Jr. "Just before *Away We Go!* opened at the Shubert, I had a long-distance call from my father, who was down in his winter home at Hobe Sound, Florida. It seems that Terry had called Dad—remember, he'd had a long association with the Guild, and his plays had often made big money for them, especially *The Philadelphia Story.*

"Terry reminded Dad that there was a royalty account in a New York bank where the Guild had been channeling a considerable amount—his money from Guild productions. Just sitting there, earning interest. 'She's offered me twelve and a half percent of this new musical—it's budgeted at around $80,000—if I'll let her have $10,000 from the royalty account,' said Dad. 'Why don't you go have a look at the show, and let me know your opinion of it.'"

Barry Jr. promptly made his way to the Shubert box office and got a fourth-row balcony seat for the Thursday night opening.

"I can remember it all so well," he recalled. "It was long; there were things that needed pruning, sure, but I was absolutely entranced by it! I loved the score—the dancing, the singing—I couldn't wait to call him the next day. 'Go ahead!' I said. 'Give them the money!' Well, alas, my father disagreed with my enthusiasm. . . . Seemed he felt that *Green Grow the Lilacs* was one of the dullest plays ever written, impossible to turn into a success, and he had little faith that the Guild could ever produce a successful musical. And so. . . you figure out how much we'd have earned from his $10,000 if he'd given it to Terry. We've long since stopped—it's too painful.

"Of course," he added, "it was consistent of him. Dad also turned down Howard Lindsay and Russel Crouse when they asked him to invest in *Life with Father*."

Friday and Saturday in New Haven were filled with rumor and contradiction. "We heard a lot of stories," said Drake:

> One of them was that the Guild was insecure about the director, and they were going to replace Mamoulian. I didn't believe that was possible until Saturday. You see, I had a habit of going down to the stage before a performance. . . . I'd go down on the stage and walk around the set; it's not as though I'm looking at it for the first time, but it's a way of getting myself into the character, I guess. And that day, in New Haven, I came down on the set, and there was George Abbott, sitting on one of the benches! I knew Mr. Abbott, I'd worked for him, so I walked over to ask him what he was doing there. He said, "Well, they're asking me to direct this."
>
> I said, "Oh, are you going to?"
>
> He said, "I don't think so. Why should anybody offer me a show like this?"
>
> I was surprised at that. "You think it's all right the way it is?"
>
> He said, "Sure, it's all right!"
>
> A pretty smart man, Mr. Abbott. Certainly made me feel a lot more secure. The Guild had somebody else up to see the show, I don't remember who. . . . But eventually they must have responded to Mr. Abbott's reaction. They stayed with Rouben; they were feeling less insecure. Which turned out to be very wise.

Mamoulian may not have been in complete control during earlier rehearsals, but after the New Haven opening he took a firm hold of the situation. "The morning after the opening he called us all together on the stage," said George Church. 'Ladies and gentlemen,' he said, 'I have to cut an hour and a half out of this show, and this means that some of you are going to be unhappy.' Well, I for one was unhappy because my second-act solo tap dance to 'Oklahoma' was axed. Moo-Moo said it was too much like 'The Farmer and the Cowman,' which opened the second act. 'Anticlimactic' was how he put it."

The second casualty was the delightful solo dance that Eric Victor had done with Bambi Linn as part of "The Farmer and the Cowman." Vivian Smith remarked, "It was a charming piece which Agnes had created, Bambi following Eric around, loving everything he did in the solo, and it ended up with a special finish, with Eric going up into a tree right there on stage!" On opening night Victor's solo had gotten a big hand. By the weekend the general analysis was that it interfered with the flow of the book.

Both featured dancers had lost their solos. By the time the company entrained for Boston, Victor had given notice. "He settled for a small sum," said Church. "He had a run-of-the-play contract, but he knew this flop show wouldn't run and figured that he'd get more money by being paid off now. . . . A colossal mistake, as it turned out."

Church also saw no future for himself in the show—no solo, nothing that would give him any involvement when they got to New York. But Rodgers would plead with him not to leave. "'Just give us the opening night in New York,' he said—'which,' he added, 'may also be our closing night.' Some indication of how we were all feeling at the time," said Church. They would resolve the question in Boston.

"At the New Haven opening," said Drake, "for some reason or other the producers had decided to cut Jud Fry's second-act solo, 'Lonely Room.'

> Perhaps it was because Howard Da Silva wasn't singing it too well; after all, he was an actor first, not a singer. But they felt it didn't work. Next day I went to Dick Rodgers and I said, "This is all wrong, that song is very important; it illuminates Jud's whole character. If you'd let me work with Howard on it I think I may be able to help him."
>
> So he agreed, and Howard and I went off by ourselves into one of those little public meeting rooms off the lobby of the Taft Hotel and we worked together on that song. . . . I did my best to coach him so that it would be a dramatic solo. That he could do. When they heard him do it again, they decided to put it back into the show. And in Boston it worked!"

"Boys and Girls Like You and Me," that lovely ballad, was blue-penciled. "The most Agnes had been able to do with it was to have the boys arm in arm with the girls, strolling up and down as they sang Hammerstein's lyrics," said Drake. "It was a sixteen-bar chorus, and within that length it was difficult to give the staging a great deal of variety."

According to singer Hayes Gordon, Mamoulian was far more assertive on the subject of that song:

> Mamoulian came onstage and said in his heavy Armenian accent, "Years from now, when I am sitting in my padded cell, someone will come in and ask, 'You are Rouben Mamoulian?' and I will answer, 'Yess,' and they will say, 'You directed *Away We Go!*?' And I will say, 'Yess.' Then they will say, 'And you staged the number "Boys and Girls"?' And I will scream, '*Yaaaaaabbbbb!*'" And with that, the number was out. He insisted it didn't advance the show; he was right.

A valuable lesson was being learned here as the troupe prepared to go to Boston. Nothing in *Away We Go!*—song, ballet, or solo—would be retained in the final version unless it was totally integrated with the libretto and, most important, unless it contributed something valid to the characters. Once that lesson had been applied (and it would include changing the show's title as well), the show would begin to find its legs.

If some of the Theatre Guild's potential backers had lost faith in New Haven, Boston audiences would restore it.

What about the cast? "All I can tell you," said Drake, "is that if anybody in that cast had had a penny they would have invested it in the show. They *believed* in it."

Boston

Theatrical legend has usually had it that *Away We Go!* not only suffered indignities in New Haven from opening-night spectators but was also mauled by the local critics. Far from true.

In fact, the locals smelled a hit long before the Bostonians and the New York big-leaguers. The perspicacious *New Haven Register* critic (he remains, sadly, anonymous to this day) who'd attended Thursday night's opening characterized the show as "a rollicking musical . . . jammed to the hilt with tuneful melodies . . . ideal escapist entertainment, long anticipated." He loved the de Mille dances, had high praise for the new Rodgers and Hammerstein partnership, and heralded their work as "an excellent theatrical tonic to greet the approach of spring!"

Variety's resident New Haven critic, Harold M. Bone, did not file his review until after the show departed for Boston. Bone (as he signed himself), a jovial New Havenite and a fixture at the Shubert, was a fair-minded critic who truly loved the theatre and bent over backward to be fair to the various talents who arrived in town. Rather than rely on what happened on those hectic opening Thursdays, he always made it a point to return on Friday and Saturday as well. He would talk to the creative hands to get some sense of how they planned to repair, revise, or make changes. His contribution to the cause was understanding; a caring review in *Variety* from Bone would be a big help to an out-of-town show, especially one already being bad-mouthed in Manhattan.

On Wednesday, March 17, St. Patrick's Day, Bone's review appeared. By that time, *Away We Go!* had opened in Boston, at the Colonial Theatre. His assessment of the show's possibilities was optimistic:

> Paced on a par with the fine music are the superb dance creations of Agnes de Mille. Though dance angle absorbs a bit too much running time, it's all sterling stuff. . . . Although not so sumptuous as the golden-era extravaganza musicals, there's quality in the trappings for *Away.* Songs are appropriately sentimental, peppy, and comic, as situations require, and the score as a whole comprises a succession of melodious moments. Overall high calibre of score augurs well for future possibilities of the new tunesmith duo. It got off to a good start here, and should stretch into a sizable stay on Broadway.

If anyone in the cast or crew had hoped for a breathing space between Saturday night's closing and the arrival in Boston, he or she had not counted on Helburn and Langner's desperate determination to make the show a success.

"I'd hoped to spend the trip to Boston reading a detective story," remembered de Mille, "but I'd reckoned without the Guild. They hired a dressing room on the train. We all crowded into it and in three and a half hours rewrote the play, chiefly the second act. I was ordered to produce a small three-minute dance in twenty-four hours. I did. But the skin came off the dancing girls' ribs from continuous lifting, and I couldn't seem to stop throwing up."

"Cuts and changes were made, and we worked constantly," said Holm. "Oscar gave me an encore, which was the funniest chorus of all to 'I Cain't Say No' . . . but what I was so impressed with, working with Oscar and Dick, was to see the skill with which they knew what to put in and what to take out. That's when most people doing a new show get into trouble. The show's opened and now they're not sure what should be changed. But Dick and Oscar *did*.

"I could see Oscar standing in the back of the theatre with his back to the stage," she continued. "He'd stand there during the performance and *listen*. . . . Why? The minute anybody in the audience at the Colonial coughed, Oscar would check the spot in his script which came thirty seconds *before* that spot. That's how he finally came to see that there was an emotional sag near the end of the second act . . . right after the murder."

She added with a smile that people forget there's a death in *Oklahoma!* "All they usually talk about is that sunny sweetness and light coming off the stage . . . and I tell them, 'Yeah? Look again.'"

So by the time the Boston reviews hit the streets, Hammerstein and Rodgers were already aware of the trouble spots in the second act. And the reviews were helpful. Elinor Hughes, of the *Herald*, the city's most important critic, was very optimistic:

> The Theatre Guild has gone into the musical comedy business with *Away We Go!*, which opened last night at the Colonial before a packed and enthusiastic house . . . and the results were so satisfactory that I can't think of any reason why they shouldn't keep right at it. Big, handsome, picturesque and generally entertaining, the production isn't quite ready for Broadway, being as yet on the lengthy side and having some first-act doldrums, but the virtues are numerous and the failings can be remedied. Meanwhile, Boston has a fine new musical to take to its heart—and you know Boston. . . .
>
> A special paragraph must go to Agnes de Mille's dances, which are an outstanding feature of the show and at one point come close to turning *Away We Go!* into dance drama rather than musical comedy. . . . In Oscar Hammerstein, Mr. Rodgers has found an admirable lyric and libretto writer. . . . Broadway has a very agreeable experience in store for it. . . .

But in the *Christian Science Monitor,* L. A. Stoper was far more critical:

> At present, the piece is too long for its matter, and contains too much rural humor and homely sentiment. Mr. Rodgers has been careful to make his songs simple, in keeping with the time and place, but unfortunately their simplicity, in common or in waltz time, becomes tiresome as the first scene drags on. . . . The Guild has followed the original play pretty closely, but a less faithful treatment of the disposition of Jud would make a better prelude to the departure of the bridal couple.

This first week in Boston, Hammerstein and Rodgers cut "Boys and Girls Like You and Me," and put "Lonely Room" back in. If Mr. Stoper of the *Monitor* had done anything in his review, he had fortified Hammerstein's understanding that the last half-hour of the show wanted something, something musically solid and exciting, some sort of blockbuster.

Blockbusters are not easily come by. Yet, as any seasoned veteran of musicals will testify, some of the most exciting changes in a show out of town take place under the gun.

Under which it now most certainly was.

"Lawrence made a list of everything to be done on a yellow pad, with a program," remembered de Mille. "The various departments were allotted time onstage, exactly like astronomers scheduled for the hundred-inch telescope. Lawrence policed the theatre with a large watch in his hand and there was no reprieve possible from his 'I'm very sorry, my dear.' Every night after the show, sharp councils were held. I have never seen a group of people work harder and faster, except perhaps the same group during my *Carousel* tryout. The entire play was reorganized in two weeks."

A phenomenal course of obstacles had to be overcome. For instance, the measles.

"That's where they really broke out," said Bambi Linn. "I don't know about other cities, but up in Boston, evidently, if you had more than a certain number of people having measles they'd shut down the show and you'd be quarantined. Naturally, the management was petrified! I think five people already had the measles, and we knew that if five people had it, it would go right through the cast. . . .

"Diana Adams and I were staying at a girls' club—the Charlotte Cushman Club. I ran home and I said, 'I've had the measles, so I probably won't get it.' But Diana hadn't had them, so we put her in a hot tub and we watched the measles come out! And then Maria Harriton got them. She was the girl in 'Many a New Day' who ran across the stage, wearing red petticoats."

"In pure exhaustion," said de Mille, "I decided one night to forego dinner and have a nap instead. I was barely bedded when the phone rang. Maria had broken out in spots and no understudy was ready. An hour later I was onstage in Maria's dress and bonnet."

"Next, one of the girls in the dance hall scene got the measles," said Linn, "and Agnes went on for her! For a time up there in Boston she became our 'swing girl,' filling in for anybody who was out sick. . . . She replaced all the measles cases! She was wonderful, of course. She had her own special way, she was the choreographer, she knew exactly what she wanted to do onstage, and as one of the dance hall girls she was marvelous. Exhausted at the end of the week, of course."

"Even though we got better reviews in Boston, I gave my two weeks' notice," said George Church, whose virtuoso tap-dance solo had been cut. He talked to Rodgers, who wanted him to agree to perform on the opening night in New York.

I knew very well that the first-act ballet, in which I danced the role of Jud and Marc Platt danced Curly and in which I ended up choking him, was very important to the show. . . . so we came to a compromise. I'd do "Laurey Makes Up Her Mind" for the first week in New York without any billing either in the program or outside the theatre, and that way nobody would know it was me and it couldn't hurt my future.

That settled, we proceeded to play Boston, and by the second week *Oklahoma!* was totally transformed, without my solo.

Jay Blackton still hadn't settled his situation with the St. Louis Municipal Opera. Dick Berger, his boss there, had promised he'd wait to see what happened to the show in New Haven. But after that opening, Berger still had doubts, and decided to wait until the Boston tryout to decide; in fact, he came to the Boston opening. "We went out to have lunch in Faneuil Hall Market," Blackton said. "'Well, Jay,' he said, 'I'll give it six months. . . . April, May, June—I've got to get somebody to replace you, so would you please suggest somebody?' And I went back to the hotel, and I said to my wife, 'Well, we can eat for the next six months!'"

In Boston, the "Oklahoma" number metamorphosed from a pleasant second-act dance number (too similar to "The Farmer and the Cowman" was Mamoulian's correct appraisal) in which Church had done his solo into the smashing chorale showstopper. It started with an inspired guess by one of the show's singers, Faye Elizabeth Smith. "She had the loveliest voice in the show, incredible voice," said Holm. "All I do is just think of her, even today, and it makes me sing better.

"It was *her* suggestion. She went up to Rodgers—and she said, 'Richard' (we all called him Richard—it was before he became a living legend; he was simply a darling guy who wrote wonderful music)—and she said, 'You know, with the voices you have in this show, why are you having us do this song in unison? If we did "Oklahoma" in *harmony* we could take the roof off every theatre in this country!'

"And Dick said, 'You're right!'"

Arranger Robert Russell Bennett had returned to New York; most of his work was completed, but he was on standby. "If we needed him to do anything he could hop the train to Boston and come right up," said Blackton. "He'd fix things for Rodgers, and then go home. So we phoned him and told him the problem. 'Robert, we need a full chorale arrangement for the song "Oklahoma." Everyone onstage, singing. Can you get it up here as soon as possible?'

"Now this is a major piece of work," Blackton continued. "Because from one master copy of such an arrangement we would need all sorts of copies, for each member of the orchestra. But Bennett was a helluva guy, and a hard worker. He started in immediately down in New York, got on the train, and I believe he finished some of it as the train was pulling into Boston!"

Bennett hopped a cab to the Colonial Theatre—with his one precious copy of the vocal arrangement in hand. "This was Sunday, our day off—there weren't any copyists available to go to work on it," said Blackton. "But it had been decided we had to put this new number into the show as soon as possible."

What ensued was a screenwriter's dream, a climactic moment that would have thrilled any audience. In came the cast, eager and willing to learn the new arrangement, and from improvisation there would emerge pure theatrical gold.

"Margot Hopkins, who usually worked with Dick, couldn't read Bennett's arrangement, so I had to sit at the piano," Blackton recalled. "They hauled one into the lobby of the Colonial, which was closed. Everybody—all the dancers and singers—piled around me in this very small space, and there was I, at the piano, with Russell's new arrangement on my music stand, plunking out the parts!"

Giving up their one day off, the ensemble piled in. "I was the conductor, so I had to assign the parts to the various singing groups arbitrarily. I'd say, 'You sing tenor; You sing bass here,' just by rote. I was banging out the melody and the harmonies. . . . The people were learning it on their feet, or on their haunches, or wherever they were perched on stools, whatever—everybody! Alfred Drake stood by, he had the first chorus, and of course Betty Garde was in it—that was the first part, which was easy. But the second part, that fancy part with all those countermelodies and so on—I had to teach it all!"

Little by little the Bennett arrangement came to life, growing in strength, with all the harmonies coming together. A showstopper was being born.

"Now, while I'm rehearsing all this," continued Blackton, "waiting behind us there were Mamoulian, and de Mille, Rodgers and Hammerstein, and the producers, impatient to have me prepare the cast well enough so it could be staged. The kids were marvelous . . . . some of them were such good sight readers that they'd peek over my shoulder, get the notes, and then pass it around.

"So finally . . . we all went upstairs, and we sang it, with me leading, and it sounded marvelous. But it had to be staged. Mamoulian was our director, so it was up to him to do it—but evidently he couldn't handle chorale numbers, they just weren't his thing."

"I remember exactly what happened after that," said Vivian Smith. "Agnes said, 'Wait a minute, I know how to do this,' and she got us all positioned, assigning us places in a sort of a wedge-shaped formation, in rows—she had us starting upstage, and then we moved down, in that V-shaped formation—we called it 'the flying wedge' because it came straight at the audience. You knew when you moved because it was your group which moved. We started in the rear, and came closer, and closer, and then we came together, at the footlights. A marvelous effect!"

"There I was," Blackton said, "holding on to that one copy of the score as de Mille worked with the people, making sure the right singer was in the right place melodically—guarding Russell's arrangement. There was Alfred, standing in the middle at the apex of the V, and the kids all singing this complicated thing, half doing the melody, the other half doing countermelody. . . ."

Out of a Sunday creative explosion would come true theatrical excitement. Anyone who's ever seen a cast perform that great number, assembled that March 21 afternoon, will testify to that. The revised "Oklahoma" went into the show in the second week in Boston, and the effect was immediate.

"The first night we did it, I was conducting, and so I couldn't see the audience behind me," Blackton said. "But I certainly could *hear* them. They went wild! The number stopped the show, dead. The applause was so great that first time we did it that right after the performance Dick came to me and we decided to establish an encore chorus of the song; that meant going back and repeating the ensemble part—the one I'd taught them all."

"I had only one problem with it," said Drake. "When Dick asked me to do the encore solo, I asked him, 'Richard, may I take it down a half a tone? I think it will sound better.' He agreed, Jay and I made the adjustment, and from then on that's how we did it. We did the number, down came Agnes's flying wedge, and we did the finish with the cowboy yell—'Yee-ow!' and then came the applause. And *then* the encore—and we had our showstopper!"

This eleven o'clock high point would invariably bring down the house; it also propelled *Oklahoma!* into a smash hit and performed a critical service: It wafted the second act past the sagging spot after Jud Fry's death and carried the audience happily into the finale, the reprise of "People Will Say We're in Love." "It gave the show a *punctuation*," Blackton explained. "A real exclamation point. In fact, I'm certain that's where the exclamation point in the title came from that same excitement we'd generated."

"Funny thing," de Mille reported in her diary. "People went home, down the sidewalks singing, and they wanted to come back. No one seemed very excited, but suddenly we were sold out."

The audiences were humming on their way out of the Colonial, but behind the scenes there were serious problems. Now de Mille fell victim to the measles. Helburn went to bed with icebags on her head to quell a fever, but left her hotel room to attend rehearsals with a trained nurse. Dorothy Hammerstein was taken to Peter Bent Brigham Hospital with a raging fever, and her husband commuted back and forth from her hospital room. Marc Platt hurt his foot and was ordered not to dance for a week; he ignored the doctor's warning and continued to perform. "Margit DeKova fainted every time she jumped," recorded de Mille. "Two of the leads and one of the best girls out of every number. The matinee [March 27] went on in good order. This," she proudly concluded, "is a remarkable troupe. The actors are dumbfounded. They've never seen such stamina before; they've never worked with real dancers."

"I think we did as good a job on *Oklahoma!* as I've ever done on a show," mused Elaine Steinbeck. "Everybody pulled together. They took out a number, and they added a number, but most of all they added *authority* to the show. They tightened it. They gave it a viewpoint. I think Mamoulian was superb in Boston. He saw what he had in New Haven, and then he went to work and put it into operation at the Colonial.

"And as for Oscar," she added, "well, he was brilliant. I certainly think you have to give Dick Rodgers enormous credit for having chosen exactly the right man to be his collaborator."

There exists a certain amount of understandable confusion as to who actually came up with the idea of retitling the show at the Colonial. Helburn remembered that Hammerstein had originally titled his libretto *Oklahoma*, but the title had been turned down, "as people might confuse it with *Okies*. Armina, who was born on the Cherokee Strip, suggested the name *Cherokee Strip*, but there were objections to this, too. People might think of striptease.'"

Agnes de Mille was equally uncertain. "*Oklahoma* was suggested," she said, "but it didn't seem like a very good title. Lawrence declared himself satisfied if an exclamation point was added. Would people go to see something with a plain geographical title? we asked. Armina had been born out there, and she thought, with great fervor, they would."

Hammerstein's biographer, Hugh Fordin, has it that the new title had been agreed upon by all when Hammerstein said, "Why don't we add an exclamation point to *Oklahoma* and be done with it?"

It's possible that the origin of the final title may lie in the emphasis that was newly placed on the song "Oklahoma." Or it may have been the reverse: that the revised title impelled the emphasis on the song—and caused it to be expanded into the chorale version that became the second-act blockbuster. We can only conjecture.

Down in the Manhattan offices of the Guild, Helene Hanff toiled away at her press department chores:

> . . . We were busy addressing envelopes and grinding out ten thousand copies of the press release on the mimeograph machine, to tell the world about the new American folk opera *Away We Go!* We had about eight thousand mimeographed when Joe came back from Boston and broke the news to us that we'd have to throw them all away and start over.

There had been a title change.

It sounds fine to you; you're used to it. But do me a favor and imagine you're working in a theatre and somebody tells you your new musical is going to be called *New Jersey*, or *Maine*. To us, *Oklahoma* remained the name of a state, even after we'd mimeographed ten thousand new releases and despite the fact that *Oklahoma* appeared three times on each one.

We had folded several hundred of them when the call came from Boston. Joe picked up the phone and we heard him say "Yes, Terry" and "All right, dear." And then he hung up and he looked at us, in the dazed way people who worked at the Guild frequently looked at each other.

"They want," he said in a faraway voice, "an exclamation point after *Oklahoma*."

Which is how it happened that, far, far into the night, Lois and I, bundled in our winter coats, sat in the outer office putting thirty thousand exclamation points on ten thousand press releases while Joe, in the inner office, bundled in his overcoat, phoned all over town hunting down and waking up various printing firms and sign painters. We were bundled in our coats because the heat had been turned off by an economy-minded management, now happily engaged in spending several thousand dollars to alter houseboards, playbills, ads, three-sheet posters, and souvenir booklets, to put an exclamation point after *Oklahoma*.

By the end of the second week in Boston, *Oklahoma!* was, in theatrical argot, "frozen." What the Boston audiences saw and cheered on that final Saturday night was what the much tougher New Yorkers would see on the coming Wednesday night, March 31, at the St. James. Hammerstein was shrewd enough to see that in all these frenetic Boston days the cast had lost the pace of the show while all the changes were added in rehearsal. But, in a letter to his son Bill, he said, "We gave them a good drilling, and the result was so successful that one night we suddenly took on the aura of a hit. . . . All this is said in the hope that a handful of beer-stupefied critics may not decide that we have tried to write a musical comedy and failed. If they see that this is different, and higher in its intent, they should rave. I know this is a good show. I cannot believe it will not find a substantial public. There! My neck is out."

A good many futures—perhaps even more than in most Broadway ventures—hung in midair. There was enough money in the Theatre Guild bank account to keep the show running in New York for a week or so. At the St. James box office there were hardly any advance sales.

The work was done. A couple of dress rehearsals away loomed Wednesday night's opening. Then it would be up to the New York critics.

In his biography of Hammerstein, Hugh Fordin recounts how the lyricist and his wife went for a walk near their home in Doylestown on the day of the show's opening. An optimist by nature (he would give the audience his credo when he wrote "A Cock-Eyed Optimist" for Mary Martin), he was also a seasoned pragmatist who'd spent the past decade or so swimming against a hostile tide. Certainly the past year had been a long pull upstream. That day Hammerstein told his wife, "I don't know what to do if they don't like this. I don't know what to do because this is the only kind of show I can write."

One member of the company was already convinced of the show's success. "We were rehearsing in the foyer, one day after the matinee," recalled Kate Friedlich. "Agnes, Joan and I, I think it was 'All Er Nothin'.' When we came upstairs, everyone had gone to dinner except Lawrence Langner. Under the arc light, on stage, he was bowing right and left and acknowledging the cheers from the balcony, and we could hear him saying 'This has never happened to me before.' Obviously he was rehearsing for the New York opening night when the audience would shout 'Producer, producer!' Happily, he didn't see us."

Oh, What a Beautiful Evening!

The scenery, lighting, and costumes left Sunday on a train from Boston, and by Monday, March 29, were being unloaded into the St. James Theatre, on West 44th Street.

"I got back to New York, picked up my mail, and found the well-known summons from my Uncle Sam ('Congratulations: you have been accepted into the United States Army!')," said George Church. "I went over to the St. James, where we were due to open in two days. There, out front on the houseboards, was my name, in large print, and in the program also, big as life!

"I ran into Dick Rodgers inside. 'Hey, Dick,' I asked, 'what happened to our deal?'

"'Looks like somebody goofed, George,' he said, and he apologized. . . . It was too late now to make a fuss. What was my problem? The word seemed to have gotten around town that this show was very shaky. Nobody really figured it was going to make it, so I could play out a few days and then I'd go off to take care of Mr. Hitler, right?"

Bambi Linn wrote to her family and told them she'd gotten them opening-night tickets. "I said, 'You have to come opening night, because we may not be running much longer than that.' Big Broadway dancer that I now was, I was talking as if I really knew what I was talking about!

"I walked over to the St. James, and I saw my picture up in front of the theatre! And then there was an article about me in the *Brooklyn Daily Eagle*, because I was a local girl making her debut—and I thought to myself, 'How can this be? I'm the lowest of the low in this production, and here they have me out in front of the theatre?' . . . Oh, for me, it really didn't matter if the show was a hit—it was just so wonderful to be there!"

As the production was being set up on the stage, Jay Blackton assembled his New York pit orchestra and ran a musical rehearsal while Jerry Whyte and his stage managers checked out every under-the-gun last-minute detail backstage.

There was precious—and rationed—heat on in the St. James, and lights on in the box office, but outside that ticket window there was no line of eager buyers, and in the cash drawers there wasn't much of a "wrap"—theatre talk for the day's take. The prospective audience for *Oklahoma!* was nowhere to be seen. Obviously, the word from Boston, the news of the second week's changes and their impact on the audience, hadn't reached New York, and if it had, it hadn't caused any groundswell. The Guild's subscription list had dwindled seriously in the past two seasons, eroded by sixteen flops.

Then came the final obstacle. On the morning of March 31, 1943, it began to snow.

Is it any wonder then that opening night was not sold out?

It continued to snow.

"I had ten front-row balcony seats, and I didn't know whom to give them to," said de Mille. "I think a couple remained empty."

"We hear they went out and started bringing people in," said Linn. "They found as many servicemen as they could; they literally went out and dragged them in . . . 'Come see a new show, come on in!' They had to do it. You know how big the St. James is, and if those last few rows were empty downstairs, they couldn't let it look like that. Not to have a full house on *opening night*?

"So they papered the house, and in fact I remember somebody said to us, 'Is there anybody you could invite?' I mean, to the cast! Of course, I'd already paid for my family's tickets, and when I heard that I said, 'Gee whiz, I could have got them in for free!'"

Helene Hanff was still laboring up in the Theatre Guild press department.

At six, that evening, the snow had turned to sleet, and the cold I'd developed now included a cough. As I left the office to go home and climb into a drafty evening dress, Joe Heidt took pity on me. "I don't need you there, dear," he said. "Don't come unless you feel like it."

I felt guilty about not going as I ate a quick dinner at a cafeteria. But by the time I'd fought my way home through the sleet, guilt had given way to self-preservation. I undressed and crawled thankfully into bed. In bed, I reached for the wet newspaper I'd brought home and opened it to the theatre page. Our big opening-night legend leaped out at me: OKLAHOMA!

Slowly, surely, with that foggy bewilderment you were bound to feel sooner or later if you worked at the Theatre Guild long enough, I saw that Terry and Lawrence were right. About the exclamation point.

. . . I switched off the lamp, thinking how typical it was of both this epic and the Guild that the notices would appear on the morning of

April Fool's Day. . . . I coughed, pulled up the blankets as I drifted off to sleep, said a silent "Good luck" to Alfred Drake . . . who was at that moment about to stroll onto the stage of the St. James Theatre to sing "Oh, What a Beautiful Mornin'."

Marc Platt's foot, which he'd injured in Boston, was still troubling him. But the young ballet dancer, who'd lately been in three successive flop musicals, *The Lady Comes Across, My Dear Public,* and *Beat the Band,* told his doctor he'd be damned if he'd miss being in what he hoped would be his first hit. So the doctor taped Marc up as best he could to protect him from further injury, and in order to make certain the dancer could go on agreed to be around on opening night at the theatre. And Marc sat backstage, preparing to go on.

"That took a lot of guts on Marc's part," said George Church. "He and I worked up a very strenuous routine in the first-act dream ballet. We used to kill each other every day out of town. We had a lot of fun, but we ended up black-and-blue."

"We used to bring gasps from the audience at some of the stuff we did; very acrobatic stunts," said Platt. "George used to throw me ten, twelve feet in the air, and then when I landed I'd slide another six. Very flashy acrobatic stuff."

"Of course," added Platt sadly, "none of that was ever seen after opening night. By that time I was out, and George had left to go into the army."

By nightfall the weather hadn't improved. Bundled in winter coats, the opening-night audience sloshed up 44th Street to the darkened marquee of the St. James and filed inside.

The audience dispensed the customary waves and greetings (New York openings were clubby affairs), the house lights went down, and Jay Blackton took his place in the orchestra pit. He raised his hands to give a downbeat (he did not yet use a baton, but would later, after a collision with a music stand gave him a permanently gnarled left pinky).

The music began.

When the overture ended, there was silence.

Outside the St. James, in a browned-out city, there were shortages, rationing, uncertainty. There were few families who were not bereft of sons and husbands. But here, inside the theatre, a thousand-odd people sat and watched the lights come up, bright and strong, bathing Lem Ayers's prairie vista in a warm, golden aura. There sat a placid lady, in simple clothing, at a butter churn, and as she did her chores there was a sense of peace and quiet and complete security. "Was there ever a more magical moment in the theatre than that one of small, early sounds that preceded Alfred Drake's song of rejoicing in the morning?" wrote Celeste Holm years afterward.

And then, from offstage, came the voice of Curly, singing.

When he finished, there was a wave of applause.

"Then they fell in love with 'The Surrey with the Fringe on Top,'" said Holm.

"Alfred had never been more wonderful. They adored Lee Dixon doing 'Everything's Up to Date in Kansas City.' And then it was my turn. I tried to remember everything that those two-and-a-half weeks of acting and reacting to audiences had confirmed. . . . My opening-night nerves really attacked; a tight band of hope around my head, and a tighter one of fear around my chest. . . ." Then she made her entrance, and soon she was enchanting the audience with "I Cain't Say No."

The laughs were delighted, and the applause hearty. If they wanted an encore, Hammerstein's second chorus was all a comedienne could dream of. "With each song," said Celeste, "the show rose higher and higher."

On rolled the first act. At the end, when the curtain fell on the de Mille ballet, "the boys started hitting each other backstage with their big hats," Holm remembered. "'It's a hit, it's a hit!'"

Outside, the lobby was buzzing with excited responses. Upstairs in the dressing rooms there was also excitement, but of a different nature. "At intermission," said Agnes de Mille, "I bucked the tide of spectators and fought my way to the stage door. Marc's leg was in a terrible state. Upstairs, Kate Friedlich was crying; she'd torn two ligaments from her heel."

"It was in the ballet at the end of the first act," said Friedlich:

I was dancing with a young man whose first show this was. I'm sure I was keyed up and nervous; he was probably even more so. . . . But he took me up in a lift, way up, he was a six-footer, and he lifted me eight feet up there, off the stage. And in his nervousness he forgot to bring me down properly, and he just dropped me—and I smashed down to the stage! And I badly sprained my ankle.

Since Marc Platt's doctor was backstage, it was decided they would shoot me full of something called ethyl chloride, which froze your foot up like a block of ice . . . so then I could go on spraining my ankle four or five more ways, without feeling it, not knowing what the hell I felt! Later a sports doctor told me that was a very dangerous treatment; they use it on athletes sometimes to kill the pain, but never allow them to go back in action afterwards. But that night, at the St. James, I didn't feel I had much choice not to go back and do the second act—I was duty bound. We didn't have any understudies.

Agnes claims she fed me and Marc both some brandy. I don't remember much about that. But by the time the second act began we were both ready, and off we went. When the show was over, I had myself six or seven sprains. I was out of the show for eight weeks; Marc was out for a long, long time. But we'd danced that opening night!

"The way it worked out, with Marc Platt and Katie injuring themselves," commented Vivian Shiers, "we only had the original cast of the show on that one opening night. After the opening, they started drafting the guys, not only

George Church but George Irving, too."

The barn dance, "The Farmer and the Cowman," began the second act. "Marc, in an ecstasy of excitement, rode the pain to triumph," de Mille recalled. "Virile, young, red-headed, and able, he looked like Apollo and moved like a stallion!"

On rolled that second act, gathering momentum and resonating to an enraptured audience that laughed and sighed in all the right places to the Rodgers and Hammerstein score and followed the fortunes of Curly and Laurey, the complex love affair of Will Parker and Ado Annie and Ali Hakim. The box social. The auction, at which Curly sacrifices all his possessions to wrest Laurey away from Jud's dark attentions. The wedding, and then, to celebrate it, that exultant cast down front, belting out to the New Yorkers a hymn to a brand new state: "Oklahoma, O–K!"

The encore, second chorus, was as powerful and exciting as all that had gone before. Or more so.

Hammerstein's brilliant stagecraft wound it all up. The shivaree on the wedding night. The struggle with Jud, who dies at the hands of Curly by Jud's own knife, that symbolic weapon we'd known about since the first act. The accusation of Curly, then the reprieve: "We ain't gonna let you send the boy to jail on his wedding night!" cries one of the Oklahomans; justice triumphs—it was self-defense! And away go the happy bride and groom in their surrey with the fringe on top, headed for a truly happy ending. . . .

During the run of *Oklahoma!* at the St. James Theatre, full-size photographs of the principals in the cast were mounted under the marquee. This one of Bambi Linn, shown here greatly diminished, miraculously survived. (Courtesy of Bambi Linn)

Applause, and more applause, roars of it! And bows from the beaming cast, to an equally exhilarated audience. Which eventually gathered up its coats and hats and reluctantly began to leave, many of them floating out of that theatre on a cloud of delight into the cold darkness of the wartime city. Away from the glow of that Oklahoma prairie and its staunch pioneer people.

After this night, with this one performance of *Oklahoma!*, the American musical theatre would never be the same. This simple story of America's growing up on the frontier, set to a wonderful score, with its honest characters and brilliant choreography, was something new. A successful vision, a prototype from which everything would now flow. But how could the St. James audience know that its opening-night tickets had given it a place in theater history? At that moment, those thousand-odd people were simply basking in the impact of the show.

But they were newly equipped with memories for a lifetime, memories set to music which they could not wait to rave about to anyone who had not been at the St. James that night.

Agnes de Mille took her mother to Sardi's for a sandwich. A thin, bespectacled gentleman crossed over to her table, shook her hand, and congratulated her. He was Wolcott Gibbs, the drama critic of *The New Yorker*, well known for his waspish reviews and acerbic tongue. But not on this night. "I want to congratulate you," he said. "This was most distinguished."

"I chewed on, in a sort of stupor," she related.

In Sardi's, as was the custom, applause greeted each member of the *Oklahoma!* crew as he or she entered that traditional theatrical watering hole. Everyone knew how important the newspaper reviews would be, especially the one being written a block away, on West 43rd, at the *New York Times* office —not by the dean of New York critics, Brooks Atkinson, who'd gone off to war, but by his replacement, Lewis Nichols.

Meanwhile there were congratulations all around. Rodgers was suddenly accosted by a small man grinning from ear to ear who threw his arms around him. It was Larry Hart, who'd seen the show from a Row B seat and roared with laughter and applauded all the way through. *"Dick!"* he cried, "I've never had a better evening in my life! This show will be around twenty years from now!"

An error on Hart's part, this time one of underestimation.

Before the *Times* review arrived, Helburn went home and turned on a radio. At midnight she heard the first commentator. "The show," he said, "won't last a week." One is forced to speculate which theatre he'd attended that night.

Probably the happiest member of that opening-night audience—certainly the most possessive—was playwright Lynn Riggs, in New York on an army pass from his post. His escort to the show was Miranda Masocco Levy, an old friend from Santa Fe who had taken a job at Bergdorf Goodman. "Lynn absolutely loved the show from beginning to end," Levy remembered. "He laughed, he applauded, he was delighted with what they'd all done with his play. When it was over we went backstage so he could congratulate everyone; what a thrill for me, a small-town girl, meeting all those performers!" The next day, Riggs euphorically hurried up to Bergdorf's, where he bought presents for the cast.

Jules Glaenzer, the head of Cartier and a veteran Broadway habitué, threw a large party after the Sardi's gathering. When he offered Rodgers a drink, the composer refused, saying, "No, thanks, I don't want to touch a drop. I want to remember every second of this night!"

Years later, in his memoirs, Rodgers summed up the experience: "I was forty at the time, with a number of hit shows behind me, but nothing had ever remotely compared to this. It was a rebirth, both in my associations and in my career."

The *Times* review appeared, and was good. "For years they have been saying the Theatre Guild is dead," wrote Nichols, "words that obviously will have to be eaten with breakfast this morning. . . . A truly delightful musical play. . . . Wonderful is the nearest adjective, for this excursion of the Guild combines a fresh and infectious gaiety, a charm of manner, beautiful acting, singing and dancing, and a score by Richard Rodgers that doesn't do any harm, either, since it is one of his best."

Howard Barnes of the *Tribune* called it "jubilant and enchanting . . . a superb musical." Walter Winchell, who hadn't made it up to New Haven, was less excited. "When the ladies of the ballet are on view," he remarked, "*Oklahoma!* is at its very best. The audience last night had a happy time." Burns Mantle gave it three stars and a plus in the *Daily News*.

The rave reviews would be joined by those in the afternoon papers, and they would mount in crescendo in the following Sunday's assessments.

Blackton, his evening chores done, left the theatre and with his wife, Louise, and his assistant ate in a nearby Italian restaurant. After a plate of spaghetti he went uptown with his wife and they retired. "We figured what must be must be," he remembered. "We could read the papers tomorrow morning. Now we needed sleep.

"In the morning, we were still in bed. Very early. The phone rings. It's Dick Berger, my patient boss from the St. Louis Municipal Opera, who's been waiting for weeks now to see how things would be with this show and if I'd be able to do his summer season or not. He said, 'Jay, did you read?'

"I said, 'Read *what*?'

"He said, 'You haven't read the papers? The *Times*—the *Trib*?' He was so excited.

"I said, 'No, we just got up-'

"He said, 'My God—you have got to read them!' And then he added, 'Jay—*goodbye!*'"

By noon the next day de Mille was back at the St. James rehearsing Marc Platt's understudy for the Thursday night performance.

The afternoon papers came out. John Anderson, in the *Journal-American*, called *Oklahoma!* "a beautiful and delightful show, fresh and imaginative, as enchanting to the eye as Richard Rodgers' music is to the ear. It has, at a rough estimate, practically everything."

Ward Morehouse, in the *Sun*, was less effusive and pointed to slowness and monotony. "But by the time they're singing the lusty title song near the finish," he said, "you're under the spell of it." Burton Rascoe, in the *World-Telegram*, enjoyed himself: "The Theatre Guild, once so austerely intellectual and aristocratic, has joined the march of democracy, let down the bars to a musical show—and has a hit on its hands." He was effusive about de Mille's ballets. "She has two numbers, danced to the music of 'Out of My Dreams' and 'All Er

Nothin','' which are such supreme aesthetic delights as to challenge anything the Met can produce this season. They are spine-tingling and out of this world."

That Thursday morning Rodgers and Hammerstein, recovered from the previous night's festivities, decided to have lunch. "Should we sneak off to some quiet place where we can talk, or shall we go to Sardi's and show off?" asked Rodgers.

"Hell, let's go to Sardi's and show off!" replied Hammerstein.

They came down 44th Street and passed the St. James Theatre. The box office was open, and there was bedlam. Ticket buyers were pushing and shoving to get to the window. A New York policeman tried to keep order.

Inside Sardi's there was another triumphal lunchtime scene as friends and pseudo-friends surrounded the pair, offering handshakes and hugs and, of course, requesting house seats for the first available date. "All the while assuring us that they'd known right from the start that the show would be a hit," commented Rodgers sardonically.

The strongest form of advertising in show business is word of mouth. A scant twelve hours after the curtain had fallen the night before, the word was spreading all over New York, and by telephone out to California. By the end of the week everyone was writing about this newly arrived smash hit. *PM*, Ralph Ingersoll's innovative tabloid, summed up the various physical problems which had beset the cast out of town—the measles, injuries, and so on. "The casualties were not suffered in vain," the paper reported. "The Theatre Guild, which seems a bit bewildered at having such a bonanza on its hands, reports in awed tones that the first five shows in New York netted $18,000 and 151 standees—capacity—and that advance sales are something like $25,000. That news makes up for a lot of sprained ankles and German measles."

Bear in mind that we are discussing 1943 dollars. The rate of inflation has been so rapid that it's safe to estimate today that $25,000 is worth at least ten times more now. Certainly not as impressive as the $32,000,000 advance sales figure quoted for *Miss Saigon*, but based on the original production cost of the Guild's 1943 production and the pay-back to its investors over the years (Miss Helburn estimated it at a staggering 2,500 percent), who, one may ask, came out ahead?

"There were a few vacant seats at the first Thursday matinee," Helburn recorded. After that, "the house sold out for the next four years."

"The real raves came in the Sunday papers," said Alfred Drake, "after they'd had time to think about what they'd seen. Florence Reed, who was playing in Thornton Wilder's *The Skin of Our Teeth*, loved the show so much that she bought tickets for the next thirty-odd Thursday matinees! Hers were on Wednesday, so she had Thursdays free, and she'd sit out there in the mezzanine every week; every time she was there, I'd know. I'd finish singing 'Surrey,' and this deep bass voice, unmistakeable, would boom out from the mezzanine: 'Bravo!'"

Shortly afterward, the Guild exercised its option on the screen rights to

Green Grow the Lilacs from Metro-Goldwyn-Mayer. The film version of the show would not be produced for many prosperous years during which the Broadway company ran at capacity, and the national and other touring companies crisscrossed the United States.

In England, *Oklahoma!* would be a tonic for war-weary audiences. The British production, mounted by the Guild, opened at the Drury Lane Theatre, in London on May 1, 1947. Some thirty-six hours before the curtain rose, lines of ticket buyers formed at the box office; they packed that huge theatre for the next three and a half years—the longest run of any show that had ever opened at that venerable theatre. The gross "takings" would reach an astonishing £1,324,500, paid in by nearly three million British theatregoers grateful for the opportunity to bask in the glow of the sunlit plains, exported to them from the colonies.

After the war there would be other productions in Europe.

There were only a thousand-odd seats in the St. James, and the show played eight performances a week. (A ninth was played for which the seats were reserved during the war for servicemen only.) It doesn't take a mathematician to figure out the odds involved in the availabilities of those St. James seats: tiny supply, untold-of demand. Getting a pair for *Oklahoma!* would be like winning the lottery. The Theatre Guild archives, stored away for posterity in the Beinecke Library at Yale, include cartons of correspondence files from the *Oklahoma!* years. Dozens of them deal with the problems involved in the show's preparation and production. But there are two bulging cartons that deal with one particular subject—requests for precious "house" seats to the show.

Day after day, from 1943 on, Langner and Helburn (as well as Rodgers, Hammerstein, Mamoulian, and de Mille, certainly) received a steady stream of begging letters from friends, relatives, friends of friends, friends of relatives, in-laws of same, business acquaintances, anyone with whom they might have had, somewhere in the past half-century, a brief chat, a cup of coffee, or shared a train seat—the entire world seemed to want only one boon from Helburn or Langner: a precious pair of on-the-aisle tickets!

An entire body of legends grew up on the subject of ticket-seekers.

In Doylestown, Hammerstein's tenant farmer asked for a pair of seats for his son and his future bride, to enable them to see the show after their wedding reception. Hammerstein promised to arrange it and asked, "When's the wedding?"

"The day you can get us the tickets," promised the farmer.

The St. James box office reported threats, cajolery, and out-and-out bribery offers from determined theatregoers. One of the treasurers refused offers of steaks, nylon stockings, and similar wartime rarities for valuable two-on-the-aisles. Al Hildreth, the head treasurer at the theatre, finally had enough of the daily stress of dealing with the crowds, and in September 1944 he turned in his resignation.

One day there came to the box office a letter mailed from a German prison camp. It read, "Please reserve tickets for *Oklahoma!* for the following prisoners of war," and it then listed the thirteen names of the senders, with their ranks.

But it was the impact on those fortunate audiences who did manage to get scarce tickets to the show, who nightly sat back and savored the love story, the ballets, that triumphant ending, and the music and lyrics of *Oklahoma!* For what also took off like a prairie wildfire was the Rodgers and Hammerstein score. Two days after the show opened, Rodgers was spending the night in a hotel off Park Avenue while his family stayed in their Connecticut home. He was awakened in the morning by the sun pouring into his hotel room window and the sound of childish voices below singing something familiar. He looked down to find a group of children singing, "Oh, What a Beautiful Mornin'." "The show had just opened and they knew the song already!" he said. "What a lovely feeling it was to realize that I was reaching not only the theatregoing adults but their children as well."

Nothing Rodgers had written with Hart had ever enjoyed such instant popularity. "People Will Say We're in Love" was the top radio tune of 1943 and sold 9,000 copies a day; "Oh, What a Beautiful Mornin'," 4,000. Less than a year after the opening of the show the millionth copy of the *Oklahoma!* sheet music was presented by the authors to Mayor Fiorello LaGuardia.

One of the side effects of this incredible success was the birth of a new kind of recording, the original-cast album. For years the Broadway theatre, which had offered such bounties of music and lyrics during the twenties and the thirties to its audiences, had been ignored on records. Major recording companies would issue singles of song hits by star vocalists and comedy performers, or played by popular orchestras of the day, but rarely, if ever, were record buyers offered the performance of a whole Broadway score by the original cast.

Right after the opening in 1943, Jack Kapp, the visionary, aggressive head of Decca Records, approached Rodgers and Hammerstein with a bold concept. He would use the original cast of *Oklahoma!* plus the pit orchestra conducted by Jay Blackton, playing Robert Russell Bennett's arrangements, and produce an album of recordings which would provide customers with an entire Broadway show. If they couldn't get precious tickets to the show, at least they could take it home in an album and enjoy it there, indefinitely!

If *Oklahoma!* would prove to be a bold watershed event in American musical theatre, Kapp's plan was equal to the event. A deal was quickly struck, and the album went into production. "We brought the whole gang into Decca's studio on West 57th Street," Blackton recalled. "Jack Kapp supervised the recording, with the help of his brother Dave. You have to remember they were making this album on 78-rpm twelve-inch records, where the length would be about five minutes. Sometimes a song we'd be recording would time out too long for the record side, and Jack would come out of the control booth and say, 'How about it, a little faster, maybe?' So I'd speed up the tempo a bit to fit the record. Take 'Surrey with the Fringe on Top.' I had to cut a whole chorus out of it so it would fit on one side of a twelve-incher."

The album went into the stores and sold steadily thereafter. By the time *Oklahoma!* closed on Broadway, Decca had sold an astonishing 800,000 copies.

And from then on, Broadway shows have been preserved for the future with their original casts.

And the financial rewards?

Those staunch souls, the backers, who'd stood up to be counted, who'd written out the precious checks that enabled the Guild to take *Away We Go!* to New Haven and bring it back to New York as *Oklahoma!* would participate in a long-term bonanza.

In 1943, for the week ending December 25 (traditionally a very poor week in the theatre financially, since ticket buyers are out shopping), the Guild books reveal the following: On the week's gross (capacity, of course) of $30,814.50, the producers paid their landlords, the Shuberts, a rental for the St. James Theatre of $8,704.00; that left the Guild with $22,110.50. After deducting all the running expenses, the salaries, royalties, expenses, publicity and advertising, taxes, crew expense, office expense, and a special item marked "Christmas Gifts," the operating profit for the week, including "Souvenir Books Income"—the product that was sold in the lobby by the same Al Greenstone who'd purchased a share of the show in the New Haven Shubert—came to a lusty $7,796.56.

Since by that month the national company was already thriving in Chicago and showing a weekly net profit of $8,058.70, the total profit for that one week would be a heartwarming $15,855.26. Multiply that sum by fifty-two weeks and we come to a total of $824,473.52 in profits, to be divided between the Guild and the investors.

According to the Guild's own recap, when *Oklahoma!* closed on Broadway on May 29, 1948, after playing 2,212 performances, it had been seen by more than 4,500,000 paying customers and grossed more than $7 million for the fortunate few who'd invested. Their eventual payoff from *all* sources was more than 2,500 times their original investment.

Translation into dollars? One thousand dollars would return a staggering $2,500,000.

A phenomenal return, indeed. Small wonder that for months after the opening, Helburn and Langner would meet with Rodgers and Hammerstein for weekly luncheons to discuss strategy and future plans. They called such get-togethers meetings of "The Three-Hour Gloat Club."

By 1944, when *Oklahoma!* was awarded a special Pulitzer Prize, a second national company had been quickly assembled and was touring. And in Chicago, the show settled down for a sold-out run of fourteen months.

At the request of the army and navy, a USO touring company went off to play *Oklahoma!* for the troops in the Pacific. The "War Company," as it came to be called, played its first one-night stand on a far-off (and unnamed) tropical island. "By floodlight," Helburn later reported. "In the steaming hot darkness. The cyclorama was a tangle of twisted banyans and cabbage palms. The curtain was a sheet of silver rain. . . . Thousands of wounded boys, stretcher cases, lay there watching at the jungle's edge. They lifted their bandaged hands in applause. The boys whistled in the dark 'Oh, What a Beautiful Mornin'.' Our youngsters played to the most distinguished first night they were ever to face. They sang with tears in their throats. . . . "

Before its travels ended, that USO company had played to an estimated million and a half homesick troops, who'd gratefully absorbed its message from home of joy and strength.

Figuring in the revenues from all these sources, plus what would eventually be derived from the film rights, stock rights, and amateur royalties, and so forth, it's a safe assumption that in the past half century no single Broadway show has ever returned as much for its dauntless investors as has Helburn's Folly.

GUTSY AND GOLDEN

What is the reason that this remarkable musical show goes on, season after season, pleasing ticket buyers everywhere, charming customers of every age group, from energetic high-schoolers to AARP members? *Oklahoma!* is by far the most popular work in the Rodgers and Hammerstein catalogue; it is performed in over 600 different theatres each and every year. New audiences keep discovering it; old audiences keep coming back to it. What accounts for this insistent popularity?

In an interview years back, Hammerstein remarked, "It has no particular message. It imparts a flavor which infects the people who see it. It's gutsy. *Oklahoma!* is youthful, and irresponsible, and not very intellectual, but it has a heartiness of life."

Richard Rodgers, who for years afterward was fond of quoting his laundry list of reasons why *Oklahoma!* could not possibly have succeeded (Hammerstein hadn't had a hit in twelve years or so; the Theatre Guild was on the verge of bankruptcy; a totally starless cast in a story that dealt with cowboys and farmers; a choreographer who'd never done anything on Broadway; no girls until forty-five minutes after the rise of the curtain, and then none of them revealing a single shapely leg, and even less showing above; no rousing number to open the show; and on and on), later tried to articulate what positive force was the core of the show's lasting impact. In his autobiography he said: "The chief influence of *Oklahoma!* was simply to serve notice that when writers come up with something different, and it has merit, there would be a large and receptive audience waiting for it. From *Oklahoma!* on, with only rare exceptions, the memorable productions have been those daring to break free from the conventional mode."

Miles White offered another reason; he looked back on the show he costumed and murmured fondly, "It has truth imbedded in it."

Certainly, during those World War II years, the magical glow that the St. James's stage gave off each evening was easy to understand. Those of us who were lucky enough to have seen the show when it was playing back then have no problem explaining our joyful, almost Pavlovian reaction to the story of Curly and Laurey. *Oklahoma!* gave us a reason to get the war over. Happier times, it promised, lay ahead. What Rodgers and Hammerstein had presented us with was a lovely two-hour promissory note set to music that we could take back home. It sent us out of the theatre charged with hope (remember those servicemen always standing in the back, ready to leave for parts unknown), it did good work in the military hospitals (where its songs were sung), and it traveled out to the tropical atolls and army camps to give a reassuring *Be of good cheer* to the men and women in the service: The time will soon come when you and your beloved will ride off to a happy ending, too.

But the war years are long over. Though in the intervening years we've traveled through several more ugly periods, and weathered dreadful backwashes from them that tore us apart, *Oklahoma!* audiences are no longer preoccupied with wartime tensions. New generations who aren't in the armed forces, separated from their families, or aren't parents waiting for them to come home, have grown up with the show. Perhaps audiences today are far more sophisticated than the crowd at the St. James that stood up and cheered on opening night. Still, they respond to the simplicity of the show, as did Hammerstein himself when he brushed away a tear watching Curly and Laurey ride in the surrey. Their innocence touched him.

It will touch others, tonight, when Ado Annie explains her sexual appetites, or when Laurey and Curly embrace, or when the barn-dancers begin to leap.

If we cannot agree on what specifically keeps *Oklahoma!* so alive all these seasons after it opened, one thing is certain. The more our world spins madly on, the more we need Curly and his pals. If factories are closing across the nation, then Will Parker must still reassure us that things are up-to-date in Kansas City. And if rock and rap are reducing love to mechanically amplified sex, Laurey and Curly can reassure us there still remains another aspect to the male and female experience, something called romance.

In a hard-edged world, *Oklahoma!* remains our promissory note on an America that most of us fervently hope will someday return, even though we know it won't. All we must do is dim the houselights, raise the curtain, and there it is: the prairie. The land that was, preserved for us. It comes floating out toward us. The magic of *Oklahoma!*, reborn each night that the curtain rises on Aunt Eller, churning, and Curly strolling on, singing, is that it gives us a permanently golden, beautiful morning.

Intermission

CAROUSEL
Shubert Theatre, New Haven	March 22–25, 1945
Colonial Theatre, Boston	March 27–April 15, 1945
Majestic Theatre, New York	April 19, 1945–May 24, 1947 (890 performances)

STATE FAIR
Twentieth Century Fox movie musical, Darryl F. Zanuck, producer
Released in August of 1945
Academy Award–winning song, "It Might As Well Be Spring"
(A remake appeared in 1962.)

ALLEGRO
Shubert Theatre, New Haven	September 1–6, 1947
Colonial Theatre, Boston	September 8–October 4, 1947
Majestic Theatre, New York	October 10, 1947–May 10, 1948 (315 performances)

SOUTH PACIFIC
Shubert Theatre, New Haven	March 7–12, 1949
Shubert Theatre, Boston	March 15–April 2, 1949
Majestic Theatre, New York	April 7, 1949–May 16, 1953
Opera House, Boston	May 18–June 27, 1953
Broadway Theatre, New York	June 29, 1953–January 16, 1954 (1925 performances)

THE KING AND I
Shubert Theatre, New Haven	February 26–March 3, 1951
Shubert Theatre, Boston	March 5–24, 1951
St. James Theatre, New York	March 29, 1951–April 20, 1954
	(1,246 performances)

ME AND JULIET
Hanna Theatre, Cleveland	April 20–May 2, 1953
Shubert Theatre, Boston	May 6–23, 1953
Majestic Theatre, New York	May 28, 1953–April 3, 1954 (358 performances)

PIPE DREAM
Shubert Theatre, New Haven	October 22–29, 1955
Shubert Theatre, Boston	November 1–26, 1955
Shubert Theatre, New York	November 30, 1955–June 10, 1956 (246 performances)

CINDERELLA
CBS television musical, premiered live on March 31, 1957

FLOWER DRUM SONG
Shubert Theatre, Boston	October 27–November 29, 1958
St. James Theatre, New York	December 1, 1958–May 7, 1960 (600 performances)

(Photo and data courtesy of the Rodgers & Hammerstein Organization)

Finale

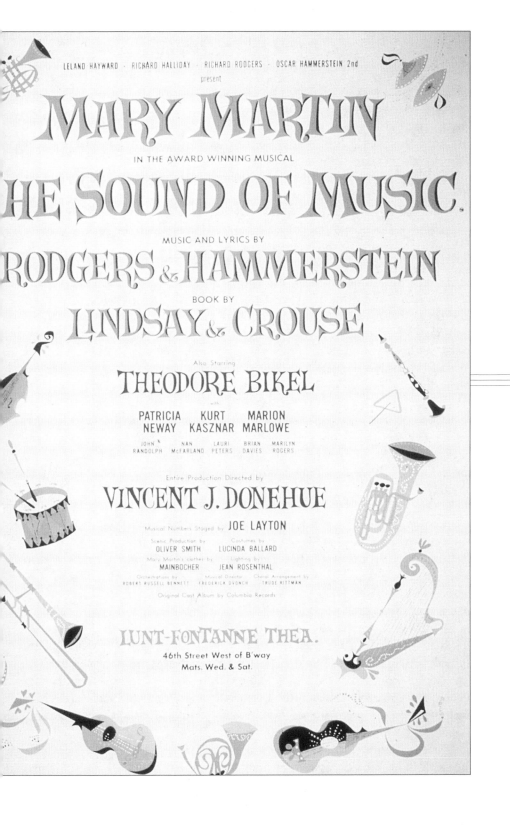

LELAND HAYWARD · RICHARD HALLIDAY · RICHARD RODGERS · OSCAR HAMMERSTEIN 2nd

present

MARY MARTIN

IN THE AWARD WINNING MUSICAL

THE SOUND OF MUSIC.

MUSIC AND LYRICS BY

RODGERS & HAMMERSTEIN

BOOK BY

LINDSAY & CROUSE

Also Starring

THEODORE BIKEL

with

PATRICIA   KURT   MARION
NEWAY   KASZNAR   MARLOWE

JOHN   NAN   LAURI   BRIAN   MARILYN
RANDOLPH   McFARLAND   PETERS   DAVIES   ROGERS

Entire Production Directed by

VINCENT J. DONEHUE

Musical Numbers Staged by JOE LAYTON

Scenic Production by   Costumes by
OLIVER SMITH   LUCINDA BALLARD

Mary Martin's clothes by   Lighting by
MAINBOCHER   JEAN ROSENTHAL

Orchestrations by   Musical Director   Choral Arrangement by
ROBERT RUSSELL BENNETT   FREDERICK DVONCH   TRUDE RITTMAN

Original Cast Album by Columbia Records

LUNT-FONTANNE THEA.

46th Street West of B'way
Mats. Wed. & Sat.

Scene Changes

Sixteen years had passed.

Sixteen theatre seasons since that memorable *Away We Go!* opening night, since the curtain of New Haven's Shubert Theatre had risen and the lights had revealed a bright, sun-drenched Oklahoma landscape where Aunt Eller sat silently churning her butter.

Not a sound. And then, the bemused Shubert audience had heard, offstage, the sound of Alfred Drake's voice singing "Oh, What a Beautiful Mornin'."

Who had known that it was not only a theatrical opening that night, but the premiere of a revolutionary era? That from then on, in the American musical theatre, the scene would keep changing?

Gone, mostly, were those comedian-driven roughhouse musicals of the late 1920s and '30s. Vanished were the opulent, slightly risqué *Scandals* and *Vanities*, and *Follies*, and other such displays, revues with their parades of beautiful half-dressed damsels, designed to please the tired businessman seated on the aisle down front. Such shows had been replaced by satire, by characterizations, set to clever lyrics-cum-melody which impelled empathetic laughter at man's foibles. Comedy was growing up, accompanied by songs which had not been dropped into a show by haphazard interpolation but which needed to be up there for a reason, usually that they served the plot.

Operettas? Those were on the shelf, or stored away in the Shubert warehouse. Perhaps you could still enjoy a Romberg or a Friml revival out at the St. Louis Municipal Opera, or encounter it on tour in the hinterlands, but as far as New York was concerned, after *Oklahoma!* innovation was the order of the day.

Where once the 45th and 46th Street musical stages had echoed to the sound of tap dancing, now choreography reigned. (Leave it to Irving Berlin to spoof the new trend with his sardonic "Choreography," in 1954.) With Agnes de Mille leading the way, choreographers of the skill and talent of Jerome Robbins, Gower Champion, Michael Kidd, and Danny Daniels followed. And later, Bob Fosse, Ron Field, and Michael Bennett—they would all become primary forces in creating musicals.

So strong was de Mille's influence that there is a satiric barb, a truly inside joke, in the book of the 1958 musical, *Say, Darling,* when a Harold Prince–type producer is auditioning dancers for a new musical production. One hapless dancer arrives for his audition and proceeds to launch into a rapid-fire tap dance. He's promptly interrupted by the stage manager, calling *"Thank you—next!"* And the poor frustrated hoofer comes down front, to yell out at us "Damn it, doesn't *anybody* want tap dancing?"

Subtext: Damn you, Agnes!

Truth in character, strong plot line, and that second-act ballet; they were the order of the day. But musical tickets were still sold by stars. So there would still be shows which harked back to the formulaic days when Ed Wynn ("The Perfect Fool"), Al Jolson, Eddie Cantor ("Banjo Eyes"), or Marilyn Miller would bring out the Standing Room Only sign.

For the producers, there were, fortunately, still a few holdover stars from the 1930s and '40s who could still carry a musical and keep the box-office telephones ringing: Ethel Merman, out there "in one"—spotlighted in front of the traveler curtain—belting out a solo crafted to order for her by Cole Porter. Or she would make the Imperial Theatre's rafters echo (unamplified, thank you) with the amazing score provided by her reliable friend, Irving Berlin. His *Annie Get Your Gun* was proof positive of her ability to carry a two-hour show and to keep the customers coming back for more—just as, a few seasons later, she would knock audiences for a loop as Rose, in *Gypsy*.

Were there still funny men? Yes, a few. Raffish, "wowoweeweewoh!" guys, such as Phil Silvers, who, equipped with a great second banana, the inexhaustible Joey Faye, could romp through such an old-fashioned exhibit as *High Button Shoes*, delivering belly laughs interwoven with the Jule Styne–Sammy Cahn score, and its vaudeville-type soft-shoe dance numbers. (Even that show's choreographer Jerome Robbins would modify his inevitable second-act ballet so that it would be pure low comedy based on Mack Sennett's classic slapstick bathing-beauties-by-the-sea two-reelers.) And we still had Bert Lahr, a remarkably gifted clown, who could keep his audiences happy by growling, roaring, gargling, and double-taking throughout such smorgasbords of shtick as *Two on the Aisle*, or *Foxy*. Sooner or later, when such vehicles disappeared, Lahr would end up going in for drama. (When he and another gifted clown, Tom Ewell, ended up in Samuel Beckett's *Waiting For Godot* sans music and lyrics, they may not have known precisely what Beckett's script *meant*, but no one who saw them could deny they knew how to *play* it.)

There were, blessedly, a few new talents around; the wonderful Nancy Walker, who brought with her echoes of the knockabout vaudeville era. (Her father had been a trouper before she'd arrived on the scene.) And for the remarkable Judy Holliday Broadway could still find vehicles; she starred in *Bells Are Ringing*, and who is to say how much further she might have traveled, had she not departed so soon from our musical stage?

Yes, echoes of the old-fashioned musical could still be encountered in the shows which leaned heavily towards comedy, as did *Pajama Game*, and *Damn Yankees*, done by the master, George Abbott. But as the seasons passed, even Mr. Abbott found it harder and harder to bring forth musical hits. With all those tried and true show-stopping elements fading away, experimentation become the order of the day . . . or of the closing night. Dozens of productions would fall by the wayside as hapless librettists and their songwriting teams labored at being smart, or clever, or satiric.

Every so often a new talent, such as Frank Loesser, who'd been working out in Hollywood, would emerge. He brashly insisted he was capable of emulating Porter and Berlin by providing both music and lyrics. And starting with his sparkling *Where's Charley?* Loesser proved he could knock them out of the ballpark for the next two decades. But for every Loesser who emerged in those confused times, the Broadway arena was strewn with the corpses of failed musicals. We weren't waiting for Godot; we were waiting for Lerner and Loewe, and until they arrived there were all sorts of high-cost attempts which began life as innovations, closed, and can only be remembered in the bins of record shops which specialize in rare LPs.

Where was the American musical headed?

Or was it headed anywhere at all? If heretofore successful practitioners such as Mr. Abbott and others of his generation, were frustrated and depressed, bewildered tyros were equally so.

One night in 1951, at a meeting of New Dramatists, a then-recently-created support group for young playwrights who'd earned their place at the table by having already written and been produced, the two sachems of the day, Mr. Rodgers and Mr. Hammerstein, came to offer their accumulated knowledge and opinions to a room full of intent listeners.

Whatever they had to tell us, it had to be valid. After all, was this not the era of successful Rodgers and Hammerstein musicals? Those Hammerstein librettos, expertly crafted, and set to the memorable Rodgers scores? Couldn't we call back those evenings—some perhaps more enchanted than others—of *Carousel* or *Allegro*? Hadn't they provided a lilting score for their movie musical, *State Fair*? Their latest show, *The King and I*, with Gertrude Lawrence and Yul Brynner, was a wonderful work. Overall, the Rodgers and Hammerstein partnership ever since *Oklahoma!* had managed to rack up a spectacular batting average.

So successful was the team, in fact, as creators and producers, that a favorite Broadway anecdote of those times dealt with an apocryphal message from the Colonial Theatre, up in Boston, where a billboard had gone up:

COMING! RODGERS AND HAMMERSTEIN'S NEW SHOW!

"We grossed twenty-six thousand yesterday," the Colonial manager was supposed to have reported. "But yesterday was Sunday! Your box-office wasn't even *open!*" protested the New York reporter. "Yeah, but when the people saw that Rodgers and Hammerstein sign," said the Bostonian, "they pushed open our lobby doors and threw in their checks!"

Hyperbole, perhaps, but based on truth. So strong had been the Rodgers and Hammerstein influence on the American musical since 1943 that the form and structure of the Broadway shows which followed would all be compared to their patterns.

During the question-and-answer period which followed that evening at New Dramatists, one of the playwrights, who'd already worked on several musical librettos and was waiting, none too patiently, for a production—any sort of production, in those pre–off-Broadway days—raised his hand: "Mr. Hammerstein," he asked, "nobody can argue, these are bleak days for the musical. Can you foresee any future for those of us who're still trying to work in that field?"

Hammerstein smiled and nodded. "Believe me," he said, "I know exactly how you feel."

And we all knew he had been there, too, in the best of times, and the worst of times. There had been all those fallow years he had struggled through, before the success of *Oklahoma!*

"The only answer I can give you," said this man who was currently half of the most successful team on Broadway, "is that I firmly believe, right now, as we're talking, somewhere, out there, in a room, there's a guy, maybe two such, working on an idea for a new show. Something exciting, something different, with perhaps a whole new vision of the way a musical can be done. I have to believe this. What he's working on— who knows? Maybe it'll shake us all up and open a whole new way to go."

There was silence as we sat and pondered his prediction of a rosy new future.

"Trust me," Hammerstein promised. "I've been around a long time. It always happens this way."

The room was still silent. His theatrical glass wasn't half-empty, it was half-full. And who could dare argue with the man who'd already written "A Cock-Eyed Optimist"?

It would take a while for his prediction to come true, but when it did, it proved to be worth waiting for. The work would be called *West Side Story*, a bold, startlingly new vision of Shakespeare's *Romeo and Juliet*, transformed by Arthur Laurents' libretto, set to a vibrant score by Leonard Bernstein, and with lyrics by a brilliant new talent, Stephen Sondheim. Brilliantly directed and choreographed by Jerome Robbins, it had the Broadway musical off and running again, leading us headlong into a bold new era of creativity.

And *West Side Story* (like *Oklahoma!* before it) would do it without a single star name on the marquee. But that was after a lot of time had passed. The Broadway tradition that evening at New Dramatists still was—as it had long been—that of the phenomenal talents who brought in the ticket-buyers and kept the shows running. Stars like Mary Martin.

MARY MARTIN

Indeed, a show business phenomenon had emerged in 1938 on the stage of New Haven's Shubert Theatre (where else?). When, in the midst of a Cole Porter musical, *Leave It to Me,* there arrived a cheerful young woman attired in a fur parka. Surrounded by chorus boys (one of whom was a young hoofer named Gene Kelly), she launched into one of Porter's cleverest and sauciest set of double-entendre lyrics, in the song "My Heart Belongs to Daddy."

By the second chorus, when this lissome actress from Weatherford, Texas, began performing a mock strip-tease with her parka, letting us know it was all in good, not-so-clean fun, the New Haven audience had begun to fall in love with her. When she finished the number, Mary Martin stopped the show—as she would continue to do so for many seasons to come. She could sing, she could clown, she could dance. And the audience remained in love with her when she later played a mythical goddess come to life in *One Touch of Venus*. Out in Hollywood, she did a batch of musical films, then she came back to the stage to co-star with Noël Coward in *Pacific 1860*.

But her finest hour would come when she merged her considerable talents with those of Rodgers and Hammerstein, to play Ensign Nellie Forbush, in *South Pacific*, opposite opera star Ezio Pinza, in 1949. Those were the evenings—and the matinees—that audiences were enchanted as she showered and shampooed and told us that she was going to wash that man right out of her hair, or doing the hilarious cakewalk to "Honey Bun," and finally, promising Pinza that once she had found him, she would never let him go.

Her fans adored her. She could do no wrong.

Especially with that brilliant libretto and score by Rodgers and Hammerstein. *South Pacific* ran in New York for 1,925 performances, and Mary Martin played Nellie for two years. Obviously, Rodgers and Hammerstein would have been delighted to create another such successful musical for her. But it would be eight years before it finally happened. Anyone in the theatre knows that lightning rarely strikes twice in the same place, if it strikes at all.

Mary Martin and her husband, Richard Halliday, and Rodgers and Hammerstein went their separate ways. But their tracks remained parallel. Rodgers and Hammerstein were busy over the next few years, producing tours of their shows, mounting British productions, and creating new shows: *The King and I*, *Me and Juliet* and *Pipe Dream*, an original version of *Cinderella* for television, and *Flower Drum Song*. Their days and nights were occupied.

So were Mary Martin's. She may not have found another *South Pacific*—it would be miraculous to find such an overpowering mixture of showmanship indeed—but she kept busy. She played opposite Charles Boyer in a tissue-thin romantic comedy, *Kind Sir*, by Norman Krasna. Even though the play had a respectable run, it wasn't precisely the sort of show the fans expected. Then such an audience-pleaser happily arrived, a new musical version of Sir James M. Barrie's beloved classic, *Peter Pan*.

With her husband as producer, and Jerome Robbins as director and choreographer; with a stage full of talented kids and Cyril Ritchard to play the villainous Captain Hook; with a score by Carolyn Leigh and Moose Charlap, plus additional songs by Betty Comden, Adolph Green, and Jule Styne, this revival provided Mary Martin ample opportunity to shine. And when she took off, to soar triumphantly across the stage, she wasn't the only one who was flying—her empathetic audiences were flying along with her. They couldn't care less that she was a trifle old to play Peter; they simply knew that they loved her.

As would millions more when she took her performance and re-created it for that then-fledgling entertainment venue, the twelve-inch television screen. It was Leland Hayward, the shrewd showman and Martin's good friend, who delivered her and *Peter Pan* to NBC as the first in a procession of what he dubbed "spectaculars." And *Peter Pan* promptly became a TV classic to be rebroadcast year after year.

Sometimes the best laid plans of producers *gang aft a-gley*, but not as *a-gley* as did Mary Martin's next venture. In 1955, someone in the State Department, in Washington, D.C., decided it would be a brilliant idea to send a new production of Thornton Wilder's *The Skin of Our Teeth* over to Paris, as part of a festival called "A Salute to France." On paper, it all must have sounded marvelous: A cast including Helen Hayes, and the legendary George Abbott returning to the stage as an actor, and, in the role originally created by Tallulah Bankhead, Mary Martin as the outrageous comedienne–maid, Sabina. No, it wasn't precisely type-casting, but in the theatre, such oddball ideas often pan out.

Not this time. *The Skin of Our Teeth* returned from Paris, where it had been less than marvelous, opened in New York, and, after three weeks, closed.

While Martin looked around for another vehicle, one which might involve her good friends Dick and Oscar, she took on the leading role of Annie Oakley in one of their early triumphs as show producers, *Annie Get Your Gun*, first to play it on a national tour, and then in another NBC "spectacular."

And then it happened.

Martin's good friend, director Vincent Donehue, went from staging her production of *Annie Get Your Gun* to working at Paramount, out in Hollywood, where he'd previously been signed to a contract. One day in 1957, he was taken into a projection room where he was shown a German film, *Die Trapp Familie*.

The story of the Baroness Maria von Trapp—who had escaped the Nazi regime with her family, left her native Austria, and come to America, where she and the *kinder* performed as the Trapp Family Singers—the film had been made in Germany a decade before. So successful had it been with German audiences that it had been followed by a sequel, *Die Trapp Familie in Amerika*.

Paramount had secured an option on the rights to these films, and, Donehue was told, someone had the idea to turn the Trapp saga into an American musical. What did he think of the possibility? He thought immediately of one leading lady. Nobody knew better than Donehue how urgently Mary and Dick Halliday had been seeking a starring vehicle. He managed to get the film back East where he showed it to both of them.

Martin, equally enthusiastic, immediately agreed with Donehue. But how should they proceed? With Paramount owning the option on the story, perhaps they should deal directly with the Baroness Von Trapp and try to secure the rights to her life story as the basis for a Broadway show.

But the Baroness was in New Guinea, involved in missionary work. And when she began to receive communications from a group of Americans she'd never heard of, suggesting that her life story might make a musical starring Mary Martin, the Baroness ignored them. Who was this Mary Martin? She wished to play her on a theatre stage? *Furicht!*

But when the Baroness returned from New Guinea, Halliday was waiting to meet her ship in San Francisco; Martin was playing *Annie Get Your Gun* in the same city. The Baroness wound up in the audience that night. Once the curtain had fallen, Halliday brought her backstage to meet the star, and from that point on, the saga of *The Sound of Music* would begin.

Theatrical fantasies always begin with someone's hypothesis—the one we know as *What if?* Most often, such fantasies arrive at the end of the runway, where some of them, like Theresa Helburn's Folly, take off and fly. But the majority of them, alas, never make it into the air. In this particular *What if?*, the fantasy was not only valid, it would prove to be solid gold.

Mary Martin, to play Maria Reiner, the nun who left her convent to tend to the children of Captain Georg von Trapp, a retired naval officer, and who'd fallen in love with the widower father, and he with her . . . and when they'd been married, she'd had more children, thus creating a large brood of talented young Von Trapps . . . and when the Nazis had overrun Austria, the parents and the children had left their homeland, escaping to far-off America, where they'd create a new career—she and the children becoming the famous Trapp Family Singers: It was a *What if* that would fly higher than any Austrian Alp.

But not until quite a few legal Alps had been climbed. For starters, Paramount's option on those two Trapp Family films had lapsed; the rights to the story had reverted to the German production company. And nobody could use the Baroness's own life story without such rights, because years back, in the original deal she'd agreed to, she'd signed a contract in which she gave over all her rights to said life story, including any and all profit participation . . . for the magnificent sum of $9,000. So, alas, it would not be up to the Baroness whether or not Mary Martin could re-create her story on a Broadway stage. It would be up to that German film company, which owned all the rights. Negotiations began, and after discussion, the Germans agreed to a deal by which they would sell the rights to Martin and Halliday for $200,000. Quite a distance from the original sum paid to the Baroness Von Trapp!

Others might have been stopped by such a price, but not Mary Martin and Richard Halliday. When you've found a project you believe is worth doing, and you also have the determination to pursue it, then you take a leaf from Oscar Hammerstein's words (the ones which were as yet unwritten)—and you climb every mountain.

Even if you don't *have* the $200,000 on hand to pay that German company.

"Dick was a very shrewd businessman," remembered Frank Goodman, who would become the theatrical press agent for the original production of *The Sound of Music*. "He and Mary looked around for capital, and guess how they figured it all out? Mary had a long-term contract with NBC Television. She'd been such a huge hit for them in *Peter Pan*. NBC could run it, year after year, and the kids loved it. In her contract, she also owed them another 'spectacular' each year, at a very good fee. So Dick went over to Radio City and asked the NBC executives for an advance on Mary's future salary. NBC, of course, wanted to keep their star happy, and they knew Mary would earn back that money for them in the future, so they agreed to lend Mary and Dick the $200,000 so they could use it to finish their deal with the Germans!"

With the NBC funds agreed to, the couple proceeded to close the deal with the German film company for the rights to the two Von Trapp films, and the rights to the Baroness's life story. And even though they were not bound to do so legally, they voluntarily signed over a royalty of three-eighths of one percent to the Baroness for the forthcoming show based on her life story. It may not sound like much on a one-week basis, but over the years, since 1959, the sum has been impressive.

Then they got in touch with a prospective producer for the project: their tried-and-true friend Leland Hayward.

PARTNERING WITH THE BEST

One of the most successful showmen of his time, Hayward had begun his career in Hollywood, as an agent for talent. In the film business, he was legendary as a specialist in class. He'd been famous for his client list; name any star of the 1930s and '40s—Henry Fonda, James Stewart, Katharine Hepburn, Greta Garbo, Fred Astaire, Ingrid Bergman, and his wife, Margaret Sullavan. Eventually, he sold his agency to Jules Stein, who founded the movie department at MCA upon it. In time to come, Hayward would regret this sale whenever he entered into a furious negotiation with MCA. "Created my own goddamned monster," he would sigh.

But Hayward had set his sights on moving to New York and producing plays on his own. "I saw all those conceited bastards I dealt with who called themselves producers out there, making so many mistakes," he said later. "I figured I couldn't possibly do any worse than they were doing."

Hayward's first shot at the brass ring was a new play based on John Hersey's *A Bell For Adano*, starring Fredric March, and it would be a smash hit.

Over the next two decades, Hayward's name went proudly onto the marquees of a long list of Broadway hits, from *Mr. Roberts*, *State of the Union*, *Wish You Were Here*, and *Call Me Madam*. He'd been partnered with Rodgers and Hammerstein as producers of *South Pacific*. And he had delivered on NBC's *Peter Pan*.

Since nothing succeeds like success, especially in show business where success is so rare, he was Martin and Halliday's first choice.

Hayward looked at the two German films on the Von Trapp family, and read their biography, too. Did he agree that the part of the Baroness was a good one for Mary Martin?

"Absolutely!" he said, cheerfully. "Let's get started!"

The rights deal with the Germans closed, Martin and Halliday were the owners, and Hayward agreed to become their partner. The project began to move forward.

In the beginning, there needed to be a script.

It was agreed the first choice for the script would be the writing team of Howard Lindsay and Russel Crouse. Hayward had been their agent ever since

Producer Leland Hayward. (Courtesy of Photofest)

his Hollywood days, and he'd continued his relationship with them during the creation of Ethel Merman's success, *Call Me Madam.* "Leland called," remembered Anna Crouse, Russel's wife. "And he said to Russel and Howard, I have three ideas for you two, and you can have your choice. One is *Gone with the Wind* as a musical, the second is Gypsy Rose Lee's book *Gypsy,* and the third is about the Trapp Family Singers, which Mary has brought me. You decide."

Lindsay and Crouse went into conference.

As a Broadway writer–manager team, these two men could not have been more respected and successful. They were also two of the wittiest men in the business. Their writing credits went all the way back to the now-classic comedy, *Life with Father,* in which Lindsay had also starred as the patriarch of the title. When they decided to become producers, they scored with such successes as *Arsenic and Old Lace, The Hasty Heart,* and *Detective Story.*

When Lindsay called Hayward back, he said, "Leland, you'll never get *Gone with the Wind* on a stage—it's not possible, it's too big!"

What about *Gypsy*? "They just didn't feel it was for them," said Mrs. Crouse. "I once had in the office a list of the plays and musicals they'd turned down, and it was quite impressive. Practically every hit you ever knew. But luckily, they told Leland they were very interested in the Mary Martin project."

Hayward promptly arranged for the two writers to read the Von Trapp biography, and to see the black-and-white German films. And they began to think about writing the book for the musical.

"Then Leland called," remembered Mrs. Crouse, "and he said, 'You know, I've been thinking about this, and I think the story needs a little *oomph*, and how do you feel about my asking Dick Rodgers and Oscar Hammerstein whether they would write a song or two for this? I mean, we know the Von Trapp repertoire is full of German classics, but maybe they ought to do something new, don't you agree?' Well, Russel and Howard said, 'That's great, go ahead and see what they say.'"

"After all," she added, "who wouldn't want Dick and Oscar writing songs for you?"

So Hayward went through the same process with Rodgers and Hammerstein; showing them the book and having the German films run for them.

"Dick called Leland," said Mrs. Crouse, "and he said, 'No way am I competing with Mozart and Brahms and Austrian folksongs—all that stuff they're singing. Oscar and I would like to write the *entire* score.'"

"And why not?" was Hayward's response.

Why not, indeed? Who could turn down Rodgers and Hammerstein?

But there was one proviso. The authors of *South Pacific* would not be available until their current project, *Flower Drum Song,* had been successfully launched—which would be at least a year.

No matter. Martin and Halliday, Hayward, and Lindsay and Crouse would certainly be willing to wait.

The Libretto

"**A**n audience must go away from your play feeling rewarded . . . or purged." Such was one of Howard Lindsay's most pragmatic rules for theatrical success.

And certainly, no libretto would prove his thesis more reliable than the one he and Russel Crouse had begun to work on during that winter of 1958–59.

For what Lindsay and Crouse accomplished in *The Sound of Music* was the creation of a truly heart-warming story, one which has charmed audiences ever since. No matter that they took certain liberties with the Von Trapp saga. Who cares that, in the show, when the Von Trapps make their final departure from Salzburg to escape the Nazis and climb the Alps to Switzerland, that the geography is askew? Facts don't make a successful show, but rewarding the audience does. The youngsters who sit home today rapt by the videotape of *The Sound of Music* in its film version or their *fort-confrères* in orchestra seats at Broadway's Martin Beck Theatre in its 1998 revival, or the performers in some little theatre company of the show this very night somewhere, all share in the same experience: total and complete empathy with Maria and her Captain, and those loving Von Trapp kids.

Small wonder that time has proven *The Sound of Music* along with *Oklahoma!* to be Rodgers and Hammerstein's two most successful musical works.

Ah, but let us pause here just a moment, and consider the anomaly of these two diametrically different Rodgers and Hammerstein musicals! One, which is grounded on the sunlit American prairie and populated with cowboys and farmers settling the brand-new state of Oklahoma—a thrilling piece which, in its primary execution, broke from most of the formulas of the Broadway of its time.

The other, *The Sound of Music*, grounded in the Austrian Alps—well, it's hard to believe that the show which would prove to be, alas, Rodgers and Hammerstein's final collaboration, could come from the same creative pair. For *The Sound of Music* is very much in the old vein, that of operetta—the very source of the formulas that *Oklahoma!* had broken away from. The noble story of a brave heroine, a nun, who falls in love with the middle-aged father of a family and renounces the nunnery, marries him, and, after they've all escaped, lives happily ever after . . . does this show not come equipped with all the virtues of the pre-*Show Boat* musical theatre relished by the audiences of the 1920s and before?

Back in 1943, on opening night at the St. James, the stage was filled with a bright golden haze, a vista of the wide-open spaces. Onto it came a brooding villain, Jud, who threatened our pair of true lovers . . . but after the dust settled, and Jud had been killed (yes, that was another broken rule, wasn't it?), we had the requisite happy ending. *Oklahoma!* filled its audience with a sense of elation and pride in the development of our new land, and it offered us a shining future, filled with hope. Whereas *The Sound of Music* would bring the curtain up on a darkly troubled Europe, and would depict characters living hemmed in by, not to mention oppressed by, Old World prescriptions of Church and State—that is, until they escape from them at the finale.

More than half a century later, *Oklahoma!* still rouses us with those dazzling de Mille dances. Just think of that next-to-closing eleven o'clock number in which the cast sings "Oklahoma!", one of the most masterly stage numbers ever devised, and how it has sent audiences out of the theatre year after year with a rosy glow of what Howard Lindsay defined as "reward." Of course, he and Russel Crouse would have rewards in store for us at the end of *The Sound of Music*, too, but there would be precious little choreography—unless you regard a bunch of beaming children bobbing up and down in their bedroom, or a line of nuns gracefully moving in and out of a cathedral, or two young lovers in a delicate love duet, as anything more than simple *movement*. (Joe Layton's credit in 1959 would read "Musical Numbers Staged by . . ." and for once, not even the most insistent agent would be able to contradict it.)

Like a Viennese operetta, *The Sound of Music* would have some pretty impressive scenery, Alpine and otherwise. At times the stage would be filled with Oliver Smith's settings. But did it break any rules, as Lem Ayers's design had? Not at all.

The similarity in these two remarkable musicals, at least the major one, is that both *Oklahoma!* and *The Sound of Music* are uplifting. The subtext of both contains the reward and the purge which are in Howard Lindsay's recipe for success. Yes, time had passed between these masterworks, and after all of Rodgers and Hammerstein's collaborative years, by the time of *The Sound of Music* they were, perhaps, no longer in the creative surprise business, as they had been back in 1943. But over the years it has never mattered. Not to any audience. The consensus is that the trip from Oklahoma to Salzburg may have been a long one, but no one minds taking it . . . over and over again.

Another similarity in the two shows is that Rodgers' score was orchestrated by Robert Russell Bennett in both, and with his customary brilliance. (Of course, if you're listening for surprises in orchestrations . . . there's something wrong with the show, right?)

In short, the one show broke every rule of its time, and the other, nearly two decades later, abided by all of them.

THE CRAFTSMEN

Lindsay and Crouse were preparing the outline which would become the script of *The Sound of Music*, and in the following months Rodgers and Hammerstein would tackle the score. Meanwhile, producer Leland Hayward had his hands full with the details of producing that same show he'd originally offered Lindsay and Crouse, the one they'd turned down: *Gypsy*.

Hayward's co-producer, David Merrick, was clearly disinterested in *Gypsy*. Even with Ethel Merman to star as the archetypal stage mother, Rose, who drove her daughters June and Gypsy through adversity to success, Merrick couldn't whip up any enthusiasm for the project. He was far more attracted to his own venture, *Destry*, which would star Andy Griffith.

Producing *Gypsy* would not be an easy task. Hayward had struggled to bring together a cadre of highly creative talents: Jule Styne to write the music, Stephen Sondheim to pen the lyrics, Arthur Laurents to craft the book, and Jerome Robbins to choreograph and stage the production.

Hayward's days and nights were filled with a constant series of wrangles and creative arguments. Director, costumer, performers, agents, lawyers—all going to the mat with seemingly endless problems, artistic, emotional, and, more often than not, financial. But through it all, he persisted. He spent long hours in meetings, trying to bring *Gypsy* together, and trying to keep his fledgling craft from being scuttled before it had even been launched. Such is the producer's task.

One of his friends asked him how could he put up with all these constant battles, even before there'd been a rehearsal? Why not move on to something else?

"Oh, no," he replied, "I have to stick with this one, because it's going to be such a helluva good show."

Once *Gypsy* was open, and he'd been proven absolutely right, it was time for *The Sound of Music*.

Lindsay and Crouse had also been busy. "While they waited for Dick and Oscar, they produced a play called *Tall Story*, a comedy about basketball," recalled Mrs. Crouse. "But they also had decided they might just as well work on the book which would eventually be ready for Dick and Oscar." In other words, without conferring with Rodgers and Hammerstein. "But," she said, "they did it scene by scene, and when they'd finished one, they'd send it on to Dick and Oscar."

"It was one of the best collaborations Howard and Russel had ever had," she added. "I can give you an idea of what a good partnership it became: Early on, they wrote a scene in which the nuns are discussing Maria, and to each other they point out how she has curlers in her hair, how she whistles on the stair . . . and all sorts of things about her. After Oscar read it, he called up and said 'I am going to ask you a very great favor: Would you mind if I made that into a song? It's a perfect lyric.'"

"They told him, 'Be our guest, because if you tell a story in a song, it's so much better!'"

Hammerstein proceeded to write, and from the Lindsay and Crouse scene would come:

How do you solve a problem like Maria?
How do you catch a cloud and pin it down?

So many different words describe Maria—
. . . A flibbertigibbet, a will o' the wisp, a clown.

It took seventeen days to complete the lyric, which ends:

How do you hold a moonbeam in your hand?"

Truly, a master at the peak of his form.

"Oscar and Dick very kindly gave Howard and Russel part of the show album royalties in return," Mrs. Crouse remarked. "Now, that was something unheard of—for book writers to share in a cast recording. How generous of them!"

Later, the give-and-take process between Lindsay and Crouse and Hammerstein would continue, this time in reverse. When the two playwrights arrived at the scene in which Maria and Captain Von Trapp come to express their mutual love, they stumbled over the problem of dialogue; none of their lines seemed to suit the situation or the characters. When they described their

A picture of collaboration: Mary Martin, flanked by Rodgers and Hammerstein on the left, and Lindsay and Crouse on the right, posed for the press photographers in 1959. (Photo courtesy of the Rodgers and Hammerstein Organization)

problem with that moment, Hammerstein would solve it for them by bringing them a lyric, which he titled "An Ordinary Couple."

By March of 1959, the work had progressed with a remarkable shortage of
problems. It was quite a different history from what usually takes place in the
creation of a Broadway-bound musical.

Hammerstein took the sixty-page treatment which Lindsay and Crouse
had completed, and went to Jamaica to work on the lyrics at a pleasant
enclave of houses called Round Hill. There was general agreement between
the four on what songs were needed and where they should go in the script.

Since it was a show for which Hammerstein had not been called upon to
write the book (a task which he would confide to his son James he'd have
given up years before had he only been able to find others capable of doing
it for him) his days passed pleasantly, and he accomplished a great deal. While
other guests lounged on the beach, he soon completed the lyrics for Maria's
opening number, "The Sound of Music."

Of course, Hammerstein labored long and hard over each lyric. He kept
meticulous worksheets of each day's work. Day after day, the lyrics developed
slowly, almost painfully. His name for that work was "woodshedding." Hour
after hour, he would remain at work, agonizing as he always had over the
choice of the exact word, the perfect choice for the thought he wished to
communicate.

He returned to Doylestown, still working steadily. Standing at his desk
each day, as he had done all those years, he completed "My Favorite Things."

One afternoon, his son William came to visit. The two ended up in the
swimming pool, where Hammerstein told Bill the story of the new show he
was working on. When he'd finished, the son was in tears.

Then Hammerstein said, "I'm planning to write a song like 'You'll Never
Walk Alone.'" He'd been thinking about it for some time. The lyric would
emerge from his correspondence with Sister Gregory, the head of the drama
department at Rosary College, in River Forest, Illinois. She had become a
good friend of Mary Martin and Richard Halliday; Martin had asked her for
advice and counsel on convent life. Over several months, she and Hammerstein and the sister would consult, by mail, on various aspects of the religious
side of the script. Why did young women choose the religious life? Sister
Gregory responded: "Everyone must find one's own answer to the simple
question, What does God want me to do with my life? How does he wish me
to spend my love?"

Hammerstein began his lyric with the title "Face Life," and then added
wrote Sister Gregory's questions onto the page. And then he wrote his own
intuitive notes, in Maria's own thoughts: "You can't hide here. Don't think that
these convent walls shut out problems. You have to face life wherever you are.
You have to look for life, for the life you were meant to lead. Until you find
it, you are not living."

Once he had begun exploring Maria's internal struggle for "Face Life"—to stay or not to stay in the convent—he wrote more notes about life, about climbing a hill, about getting to the top ". . . Which doesn't bring you much closer to the moon, but closer to the next hill, which you must also climb."

Under his own notes, Hammerstein added a warning to himself: "Don't let this be too obviously a philosophical number."

Eventually, "Face Life" would become "Climb Ev'ry Mountain." Hammerstein's lyric had a verse to begin with, and two stanzas, or choruses, to follow. When he brought it to Rodgers, who set the lyric to a very impressive musical line, the team decided that the two stanzas were strong enough, that they expressed enough to stand alone, without the verse. Which is how the stanzas have remained ever since, moving the audience as deeply as they do.

When Sister Gregory received a manuscript copy of Hammerstein's lyric, she wrote back to Mary Martin, "It drove me to the Chapel. (Relax, chums, I'm sure it will not affect your audiences in the same way.) It made me acutely aware of how tremendously fortunate are those who find a dream that will absorb all their love, and finding it, embrace it to the end." She commented on how much she liked Rodgers's music, then continued, ". . . However, it was the lyrics that sent me to the Chapel. Mr. Hammerstein's lyrics seem perfectly, yet effortlessly, to express what we ordinary souls feel but cannot communicate."

And she was also right about audiences. They don't go to a chapel after hearing "Climb Ev'ry Mountain," they come back to hear it again and again, year after year.

Gains and Losses

During the summer of 1959, Hayward and Halliday were assembling the creative cadre for *The Sound of Music*. The costumes would be designed by Mainbocher and Lucinda Ballard. Oliver Smith was at work designing the scenery, and Robert Russell Bennett was orchestrating Rodgers' score.

Casting was supervised by Edwin Blum, from the production office of Rodgers and Hammerstein. Blum's formidable task was to bring in actors and actresses whom director Vincent Donehue could audition. Since the Von Trapp brood ran from tots to teenagers, and had to be good singers, finding the right performers was a large order. (As would be replacing them when they grew out of their age-groups in the next few years.) For choreography, there would be Joe Layton.

One of the most important casting tasks would be to find a leading man who could sing, to play opposite Mary Martin in the role of Captain Von Trapp.

The first day of rehearsal: Richard Rodgers (far right) watches as director Vincent Donehue (at table) addresses Mary Martin (center right), Theodore Bikel (center) and the *Sound of Music* company on the stage of the Lunt-Fontanne. (Photo by Toni Frissell courtesy of Lauri Peters)

Toni Frissell

The name of Theodore Bikel was on the list of possibles. The actor–folksinger was then in Holland, making a film. "My agents thought I would be an ideal choice to play the Captain," he remembered, "and I thought so, too. It goes without saying that almost every leading man in the New York theatre was dying to have a crack at the part, which forced my agents to work fast."

Bikel was flown in from Holland by Hayward and Halliday; he had forty-eight hours' leave from his Dutch assignment. "They also arranged for me to work with someone on a couple of songs for the audition. I had never done a musical before. The music I was used to performing was of a different genre from Broadway tunes—not exactly audition material, they said. . . . Big question: When you audition for Rodgers and Hammerstein, do you do one of their own tunes and risk running afoul of their concept? . . . Even if you are brilliant, if you've shaped their music to your style, will it be seen as chutzpah, or even hubris?" he recalled thinking as he faced the audition.

After some thought, Bikel ended up performing two Frank Loesser songs: "Luck Be a Lady," and "My Time of Day." "I also slipped in one of my folk songs, with my guitar," he said.

"I stood waiting while I dimly saw some heads bobbing in the dark auditorium. After a while, they thanked me for having come in to do this, and said they would be in touch with my agents. Well, that's that, I thought. It won't come to anything, but the trip was worthwhile, anyway."

Bikel returned to Holland, finished his role in the film, and then went off to visit family in Israel. From New York, silence. Finally, after waiting through several more days, he managed to get a call through from Israel to New York, and reached his agents. What was the resolution of the audition? Who'd been cast as the Captain?

The part, it seemed, was his!

"Mary Martin told me later that after I had done my folk song at the audition, she'd leaned forward, tapped Dick Rodgers on the shoulder, and whispered, 'We don't have to look any further, do we?'"

In the rest of the company would be Kurt Kasznar, as Max Detweiler, and Marian Marlowe, as Elsa Schraeder. "Ironically," said Bikel, "almost all the actors who would play Nazis or Nazi sympathizers in the second act were Jews—Michael Gorrin, and Stefan Gierasch. . . ."

"One night, I was waiting in the wings for my entrance after Franz, the butler, played by John Randolph, was to bring Captain Von Trapp the telegram ordering him to report to the Nazi navy . . . He came across the stage and exited into the wings carrying the telegram on a silver tray. When he handed it to me, he said, 'Captain, *tsuris!*'—Yiddish for 'bad trouble.'"

The last week in August of 1959, the show went into rehearsal at the Lunt-Fontanne Theatre, on West 46th Street, where it would open in November. All was going well, but then. . . .

Early in September, Hammerstein went to his doctor for an annual physical check-up. When he'd finished, Hammerstein mentioned he'd been waking up hungry at night, and drinking milk to assuage it before going back to sleep. The watchful doctor suggested tests for an ulcer. The tests revealed that Hammerstein had cancer of the stomach. Surgery was absolutely necessary; it was suggested for two days later.

Before he left for his operation, Hammerstein came to the Lunt-Fontanne, and met Mary Martin backstage. Whether or not he could articulate himself verbally, he had for many years always put the right words on paper. He handed his star a folded page. "Don't look at it now," he said. "Look at it later." Then he left.

Director Vincent Donehue joins in as Mary Martin guides Kathy Dunn (kneeling) and Mary Susan Locke (at bottom) through a song rehearsal at the star's home. (Courtesy of Photofest)

When she did, she found on the paper a lyric, the verse he'd written for "Climb Ev'ry Mountain," but which had not yet been used. It read:

A bell is no bell till you ring it,
A song is no song till you sing it.
And love in your heart wasn't put there to stay.
Love isn't love till you give it away.

Eventually, these words, so touching, so indicative of Hammerstein's philosophy, would end up as the verse to the reprise of "Sixteen, Going on Seventeen."

Comforted by Rodgers, who had also had a bout with cancer and survived, and who promised Martin, "We are going to work as long as we can," she treasured those lines, her gift from Oscar Hammerstein. For the rest of her career, she would sing his couplet, in many languages, at the end of each performance, wherever she was in the world.

For her, Hammerstein was "the epitome of love for his fellow man."

Without him, the company continued rehearsing for the New Haven tryout opening. This would be the first Shubert tryout he could not attend. Hammerstein was recovering from the surgery, but the prognosis was not good. The carcinoma was large; the surgeons had removed most of his stomach. At best, Hammerstein would have six months to a year to live.

"It had all gone so well," recalled Mrs. Crouse. "Over the years I've worked on many shows, and I can't think of a happier collaboration than this one . . . with the awful exception of our loss of Oscar."

Out of Town

October 3, 1959: Opening night in New Haven.

In came the Shubert ticket-holders; for weeks they'd been waiting for this one, Mary Martin starring in a new Rodgers and Hammerstein show. A sold-out house, with standees thronging the rear of the orchestra seating. Anyone who had seats for tonight was indeed fortunate.

Here were all those gamblers—the locals, intermingled with New York people, agents, and ticket-brokers, and scouts from the movie company home offices, plus a delegation in from the Coast, here to check out whether there might be a movie in this show. And, of course, the press: Harold Bone of *Variety*, plus a couple of New York "column planters"—press agents who, by midnight, would get the word back, and then the buzz about this latest gilt-edged "R and H" offering would be out.

And there were also the squadron of friends, people who were here to cheer on Mary Martin, and Halliday, Rodgers, Lindsay, Crouse. . . .

As much as anybody knew, this show was about that Austrian Baroness Von Trapp—ah yes, the refugee lady who'd brought her family out of Europe, established them as a group of choir singers, made them all a new life here. Not exactly a run-of-the-mill subject for a Mary Martin show, would you say?

Would it make a hit musical? By 11:20 P.M. or so, they'd have their answer.

The house lights went down, the rustle of conversation stopped. In contrast to the *Away We Go!* opening, all those years ago in 1942, a spotlight revealed a conductor in the Shubert pit, Frederick Dvonch. And now he raised a baton to lead the orchestra through the "Preludium," arranged by Robert Russell Bennett. Up went the curtain—to reveal, onstage, a tree, and there was Mary Martin. . . . *Up in the tree?*

Yes, and she was singing:

> *The hills are alive,*
> *With the sound of music. . . ."*

"That song almost compensated for the fact that I never got my banister in our production," Martin wrote in her memoirs.

"In the German movie, Maria the postulant appears in her first scene sliding down a long, long banister. She is always late to her classes, always going as fast as she can, dashing madly to get places on time. So off she goes down the banister and lands with a nice clunk, right at the feet of the Mother Superior. I couldn't wait to do that. All through rehearsals, I kept asking 'Where's my banister?'

"I never got it. There were just too many sets, too many other things to think about. In our version I first appeared on a tree—on it—at the very top, gazing at the Alpine scenery and singing. . . . The tree and I went forward, from the back of the stage towards the front, as the curtains opened. I was never madly comfortable. Not until I saw my friend Florence Henderson play Maria did I really understand how effective that entrance was. I had always felt like someone's version of a saint, being swept along, teetering a little, in a procession. . . ."

The New Haven audience loved it.

And from then on, they would be treated to a first act overflowing with the sound of music: "Maria," "Sixteen Going on Seventeen," "The Lonely Goatherd," "My Favorite Things," "Do-Re-Mi." . . . Richly varied Rodgers music, all with Hammerstein's lyrics, which for the first time in a long career he was unable to hear his audience respond to tonight.

Then came the final scene of the first act, when the Abbess is confronted by Maria, who must make a decision: To stay in the order, or to leave it and go back to the Captain, whom she's discovered she has feelings for, and to the children, whom she has also grown to love.

"Climb Ev'ry Mountain," sang Patricia Neway, her voice filling the Shubert.

In three very rare images from the Shubert Theatre in New Haven, here is *The Sound of Music* as captured during its tryout performances. (Courtesy of the Shubert Theatre, New Haven, Connecticut)

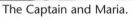

The Captain and Maria.

The Mother Superior (Patricia Neway) singing "Climb Ev'ry Mountain."

The Von Trapp children are won over by their new governess.

In the midst of the song, Maria realizes that she must abandon the religious life to respond to her emotions. She slowly removes the veil from her head as the initiation of her new life. Curtain.

No chorus, no dance number—but, truly, an emotional first-act finale. Certainly as powerful as the first act finale of *Gypsy*, Leland Hayward's latest—a thrilling *coup de theatre*.

During the intermission, the audience pushed its way up the aisle, out to the lobby, where the smokers could hold conference on the windy street. Hayward, Halliday, and assorted members of their staff prowled their way through the ticket-holders, impassively eavesdropping on the chatter, checking out the reactions so far.

Yes, the show was a little long. Well, what difference did that make?—hadn't *My Fair Lady* shown up here running fifteen minutes too long? And what about *South Pacific*, which had kept everybody in their seats way past eleven-twenty? So if this latest "R and H" seemed to be a bit slow and heavy, why worry about that? These guys knew what they were doing. Wasn't Mary Martin terrific with these kids? How could you go wrong with kids like that? In the next act, she'd be marrying the Captain and raising the family—oh, maybe she was a little old for this part, but she was doing a marvelous job with it—wasn't she adorable? The lobby lights blinked.

Now it was time for that second act.

Hayward, Halliday, and Rodgers met for a brief conference before retiring to their seats. "So far, so good," was Hayward's guarded comment. "I get the feeling they like it."

He was right. But even he, the master showman–salesman given to bursts of hyperbole (one of the people who knew him well was fond of referring to him as "a guy who could sell you smoke"), could have no idea how future audiences would respond to *The Sound of Music* tonight and for years to follow.

The New Haven people fixed their attention on the second act. Watched and listened as the Captain, and Maria, now married, staunchly resist the onslaught of the Nazis into their beloved Austria, as they announce they will not fly the Nazi banner; and heard how he would neither serve in Hitler's navy, nor bow to the invaders. Then, their inevitable decision to leave their homeland. And the final climax, as the Von Trapps finish their command performance in Salzburg, singing "So Long, Farewell," to their compatriots.

And then, for the final scene, the family bravely scaling the mountains enroute to Switzerland (not precisely true, but much more dramatic than the fact of their departure) singing "Climb Ev'ry Mountain."

And when the curtain fell, the thunder of applause. "Who could resist those ingredients?" remarked Bikel. "Seven adorable children, a chorus of gorgeous nuns' voices, and a young woman who had almost renounced any chance for a normal life."

Grateful at having been midwives at the birth of what promised to be a success, an event which in years to come they could boast about to their own children, the New Haven theatregoers went home.

The next day, the New Haven reviews were favorable—except for one notable exception. The show got its first pasting, one of the many which it would earn from the venerable *Yale Daily News*, where there appeared a review by Leslie Epstein. The headline read, "OH SISTER! MIT SCHLAGE!" and beneath that irreverent salvo was "I'm Getting into the Habit with You."

Years later, Epstein recalled that Richard Rodgers was so annoyed by the *Yale Daily News* pan that when he later encountered the young critic's mother at a Hollywood social event, he told her, "Your son doesn't know his ass from his elbow!"

With some justifiable wonder, Epstein said, "He took it as a personal insult!" But, he added, "When I came to the end of my bad review, I was savvy enough, even then, to append this prediction: In spite of all I've said, this show is going to make a billion dollars." (Such prescience had to come from the Epstein gene pool: Leslie had grown up in a show-business metier, the son of Philip Epstein, and the nephew of Julius, two icons of Hollywood screenwriting!)

Everyone involved in *The Sound of Music* knew full well that no matter how much the audience and the critics praised the show, there was work to do. "No one in the theatre ever takes success for granted," commented Bikel. "Too

often theatre people have allowed themselves to be lulled by the early appro-
bation of audiences so grateful for the chance at seeing a new work that they
refuse to be critical."

Not such old pros as Lindsay and Crouse or Martin or Donehue or
Rodgers. The October 13 opening in Boston was just around the corner, and
"there was chopping and changing scenes, a constant quest, if not for perfec-
tion, then at least for the promise of it," said Bikel. "Donehue and Joe Layton
did the arranging and the rearranging. But Dick Rodgers was also very much
in evidence during the process of whipping the show into shape." Hammerstein, having undergone his surgery, did not arrive in Boston to rejoin the
show until it was in its second week of the run.

By that time, the Boston reviews were in. Eliot Norton, the respected dean
of the critics, hadn't cared for the show very much; his *Boston Herald* Sunday
review would be another early example of a long line of negative notices:

> . . . Musically, this is one of the grandest of Broadway shows; dramati-
> cally, it is weak.
>
> In the songs they have written for Mary Martin, for Patricia Neway,
> for seven singing *wunderkind* and for a chorus of women who have
> undoubtedly come down from heaven to personate nuns, Richard
> Rodgers and Oscar Hammerstein have matched their best work. Their
> music is not only melodious, it is exultant; it runs through the show in lit-
> tle freshets of melody, or in great tumbling rivers of sound. . . . The sound
> of music is rich and fresh and magnificent in *The Sound of Music.* . . .
>
> The libretto should have been equally wonderful . . . for the true story
> of Maria Reiner is just that, and Howard Lindsay and Russel Crouse have
> all the qualities needed to make it move and amuse any audience. . . . But
> they have falsified the character of the Baron so that he is presented first
> as a ridiculously stern parent, who makes his small children march like
> little storm troopers and summons his help and everyone else with a
> bosun's whistle. He later rebels against the Nazis—as Captain Von
> Trapp did in real life—you are apt to wonder why. For in his own home,
> in those early scenes, he seems the very model of a heel-clicking, heil-
> ing tyrant.
>
> The Baron comes off badly in the play, and so do most of the other
> characters, except when *The Sound of Music* is occupied in singing one or
> another of the gay and great songs which roll over the play at regular
> intervals, inundating it in melody and in beauty. . . .
>
> Some of the silliness, the stiffness and the corny operetta falseness of
> this script can be eliminated. The truth can set *The Sound of Music* free of
> clichés, and lift it up to that high level of excitement where the best of it
> now shines and warms the hearts of the luckier playgoers of Boston. . . .
> [October 18, 1959]

(Years later, Hayward was sitting at his office desk, which was covered with checks he was endorsing—a distribution of profits for the investors in *The Sound of Music*. This batch added up to more than a million dollars. "This has been going for a long time," he chuckled. "Not bad for a show which the critics hated, ah?")

Hammerstein went to see the show. It was the first time in his long career that he hadn't been able to be an active participant in the preparation and day-to-day production of one of his works. There was *The Sound of Music*, spread out on a stage, playing to a full house.

"I remember he sat in a box, with his wife Dorothy," said Anna Crouse, "and Dorothy came out during the intermission to Russel, and she said, 'I have only seen Oscar'—Poppy, she called him—'cry once in my whole married life . . . and he's been crying.' Broke your heart."

When the performance ended, the Hammersteins went backstage to talk to the assembled company. Everyone knew of his operation; most of them knew it hadn't been totally successful. Hammerstein had his notes for them. He spoke to each member of the cast, giving them his comments. If, after forty-four shows in a long career, this one was to be his last, there would be no slackening of his professionalism.

As her Poppy went through his critiques, it was Dorothy's turn to stand behind a piece of scenery backstage, and to cry.

Hammerstein did the only other thing he knew how to do. He went to work. "With eleven days to go, we thought there could be no major additions or deletions," recalled Bikel. Rodgers and Hammerstein had decided there was something lacking in the score, and it had to do with the character I portrayed. They argued that my 'special talents' had not been fully used in the show, and that my folk background and my guitar playing could be used to better advantage."

What Hammerstein, with his remarkable acuity, was seeking was a lyric which would express the sadness in the family's departure from Austria, facing an enforced exile. He came up with the idea of what would be "Edelweiss," and for the next six days, he worked on a lyric, jotting down notes, writing phrases, seeking to express the sentiment of their loss.

One of the phrases he would set down early on was certainly the subtext of Hammerstein's own frame of mind. Sadly, he had written:

> Look for your lover and hold him tight
> While your health you're keeping. . . .

"Edelweiss" was Oscar Hammerstein's last lyric. Simply, he described a mountain flower, and by so doing, he created a remarkably strong sense of authenticity, of deep patriotism.

A piano was brought in to a private room at the Ritz-Carlton, where he and Rodgers could finish the song. Then they gave it to Bikel to sing near the clos-

Theodore Bikel with Marion Marlowe, as Elsa Schraeder, and Kurt Kasznar, as Max Detweiler. (Courtesy of Photofest)

ing of the second act. With the actor's first performance of it, the audience response was immediate. Simple, quiet, loving, Hammerstein's swan song proved absolutely necessary for the show, as it has been ever since.

Remarkably enough, "Edelweiss" created its own aura. People automatically assumed it was a traditional Austrian folk ballad. "I sang and played it eight times a week for the next two years," said Bikel. "This beautiful little tune sounded so authentic that one autograph-seeking fan at the stage door some months later said to me: 'I love that "Edelweiss"'—and then added, with total confidence: 'Of course, I have known it for a long time, but only in German.'"

The Sound of Applause

The New York opening would be on November 16, 1959.

By that night, there was a massive advance sale already "wrapped"—the theatrical term for tickets bought and paid for— almost two million dollars' worth of seats reserved by expectant theatregoers who wanted to see Mary Martin in whatever Rodgers and Hammerstein had created for her.

Such a large sum of faith-money was almost enough to ensure that Martin and her partners would recoup their original investment. The production's budget had been originally set at $400,000, and so shrewdly had the management put the show together that its final cost was only $20,000 over budget.

"That overage was the cost of a replacement sofa in Captain Von Trapp's living room," said Frank Goodman, the production press agent. "Dick Rodgers didn't like the original one, and he insisted it be replaced."

That November night arrived, and so did the opening-night audience— into the Lunt-Fontanne they flocked. "There was incredible tension in the cast before the curtain rose," remembered Bikel. "I shared in the excitement, but felt none of the fear that seemed to grip the other cast members, including the children and the chorus. Everyone had gotten flowers, telegrams, and presents. I received a solid gold whistle as a tribute to my bosun's whistling onstage. Mary gave me a silver-framed photograph in which she wore the dress from our wedding scene. . . . I gave gifts and went around the dressing rooms trying to calm everyone down. . . . Then we opened."

Years later, Mary Martin remarked, "I knew that my part required perfect pitch—and I'm not talking about music now. The treatment had to be very skillful, totally controlled. It was one of the most disciplined shows I ever did. You could never do a kidding thing, never play it broadly. I had to remember the character always, keep a tight rein on my emotions and my performance."

She would certainly do so that night. The audience loved her; they were enraptured with her, with the Von Trapp children, with her romance with the

Captain, and with the triumphant second act closing. And, as Rodgers and Hammerstein had predicted, they were deeply moved by "Edelweiss."

The cast received a standing ovation.

"We'd gone to Sardi's for the after-theatre party," remembered Anna Crouse, "and we got to the room where the party was being held, and we were all enjoying ourselves until the word got out: Both major reviews were absolutely terrible. . . . And there we all were, trying to be up and gay and cheerful, knowing that the show had been damned."

Soon enough, the early editions of the next day's papers hit the newsstands, and the reviews were there to be read.

Walter Kerr of the *Herald Tribune* said:

> I only wish that someone had not been moved to abandon the snowflakes and substitute cornflakes. Before *The Sound of Music* is halfway through its promising chores, it becomes not only too sweet for words but almost too sweet for music. Is it director Vincent Donehue who has made the evening suffer from little children? There are seven tots necessary to the narrative, and I am not against tots. But must they bounce into bed in their nightgowns so often, and so charmingly? Must they wear so many different picture-book skirts and fluff them so mightily, and smile so relentlessly, and give such precocious advice to their elders? The cascade of sugar is not confined to the youngsters. Miss Martin, too, must fall to her knees and fold her hands in prayer, while the breezes blow the kiddies through the window. She must always enter as though the dessert was here, now. The pitch is too strong; the taste of vanilla overwhelms the solid chocolate; the people onstage have all melted before our hearts do.

If Kerr had had himself a bad night, he was not alone. Brooks Atkinson, the most powerful of the New York critics, wrote in the *Times*:

> Although Miss Martin has longer hair than she had in *South Pacific*, she still has the same common touch that wins friends and influences people, the same sharp features, good will and glowing personality that makes music sound intimate and familiar. . . . Mr. Rodgers has not written with such freshness of style since *The King and I*. Mr. Hammerstein has contributed lyrics that also have the sentiment and dexterity of his best work. But the scenario of *The Sound of Music* has the hackneyed look of the musical theatre they replaced with *Oklahoma!*, in 1943 [sic] . . . It is disappointing to see the American musical stage succumbing to the clichés of operetta. The revolution of the Forties and Fifties has lost its fire. . . .

The other critics were less captious and negative. Richard Watts, Jr., of the *Post*, wrote: ". . . The new Rodgers and Hammerstein show has a warm-hearted, unashamedly sentimental and strangely gentle charm that is wonderfully

Stagehands hanging the show: The Lunt-Fontanne Theatre being readied for the Broadway opening of *The Sound of Music*. (Photo by Toni Frissell courtesy of Lauri Peters) endearing." And John McClain, of the *Journal-American*, remarked ". . . The most mature product of the team and it seemed to me to be the full ripening of these two extraordinary talents."

But it was perhaps left to Whitney Bolton, of the *Morning Telegraph*, to make the most sagacious remark. ". . . With better than two million dollars sacked up in the tills," he commented, ". . . it couldn't matter less what a critic might think."

It did, however, matter a great deal to those who'd worked so long and hard to bring Mary Martin's *What-if* to full-scale life on the Lunt-Fontanne stage. The Hammersteins went home; for Oscar and his wife Dorothy those reviews were especially depressing. "They went with Herb Mayes and his wife," remembered Mrs. Crouse. "The Mayeses lived up above the Hammersteins; they shared an elevator up to the apartments. Herb told me later that, as they were going up in the elevator, they heard Oscar give a heartfelt sigh of despair. 'It just broke my heart,' he told me later.

"Here was Oscar, who'd been through so damn much in this past summer. . . . It was a real shock to all of us—to all four of the men who'd created the show. But for Oscar, it was worse. He'd come to see the show in Boston, and sat with the audiences loving it, and then that negative review from Eliot Norton. . . . Perhaps he could have shrugged that one off, but here were the two most important critics in New York—Atkinson and Kerr—and they'd both given us bad reviews. Too much."

But the following night, everyone was back at the Lunt-Fontanne.

In came the audience, down went the lights, and, the "Preludium" concluded, up went the curtain. There was Mary Martin in the tree, and from the moment she began to sing "The Sound of Music," there was electricity in the theatre. The second-night audience responded with laughter, with applause, with total empathy.

"It was remarkable," said Mrs. Crouse. "We all went out into the lobby during the intermission, and Oscar came over to us. 'Make no mistake about it,' he told us. 'This is a hit!'

"And we looked at him. 'Do you really think so?'

"'Just look and listen to that audience!' he insisted. 'They couldn't care less about the reviews. I promise you, this is a *smash* hit!' And by the time the second act curtain came down, we knew he was right," she said.

It wasn't hyperbole, or Hammerstein doing his best to bring himself out of depression. It was a master's innate perception of what an audience wanted.

The box office response was healthy. There were lines each day at the Lunt-Fontanne, but in those first few days of the Broadway run, nobody, not even such a dedicated optimist as Hammerstein, could dare to envision the incredible success which the final Rodgers and Hammerstein collaboration would become. "They came in droves," Mary Martin remembered, years later. "I was given many gold medals during *The Sound of Music*, was blessed twice by monsignors, kissed by priests, and even received a special blessing from Pope John in Rome." And with a certain amount of personal satisfaction, she commented:

> If there ever was a triumph of audience over critics, it was *The Sound of Music*. . . . From beginning to end, and all over the world—the United States, Australia, England, wherever it played—most of the critics and the intellectuals in the audience found it impossibly sweet. Some of them absolutely loathed it. But audiences loved it. No matter how critical the reviews were, they didn't keep the people out—they pulled them in. . . . They kept finding a message in the show. They become quite passionate about it. People brought their children, reserved blocks of seats in advance. Some saw it over and over again; that was one reason why there was never an empty seat.

While those audiences responded with fervor eight times each week to his show, Hammerstein's physical condition did not improve. Always a pragmatist, he prepared himself for his demise.

"Oscar asked Dick to meet him at the Oak Room of the Plaza for lunch," wrote his biographer, Hugh Fordin.

> He told him matter-of-factly that he knew he would die soon, that he had decided against treatments that would leave him to die in comfort but could not cure him. He discussed Dick's future and suggested he find a younger man to work with. "We discussed many things that day, two somber, middle-aged men sitting in a crowded restaurant talking unemotionally of the imminent death of one and the need for the other to keep going," Dick recalled. . . . A man seated a few tables away came over to ask them to sign his menu. The stranger told them that he couldn't imagine why they looked so sad—they were so successful they couldn't have a worry in the world.

Ironically enough, his chance remark had been echoed in one of Hammerstein's earlier lyrics: "I Haven't Got a Worry in the World."

Hammerstein returned to Doylestown, where he could spend his declining days surrounded by family and friends. And with one final mountain to climb.

By August, the climb had ended. In tribute, on the evening of his passing all the lights of theatre marquees in midtown Manhattan were dimmed.

His works would go on, with delighted audiences applauding. But even Oscar Hammerstein, the dedicated optimist, could not have foreseen his last show's remarkable future history.

Martin stayed with *The Sound of Music* for the next two years. During that run, she would miss only one performance. The cause? "For the life of me, I can't remember what it was," she remarked later. "Something must have been sprained."

Her understudy, Renée Guarin, who'd been faithfully standing by month after month, was so excited that she'd finally been called to go on that she insisted Martin should listen in. She and the stage manager arranged to have the stage amplifiers turned up, and had the backstage telephone taken off the hook. In her backstage apartment, Martin, in bed, was able to listen to her understudy's one and only performance.

"She was just great," the star declared. "Later, she played Maria in an Australian production, stayed there for a while and married her stage manager."

Such lack of jealousy was merely one of her traits. "How do I remember Mary?" Bikel mused. "In the first instance, you have to understand that Mary Martin was first and foremost a professional with an awesome talent. She worked at her craft and she never let up, even after hundreds of performances. Working with her was a very rewarding experience."

His leading lady was refreshingly modest. "*The Sound of Music* was not a demanding show physically, except for the sheer distance I had to cover," she remembered. "The theatre was built on two stories, and we had a two-story set. My main dressing room was on the second floor of the theatre itself, but I also had a quick-change room on either side of the stage itself, in the wings. Just for fun, Richard, who loves statistics, put a pedometer on me once, and we found that I walked—ran—three miles at each performance, six miles on Wednesday and Saturdays!"

Stamina was one of her strongest suits; it had to be. But she did develop another problem. "For the first year, I was almost as blind as if all the lights had been out. I wasn't even aware of it. I knew all the children by their sizes and the color of their hair, and I knew Theo, as Captain Von Trapp, by his comfortable presence and his marvelous voice. Then I became painfully aware that I always had headaches on Thursdays and Sundays. I went to a doctor, who examined me and explained that it was because I strained my eyes so much doing two performances on the matinee days."

The doctor would prescribe a simple solution: contact lenses.

"The first time I wore them was a matinee," she remembered. "I had put them in . . . then came the scene in which I entered, alone, with my back to the Captain. His line, very stern, was 'What is your name?' I was supposed to say 'Maria Rainer.' That afternoon, onstage, I turned and saw Theo, really saw him—for the first time. He was so handsome, but much larger than I thought before. I blurted out 'Luise Rainer'" [a film star of the 1930s].

"*Luise Rainer?* I couldn't believe my ears. Theo couldn't believe his, either. He said, 'What?' and I got so completely out of my Austrian character that I drawled, in Texas style, 'Oh, ah mean . . . Ah mean, my name is *Maria* Rainer.'"

"This little postulant nun, who is supposed to face the Captain bravely at their first meeting, was smiling all through the scene!" remembered Bikel. "In fact, she was smiling all through the first act, unaccountably. At the intermission I went to her dressing room, and I asked, 'Is anything the matter? You are giving a different performance.' Mary said, 'Why, what am I doing?' I said,

Lauri Peters, as Leisl, in scenes with Mary Martin (opposite page) and Brian Davies, as Rolf Gruber, her romantic interest. (Courtesy of Lauri Peters)

'You are *smiling*. A lot.' She said, 'I am? Oh, oh, I know why that is—contact lenses! You know something? I could see what you were doing; that was so lovely!'"

She had seen it all: the childrens' faces, the Mother Superior . . . everybody.

"She had never seen me before," marveled Bikel, years later. "Only a blur. . . ."

"We did it, we loved it, and we loved each other," recalled Lauri Peters, the young dancer who was selected to play Liesl, the oldest Von Trapp daughter.

"I'd trained with Balanchine," she said, "but after a while, ballet becomes an expensive proposition. All those toe shoes . . . and if you're not working, it can add up for your family." So Peters decided to find a job which could help her support herself; she was promptly hired to join the chorus in *Say, Darling,* an Abe Burrows–Comden and Green musical version of a novel by Richard Bissell.

From there, she had gone into *First Impressions,* and that is where Richard Rodgers saw her and suggested she audition for him. Without knowing she would be trying out for the role of Liesl, she arrived at his office. "I went determined to impress him," she said. "I was dressed to the nines."

Rodgers took one look at her, shook his head and said, "Go home, take off the lipstick, and the high heels, and come back tomorrow."

"I was so remarkably lucky," Peters said. "Not only to get a second chance, but to be part of that show for two years. It was a very, very special experience. All of us felt it, that morning when we arrived for the first rehearsal. We knew—we had to know—even someone as young as I, that these people we were going to work with were titans. All of them, Rodgers and Hammerstein, Lindsay, Crouse, our director Vinnie Donehue, and, of course, our star, Mary Martin. What an experience it was to work with such a group of total professionals, such craftsmen, all of them, who did it for the love of their work!

"Somehow, their professionalism extended itself to all of us in the cast—down to the youngest of the kids, and even their mothers. There was none of that usual stage-mother nightmare," she insisted, "with all the back-biting and competition. Those children who played the Von Trapps were chosen with such care. They were loving and involved. Throughout the run, for all those two years' worth of performances, all of us were having such a good time!

"I wasn't even aware of a bad press. You see, we always relied on the audience reaction. The show was—and is—such a simple tale of good and evil; we could tell from our audience out front how they were palpably involved. Of course, there was a wholesomeness in our show, something which doesn't seem to exist in most of the current shows," she explained. "And there's that incredible score. Audiences . . . leave the theatre humming the songs, and then go home and teach them to their kids. And that's going on today, isn't it?

"And there was Mary. There was such an electricity with her, an immediate accessibility. When she appeared in that tree at the opening, in the fork of those two branches, and began to sing." Peters shook her head fondly at the memory. "There she was, reaching out to them, and they immediately reached back. People got chills from that moment. And it was exactly that way, with the same reaction, for the entire two years. Every performance! . . . People stop me, even now," Peters said (some thirty-odd years after those first audiences saw her), "and they tell me how much they liked it, and how fondly they remember me doing 'I Am Sixteen, Going on Seventeen.' It's truly amazing!"

And what were the ex-ballerina's memories concerning the choreography? "The dancing?" she asked. "I did all there was!"

"There is something wonderfully timeless about the show," she mused. "I guess it's because we've been through so much—and we come back to this show to get a sense of love, and good triumphing over evil—that 1950s sense that there is good, and there is love. The show presents that to you, and makes no apology for it."

Week after week, they played to sold-out houses.

Nothing seemed to faze Martin, not even the accident she had while doing the TV performance of *Peter Pan*, which she filmed in the NBC television studios in Brooklyn during days she wasn't playing matinees. She survived a schedule which would have dismayed most leading ladies, and then, at one disastrous day, she slammed into an NBC studio wall and broke her arm. That night, she had to play a show. Should her understudy replace her? No, indeed; with her arm in a sling, Mary Martin went on.

In the first act of the show, it didn't matter much; her arm was folded in a sling, and since, as a postulant, her arms were meekly folded to her sides most of the time, nobody seemed to notice anything amiss. The sympathetic backstage crew had prepared slings for their star in the proper colors which would match the rest of her costumes. But the true crisis came when Mary had to play the guitar. "I stuck my guitar between my sling and left side, and pretended to strum with my right hand while a musician in the orchestra pit filled in the guitar music," she remembered. Later, she performed an Austrian folk dance in the "Edelweiss" number: "Theo Bikel did his part of the dance with even more than his usual enthusiasm, waving his arms like mad, and never seemed to notice that I was waving only one arm!"

Rodgers also wrote admiringly of Martin: "Working with Mary made me appreciate even more what an extraordinary trouper she is. During rehearsals and during the run of the show on Broadway, she was constantly in training, both vocally and physically. Nothing we ever suggested was ever considered too demanding. Even after it seemed impossible to do anything with her part, Mary was still working to improve her interpretation. In all the years I've known her, I have never seen her give a performance that was anything less than the best that was in her."

From a man known for his sense of perfectionism, high praise indeed.

There would be extraordinary examples of audience loyalty to the star and her show, such as the memorable night in July of 1960, when Manhattan suffered through a power failure. Shortly before curtain time, all the lights on Broadway and its environs went out.

But the audience for that night's performance of *The Sound of Music* had no intention of leaving. They stood quietly under the darkened Lunt-Fontanne marquee, holding their precious tickets, waiting for the theatre doors to open. The theatre managers came out to inform the people that there were no lights inside. There could be no show; musicians couldn't read music in the dark, scenery could not be moved without power, nobody could perform on a darkened stage.

Still, nobody moved.

"They had come to see *The Sound of Music*, and they were going to stay there until they saw it," remembered Mary Martin. Power or not. This proved to be

Mary Martin teaches "Do-Re-Mi" to the youngsters in the cast. (Top:) Lauri Peters (Liesl); (second row:) William Snowden (Friedrich), Kathy Dunn (Louisa), Joseph Stewart (Kurt); (bottom:) Marilyn Rogers (Brigitta), Mary Susan Locke (Marta), Evanna Lien (Gretl). (Courtesy of the Shubert Theatre, New Haven, Connecticut)

an extreme case of that old show-biz adage "The show must go on." Halliday quickly sent stagehands out to buy flashlights, as many as could be found. While they were out scouting for the hundred or so they returned with, Halliday consulted with the musicians and the rest of the backstage crew. "They caught the spirit," Martin said, ". . . and they said they'd do their best. And away we went!"

The theatre doors were opened, by flashlight. Then the ushers, with flashlights, led the audience inside. When they were seated, the star came onstage and explained the problem. "And I told them we'd carry on if they wanted us to. They did!"

What transpired then certainly deserves a place in the *Guinness Book of Records*, as one of the most amazing theatrical performances ever recorded: a full-scale Broadway musical being done by a cast by flashlight on a bare stage. Mary Martin recalled:

"I sang my opening number wearing my dressing gown, and sitting on a stepladder, instead of up in the tree—and I held a flashlight to my face. Those darling children, in the wings, were watching me do it, and when they came on, they too held flashlights to their faces so the audience could see them, see their mouths, and understand their lyrics better.

"We had no time to rehearse what we were going to do; those children simply watched me, and every single one, so quickly, did the same thing. What pros they were!"

The audience in the dark theatre gave the cast a roaring round of applause—"the sound of music to our ears!" she said proudly.

Half an hour later into the performance—*click*—the lights abruptly came back on again!

"We must have looked pretty funny up there, in our dressing gowns or street clothes. . . . We stopped, everything stopped," Martin remembered, "and I walked down to the footlights and asked if they would like to wait a few minutes while we put on costumes and set the stage." The audience agreed enthusiastically. So, back went the cast to their dressing rooms to get into their costumes; the stagehands went to work setting up the scenery; and then, *sans* makeup, the cast returned to the stage to pick up where they'd left off—now in a regular performance.

When the curtain finally fell, there were cheers, and calls for encores!

"But I think it was almost a letdown," commented Mary Martin, a bit ruefully. "I think they'd probably rather have watched us finish up the entire show by flashlight. . . . That audience had never experienced anything like it; that night, they felt as if they were part of the show. . . ."

Finally, the star's two-year run was almost over; eight times a week she'd enchanted the audiences. Meanwhile, the producers had cast the touring company, which would star Florence Henderson as Maria von Trapp.

"I remember that the night before the company left New York to open in

Detroit was a Sunday," said Anna Crouse. "So it was decided to use the Lunt-Fontanne sets to do a run-through, and they invited a preview audience, including Mary, who, of course, had never seen the show from the front of the house. And at the intermission, we couldn't find Mary. She was down on all fours, feeling around the floor where she'd been sitting. Russel said, 'Mary, what is the matter?' And she said, 'I've cried my lens out.'

"Isn't that wonderful? Because she'd been playing it night after night, and she never knew what the effect was on the audience."

Maria weds the Captain at Nonnberg Abbey surrounded by familiar faces and a set designed in the grand tradition by Oliver Smith. (Courtesy of Photofest)

The Passing of the Torch

The *Sound of Music* would eventually run for 1,433 performances. When it finally closed, it had been almost five years since the day when Mary Martin had first been approached by Vincent Donehue, to suggest the idea of her playing Maria von Trapp. Five years since she and Dick Halliday had borrowed enough money to buy the rights to the German Trapp Family films and start the project. Five years since all the rest of that remarkably creative group, Leland Hayward, Howard Lindsay and Russel Crouse, Richard Rodgers and the dear, departed Oscar Hammerstein had joined her and Halliday and Donehue to make the whole thing happen to create a classic American musical—one which withstands all sorts of bad reviews.

"Mary and I left the show on the same day, two years in the Lunt-Fontanne and one month on the road after we'd started," said Theodore Bikel. "I had wanted out earlier, or at least to be sprung for a film job with a promise to return to the show. No dice. For all our friendship, Mary insisted that I stay with the play. She hated change of any kind.

"But in some cases, change could not be helped. For example, some of the children had to be let go because of the difference in their growth rates. The idea was that when standing in line, they should look like organ-pipes, in an ascending or descending order. . . . Some of the kids simply grew too fast, and two of the children suddenly would be the same height. The faster-growing kid had to be replaced."

And that was not all. "Mary was used not only to their height, but also to the color of their hair. When she sang 'Do-Re-Mi,' she tapped the kids' heads for different notes. Once, they replaced a blonde-haired child with a dark-haired one, and Mary insisted that they dye the new child's hair the exact color as the old one's, so she wouldn't get mixed up!

"After two years," concluded Bikel, "both Mary and I were quite prepared to say goodbye. . . but when the actual night came, it was a surprisingly difficult thing for all of us to face. There were places in the performance that had us all choked up and almost unable to continue. The children singing 'So Long, Farewell,' which we had heard so often, suddenly took on a personal meaning and touched us, not as the Captain and Maria, but as Mary and Theo."

The end of their last performance arrived. "After the final curtain, Mary and I stood onstage amid grown-ups and children, all with tears in their eyes, and we did not want to leave. Finally, Mary's dresser pulled her away. I stayed and shook hands, hugged stagehands, nuns, and children. Then I left to take off my makeup and clear out my dressing room, which would be occupied on Monday by a stranger.

"On the next Sunday," he said, "I was all right—that had been my day off all along—but on the Monday, I was frantic, and could not bear to be in New

York. I went to spend the day with friends in Poughkeepsie, but even there, when seven-thirty rolled around, the time for the half-hour call, I was itching all over. This is what a junkie feels like, I thought, when he needs his fix!"

Bikel was far from alone in recalling such a conditioned reflex. Thousands of others have been affected by *The Sound of Music* over the last few decades in similar fashion.

SOGGY NOTICES

Given the success of the show, what about those bad reviews?

Kenneth Tynan, in his review for *The New Yorker*, had sniffed, ". . . for children of all ages, from 6 to 11. . . . The book is damp and dowdy, like a remaindered novelette."

Audiences didn't seem to agree. The touring company went out on the road for two and a half years, and when it closed in November of 1963, it had played a total of thirty-five cities.

"Instead of offsetting sweetness with lightness, it turns sticky with sweetness and light," wrote Louis Kronenberger in *Time*. "[It] ends by making its warmheartedness as cloying as a lollipop, as trying as a lisp."

That was not the opinion of the show's press agent, Frank Goodman. "They gave me a small piece of the show out of friendship," he said of Hayward, Halliday, Rodgers, and Hammerstein. "My share was worth $1,000. For years I've been getting checks. I think by now my share adds up to about $25,000 or more."

In 1961, *The Sound of Music* opened in London, at the large Palace Theatre. In England, recalled Anna Crouse, the performing company was truly not a good one: "In those days," she explained, "the British laws wouldn't permit you to have children on a stage—some old regulation against the exploitation of under-agers. And so we had to have gnomes playing the children of the Von Trapps—midgets! Which was awful!

"We went to the opening night, and then Russel and I went back to Claridge's. We were in a little back room—I think they'd cleaned out some maid's room, or something, but it was fine. We had a lovely room waiter who brought us breakfast after the opening night, and sat there and read the notices":

Only Rodgers' almost infallible ear for a tune saves the evening from foundering in a marsh of treacle, bathed in a dim religious light. . . .

[Bernard Levin, in the *Express*]

It is a mistake to treat the Von Trapps as heroes. This falsity of feeling undermines the whole entertainment. . . .

[Harold Hobson, *Sunday Times*]

Take the basic story of *The King and I*, scrape the oriental spicing and substitute Austrian sugar-icing an inch thick. Add a little bit of drama at the end. Serve—and sit back and listen to the praises of the flavor. . . .

[W. A. Darlington, *Daily Telegraph*]

"I have never read such notices in my life!" Mrs. Crouse exclaimed. "We're sitting there, with all the London papers knocking the show, and our waiter comes back and he says, 'Oh, congratulations! You have that marvelous hit.'

"And Russel said, 'What?' He held up the papers. 'These?'

"And our waiter said, 'Oh, don't pay any attention to those notices!'"

Prescient waiter, indeed.

The English production would finally close in January of 1967, after a remarkable run of 2,385 performances. In the special *Variety* show-biz lingo, it was celebrated as "LONDON 'SOUND' LONGEVITY CHAMP."

"We had another review in London," said Anna Crouse. "One of the critics referred to the show as a 'soggy old plum.'"

So much for the British critics.

There is an old and trusted show business saying, one which probably may help to explain the incredible appeal of *The Sound of Music* in the face of all the derogatory reviews it garnered over the years. (Remember, we haven't even come to the ones which awaited the motion picture version.) It's simple enough: "Nobody liked it except the people."

How is it that *The Sound of Music* goes on ticking, providing audiences with satisfaction?

"First of all," mused Theodore Bikel, decades later, "it has to be the reverence for the material by all those people who worked on the show."

"This show," said Anna Crouse, "was put together by four men who knew what they were doing. Russel and I were married twenty-one years, and I've heard him talk about his earlier shows, and I never remember anything he and Howard did that went so smoothly and happily. I don't mean they didn't argue, or change things—of course they did, but it was all created in such a professional manner."

"It's a show about individualism," said Bikel. "On the one hand, you have a young nun who breaks away from the rigidity of convent life . . . and so does the Captain. He could stay behind in Austria and become a Nazi, but no, he wants his freedom. They both break free, one for love, the other for principle. They risk all sorts of dangers for themselves, and for their family, and in the end, good triumphs over evil. What could be more satisfactory?"

And not only to audiences here in America, but all over the world.

"Did you know that when the movie came out in China, it was a huge success?" he added. "The film ran and ran—they loved it! Now you tell me, what do the Chinese know from nuns, or Nazis, or Austrian noblemen?"

LEHMAN AND LAZAR

Any Rodgers and Hammerstein opening night was certain to draw an in-crowd, those socialites and business people, movers and shakers from uptown and downtown—and from Hollywood. That November night in 1959, when *The Sound of Music* opened, down front in a pair of the best seats were two very important audience members sitting and watching the musical version of Maria von Trapp's saga.

One of them was Spyros Skouras, the head of Twentieth Century-Fox. His company had been a comfortable partner with Rodgers and Hammerstein over the years since they had agreed to work on *State Fair* back in 1945. In the mid-1950s three of Rodgers and Hammerstein's major musicals, *South Pacific, Carousel,* and *The King and I,* had been made into successful Fox films. When Fox had made the deal for *The King and I,* the studio secured the right of "first refusal" on any forthcoming Rodgers and Hammerstein musical.

Next to Skouras sat Irving "Swifty" Lazar, the archetypal agent, who'd built his career by specializing in selling the highest quality merchandise to the highest quality purchasers at, needless to add, the highest prices. In such matters of quality, Lazar was the lineal heir to Leland Hayward. Tonight, he represented not only Hayward but also Lindsay and Crouse and Rodgers and Hammerstein.

According to the legend, on this opening night, while the Von Trapp story unfolded, Skouras could be seen weeping at what he saw and heard. When Lazar took notice of the old titan's reaction, the sight of Skouras giving way to his emotions told him everything he needed to know: He had hooked himself a "live one."

But not quite yet. Lazar knew that Fox had not exercised its right of first refusal on buying the rights to *Flower Drum Song.* That show had been sold to Universal. And since the New York reviews of *The Sound of Music* weren't written yet, who could be certain that Skouras would dip into Fox's diminishing supply of cash to pay the very high price which Lazar was preparing to ask?

It would be a while before such a deal was struck, especially after the two most important New York critics, Brooks Atkinson and Walter Kerr, proved—as we can now recall—to be no big fans of *The Sound of Music.*

Two weeks after that opening night, the very talented screenwriter Ernest Lehman came to New York on assignment. At the end of a day's work, he took his wife to see *The Sound of Music.* Lehman, an ex–Broadway press agent who had turned his experiences in that exotic trade into the classic screenplay *The Sweet Smell of Success,* had followed it with a string of impressive screenplays—for *Sabrina,* then the Alfred Hitchcock thriller *North by Northwest, From the Terrace,* and *The King and I.* He'd worked closely with Robert Wise, who had directed Lehman's script of *Executive Suite,* as well as his *Somebody Up There Likes Me.* And now he was at work on Wise's production of *West Side Story.*

During the intermission of *The Sound of Music,* Lehman remembers racing with his wife to the nearby Howard Johnson's for a bowl of chowder. There he told her: "I know the critics have beaten this show around the head, but I don't care what they say; someday this show is going to make a very successful movie." It would be several years before Lehman's prediction could begin to come true, but how could he have foreseen that, when it did, he himself would be one of the linchpins in the successful production of a classic musical movie? Before he left New York, Lehman repeated his opinion to David Brown, one of the key Fox executives in Manhattan, and then, back in Hollywood, he gave his enthusiastic recommendation to Buddy Adler, then the president of Twentieth Century-Fox.

By that time, the weekly box-office grosses were being reported by *Variety*; the word was out: *The Sound of Music* was a hot ticket, very definitely a commercial success. So, by the following June, in 1960, the persistent Swifty Lazar had closed the deal with Fox. The studio exercised its right of first refusal, and bought the screen rights. The price? One and a quarter million dollars, against 10 percent of the gross. (Pay attention to that innocent-seeming word "gross," please. We did not say "net," which translates as an invisible profit, never seen in the film business. No, Lazar had negotiated 10 percent of what is known in the film business as "the first dollar," that is, the audience's cash money collected at the ticket window.)

It would be the largest sum paid for a property by a film studio up until that time.

Anna Crouse vividly recalled those negotiations, as well she might: "Swifty sat and explained to Howard and Russel, 'I have gotten them to put a clause in this contract which stipulates that you'll also get a percentage after the film has made $12 million.' Howard said, 'Swifty, that's just wasting ink. Nothing has ever made $12 million profit.'

"Well, of course, Howard was right—in the 1960s, no film had ever earned that much," Mrs. Crouse declared. Thirty-odd years after the release of the film, she added fervently, "All I can say today is, thank God for Swifty!"

Part of the deal Lazar negotiated also stipulated that Twentieth Century-Fox would control the rights to the original two German films about the Von Trapps for a period of six years. Fox would combine the two films into one, and have them dubbed into English. They would be released in the United States a year later. Does it surprise anyone to know that the reviews in 1961 were negative? "Uncompromisingly sentimental nature has a tendency to slop over into naiveté," said the *Variety* critic.

The Filmmakers

The Twentieth Century-Fox agreement with the *Sound of Music* partnership stipulated that no film of the musical could be released before December 31, 1964, or until all first-class presentations of the musical had closed, whichever came first. So, for the next three years, the Fox accounting department would issue six-figure checks, in installments, to maintain the studio's rights. Unfortunately, that same Fox accounting department was faced with dwindling revenues.

Darryl F. Zanuck, the powerful head of the studio's production, had decamped Hollywood in 1956, to set himself up as an independent producer in Paris. Control of the company passed on to Spyros Skouras, in New York. The studio would be run by a series of executives, with varying results, in a downward spiral of success.

The movie business was far from what it had been during its glory years. That twelve-inch TV screen in our living rooms, which heretofore had seemed only an interesting toy, had grown into an all-pervasive monster. Executives who'd shrugged off the video screen as trivia which would pass found the TV networks treading more and more on their Achilles' heel, the audience.

Then came *l'affaire Cleopatra*.

It didn't begin as one of the largest projects Fox had ever attempted. Like Topsy, it just grew. And grew, and grew—until the film, which starred Elizabeth Taylor, Richard Burton, and Rex Harrison, became a cash-eating monster. By the time that barge had floated down the Nile to completion, it would almost sink the entire studio beneath its weight of nearly $40 million in costs.

A shrewd observer of the motion picture scene once remarked, "The Hollywood studios are just like someone who tries to commit suicide in public, but never quite succeeds." In order to find the money to pay for the Italian production costs incurred by *Cleopatra*, Skouras sold off the studio's vast back lot, a choice tract of 260 acres. It eventually became the great urban sprawl of buildings, hotels, theatres, and malls known as Century City.

But the losses continued to mount, and the various heads of production whom Skouras had installed to replace Zanuck weren't savvy enough to bring forth box-office winners.

Fox reissued all its previous Rodgers and Hammerstein film versions, *Carousel, South Pacific,* and *The King and I,* in an effort to generate cash. But in the face of the problems incurred by the behemoth *Cleopatra*, who could contemplate investing money in a film based on *The Sound of Music*?

Eventually, in what must be compared with a cliché climactic ride to the rescue, Zanuck returned from Paris, bringing with him his film, *The Longest*

Day, a blockbuster packed with stars re-enacting the events of D-Day, in 1945. The film would bring in desperately needed grosses. But before he handed it over to Fox, Zanuck took over the reins of the company again. After all, he was the major stockholder, and he wasn't about to permit the company to go under. He'd gambled with *The Longest Day.* His gamble paid off.

Before Zanuck returned to Paris, he installed his son and heir, Richard Zanuck, as head of the daily operation of the Westwood studio. and to bring the company back from the brink.

Pictures were still in the Fox pipeline. Director Robert Wise was to go to Asia to make *The Sand Pebbles,* and in England and Italy, Zanuck had arranged for *Those Magnificent Men In Their Flying Machines,* as well as *The Agony and the Ecstasy.* But the once-thriving Westwood lot was almost dormant. It was time for desperate measures; young Zanuck was forced to lay off most of the personnel and to shut down the plant temporarily while he planned its future. The place became a near ghost town. Even the commissary had to shut down, while Zanuck searched for a prospective life-saver.

What would make a blockbuster for the future?

Down in the story department files, gathering dust in the empty offices, there was a manuscript by Howard Lindsay and Russel Crouse, set to the music of Richard Rodgers and the lyrics of Oscar Hammerstein. A manuscript of a show which was still packing in audiences, now at the Mark Hellinger Theatre, in New York. Why hadn't anyone in the Fox studio thought of having a film script prepared of the property which Lazar had sold them?

"Even though we couldn't release the picture until the show had closed," commented young Zanuck, "they could have put a writer on it. What you want to do is have your movie ready for release when your date comes."

And what writer could that be? One who'd already gone on record with his opinion of the show as a potential hit film, Ernest Lehman, who'd recently been working with Robert Wise on the screenplay for *West Side Story,* and was completing another major film at MGM, *The Prize.* Was he still enthusiastic about writing a screenplay? He was, and he would.

Very shortly, the *Variety* headline read: "SOUND" OF 20TH PROD'N HEARD; LEHMAN INKED. And Lehman arrived at the sprawling, empty Fox studio to meet with his new employer. Zanuck had chosen a small bungalow as his headquarters—no lavish suite for him, unlike his father. Where to house Lehman? The studio manager, one of the few employees left, told him, "You can have any office in the place." He then took Lehman on a guided tour of deserted office spaces. There was first the studio chief's suite—no phones ringing, forsaken desks, silence. The suite assigned to the story department head? Also vacant. A series of producers' suites, all available. Which one did Lehman fancy?

"It was the same as that old story: A guy calls up the movie theatre to ask, 'What time does the movie go on?' and the manager says, 'What time can you get here?' " observed Lehman. Eventually, he settled for a small office in the production department, there to begin the task of adapting *The Sound of Music* into a future Fox film, one which had yet to be approved by the board of directors, but one which was desperately needed to bring life back to the dormant studio. Each morning, Lehman would arrive at his quiet quarters after a walk down studio streets where rows of empty parking spaces were mute evidence that no one was working on the nearby sound stages. Then on into the production building, its hallways once filled each day with Zanuck's busy staff of technicians, messengers, film crews, actors hurrying to meetings, agents hustling jobs at the casting department for their clients, cadres of assistants busily working out costs in endless production meetings. . . . Now all of them had vanished, dissolved, faded to black. Where were they? Sitting hopefully at home, on unemployment insurance, waiting for a phone call which could bring a welcome summons back to work.

Not for nothing is Hollywood known as the dream factory.

How could they know that their future was now in the two hands of a single talented screenwriter, seated in an office with a secretary to do his typing? It was almost a surrealist image, dreamed up by someone like a Luis Buñuel or Federico Fellini: An entire studio, once mighty and thriving, now teetering on the edge of the cliff, below which awaited bankruptcy. Its future totally dependent on one writer, a lone producer . . . a small but determined team, using each hour to try and snatch Fox back from the brink.

A true, traditional ninth-reel climax, with precisely the sort of suspense which keeps paying customers coming in, to sit on the edge of their seats and pray for a happy ending.

"Dick Zanuck and I met for our first lunch at Romanoff's, to talk about the project," Lehman recalled. "He didn't get to our table directly because he was accosted by Swifty Lazar. I watched them as they talked for about five minutes, and then finally Dick shook his head, walked away from Lazar, came over to our table and sat down.

"He said, 'You know what just happened? Lazar, on behalf of an unnamed client, just offered me $2 million—a $750,000 profit for Fox—if I would turn *The Sound of Music* over to him. I told him no. I said, 'That's great news. I wonder who it could be?' We speculated, but we didn't come up with any names.

"When I got back to my office, the phone rang; it was Lazar. He said 'Ernie, what are you doing over there, working on *The Sound of Music*? They're kidding you. They're never going to make the picture. They have no money! You'll never even get paid!' I said, 'Irving, you just offered Dick Zanuck a $750,000 profit, and he said no!'

"Lazar just kept right on talking. . . ."

It would be a year later before Lehman *et al* could discover that the unnamed Lazar client who'd made that offer for *The Sound of Music* was the rival studio head Jack Warner. Did Warner wish to produce the film? Ah, no—he had a musical project of his own in progress, *My Fair Lady*, and he had shrewdly perceived *The Sound of Music* to be a threat to his own film!

And he would be absolutely correct.

The Fox board of directors eventually gave Zanuck the green light for production. But the actual task of turning the Broadway musical into a successful motion picture, which could revive Twentieth Century-Fox, would prove to be a classic uphill struggle.

As is customary, most of the Hollywood colony were nay-sayers. In that arena known as the movie business, if you are down, even temporarily, you are automatically out. The game goes on without you. One day, when the Fox commissary had reopened to serve the technicians who'd been brought back to work on two other projects, Lehman came in for lunch. There he would meet Burt Lancaster, his old friend and the star of his *The Sweet Smell of Success*. What was Lehman currently working on? Lehman told him about the screenplay of *The Sound of Music* which was in his typewriter. Lancaster shook his head sadly. "Jesus," he remarked, "you must need the money."

On another evening, Lehman was a guest at Jack Lemmon's home; another guest was Billy Wilder. When, as is traditional in Hollywood soirees, there came the discussion of forthcoming projects, Lehman mentioned *The Sound of Music*. Wilder shook his head. "Believe me," he predicted, "no musical with swastikas in it will ever be a success!"

Another negative reaction would come from director Stanley Donen, whom Lehman had thought of as a potential co-worker on the film. Donen had considerable experience in musicals at Metro-Goldwyn-Mayer; Lehman called him in Switzerland to suggest he take charge of the project. Donen's reply was totally negative. "Ernie," he said, "I'm an investor in the show, and that is enough for me. Thanks, but no thanks."

Lehman's next choice was Gene Kelly, who'd directed the New York production of *Flower Drum Song*. "I went to Gene's house in Beverly Hills," recalls Lehman, "and I pleaded with him to direct the picture. He led me out the front door, and on the front lawn he said 'Ernie, go find someone else to direct this piece of shit!'"

Then came another possibility: Bob Wise, who had done *West Side Story* with Lehman. But Wise was preparing *The Sand Pebbles* for Fox. He did not wish to abandon that project; besides, in the opinion of his agent, Wise was not particularly interested in doing *The Sound of Music*. Whether or not he'd heard all the Hollywood predictions of its future failure, according to his agent Wise didn't feel it was something for him.

At least, not then. (Everyone in the movie business reserves the right to change his mind.) So Lehman continued working away at the screenplay, and the search for a director went on.

Young Zanuck hadn't yet actually seen the musical, so both men proceeded to New York. "I hadn't seen it in two years," recalled Lehman. "Mary Martin was no longer in it; she'd been replaced by Nancy Dussault, and the night we went, I remember I sat there thinking, 'This is what I said two years ago would someday make a successful movie? This is what I've agreed to do?' . . . Now it's one thing to say a show would make a great movie someday, but it's another thing to know you're now committed to do it!"

The curtain fell. Lehman and Zanuck left the theatre. "Dick and I were sort of not saying much to each other as we walked out. We were in deep dismay."

The following day there would be a meeting at the summit with Darryl Zanuck, who'd arrived from France to confer on possible directors and stars.

Thus began a round of Cast-O, the game which is constantly played in executive suites when a film is being readied for production. Zanuck threw out the first pitch; as Maria von Trapp he suggested Doris Day. It seemed Marty Melcher, her husband, had been lobbying on the star's behalf, and Zanuck was partial to the idea of the cheerful blonde singer joining the Trapp family.

Lehman was negative about the suggestion; in his opinion, Doris Day would be typical old-fashioned Hollywood typecasting. Besides, wasn't it a bit previous to start casting this film without a director? Eventually, the conversation got around to William Wyler. Who could fault such a prospect? Wyler was an icon, not only capable of doing such romantic classics as *Wuthering Heights* but also *The Best Years of Our Lives* and *Mrs. Miniver*. And lately, he'd directed the charming romantic comedy *Roman Holiday*.

Impressive credits; yes, indeed, Wyler would be perfect. Zanuck called California, suggested the project to Wyler, and immediately arranged for the director to come East and see the show with Lehman.

"I waited in New York, Willy arrived, and I took him to see the show," said Lehman. "This was now the third time I'd seen it . . . and this time I was even less sure of my original judgment."

Zanuck was waiting for the two men at "21."

"We're walking out of the theatre and Willy says, 'Ernie, I hate to tell you this, but I hated the show, and I'm not going to meet Darryl!' I said, 'You have to; he's waiting for us!'"

The car arrived at "21," but Wyler refused to get out. Lehman told the chauffeur to go inside and tell Zanuck that they would not be there to meet with him, and then suggested to Wyler they go for a walk.

"It's late at night, and he keeps saying 'Ernie, I can't tell you how much I hated the show, but please, keep telling me why you think I ought to do it.'"

Lehman and Wyler walked the Manhattan streets while Lehman explained all his plans for the projected screenplay, the character changes he proposed, and the climactic moments he'd begun to strengthen visually for the screen. As if in a litany, Wyler's response was, "I hate the show, Ernie, but keep talking. Explain to me why I ought to do it."

This roving "pitch-meeting," in which a writer tries to sell a project, continued until after 2 A.M., at which point the exhausted Lehman said, "Willy, I've got one question for you. Remember that moment where Captain von Trapp begins to sing "The Sound of Music" with his children?'"

"Funny you should mention that," said Wyler. "I almost cried."

"That's it, Willy!" said Lehman. "That's why this is going to make a very successful movie. That moment!"

"Keep talking," said Wyler.

When Lehman reported this to Darryl Zanuck the following day, to explain why Zanuck had been stood up at "21," Zanuck's immediate response was, "Okay, Ernie, your job is not to work on the screenplay. Your job is to stay with Willy Wyler and keep twisting his arm until he agrees to do the movie!"

Lehman would carry out his assignment from Zanuck for the next few weeks in California, continuing to confer with Wyler, day after day.

"Willy was well known for agreeing to make a picture, and then changing his mind," said Lehman. "So I kept on offering him all my suggestions for strengthening the screenplay, and eventually, as I was about to run out of ideas, Willy said okay, and we had ourselves a director!"

At least, for the moment.

For Wyler still hated *The Sound of Music*. Lehman was far from certain the arrangement with him was a lasting commitment. "I was still very leery. All I could remember is that he had hated the show, and I'd talked him into doing it. Which was far from a firm commitment."

For the next four months, Lehman worked on "treatments," carefully plotted drafts of sequences for the screenplay, with descriptions of the action therein, and proposed dialogue. Meanwhile, he and Zanuck had hired Roger Edens, the veteran musical man-of-all-work, who'd been involved at Metro for many years working on Arthur Freed productions. Eventually, all three, Lehman, Wyler, and Edens, would fly to Austria to search for locations in and about Salzburg.

There would ensue a truly comic-opera sequence in Austria. Most of the time the trio were there, it seemed Wyler would spend much of his time accepting long-distance calls from other studios, to discuss other film projects. And since Wyler had suffered a hearing loss during his service in the Air Force in World War II, he would often ask Lehman to act as his go-between. Thus Lehman became aware that Wyler was in the midst of discussing an MGM project, *The Americanization of Emily*, which was being prepared for the cameras. To top that off, the film was to star Julie Andrews, the same Julie Andrews whose name had come up as a potential Maria for *The Sound of Music*. "The same Julie Andrews," said Lehman, "whom Willy felt was wrong for Maria!"

169

F
I
N
A
L
E

A comic opera, perhaps, but it wasn't funny. Certainly not for Lehman, who'd been working on the project for all these months, doggedly attempting to get the film ready for a possible production.

Wyler suggested Lehman join him in a flight over the Austrian Alps, to seek out opening shots. Lehman refused; Wyler was adamant. Lehman dug in his heels. "I guess it wasn't just the ride I was afraid of; I don't know why I didn't want to go. I guess it was my mistrust of Willy."

Later, Lehman would realize he'd been right not to go. Roger Edens, who'd gone along on the flight, reported that they'd discovered their pilot had been a Nazi. "When Wyler discovered that, all hell broke loose!" said Lehman. "There they were, flying over the Alps, screaming at each other about Nazism! Boy, was I lucky I hadn't gone along!"

One cannot totally fault Wyler for his attitudes. He, of Austrian parentage, had spent the early Nazi years making films in Hollywood. Many of his relatives had not been so fortunate; they'd ended up in death camps. Even though Wyler had joined the Air Force and made the remarkable documentary *Memphis Belle*, he was still determined to reveal the evils of the Nazi regime. Later on, in his own autobiography, he would admit: "I knew the movie wasn't really a political thing, but I had a tendency to want to make it, if not an anti-Nazi movie, one which at least would say a few things."

Richard Zanuck would later remember: "Willy was going to make it very heavy-handed at the end. He wanted tanks, he wanted the Germans marching into Austria, blowing up the town, a true militaristic climax." That is, a vision opposed to Lehman's adaptation of the original Lindsay and Crouse script.

Once the trio returned to California, Zanuck and Lehman went into conference. Lehman said he was concerned about Wyler's attitude. It wasn't about Wyler's method of arguing, debating, questioning, scene after scene. "I knew he ate writers alive," said Lehman. "It was that same bulldog tenacity which indicated Willy's true attitude towards a project. The tougher he was on a script, the more he really respected it." No, what was making Lehman nervous were the stacks of books in Wyler's office; they all seemed to deal with the Anschluss, Hitler's annexation of Austria. And then there were the endless phone calls from MGM, involving the imminent production of *The Americanization of Emily.*

In the interim, the long-awaited monster production of *Cleopatra*, in which was invested most of Fox's capital, had sailed into theatres, and wonder of wonders, it was doing business! In fact, so many ticket-buyers had shown up to put down cash and sit through the mammoth spectacle that they were providing a welcome infusion of capital into the depleted Fox bank accounts. Once again, suicide had been avoided.

There was so much gross coming in that the company would now be able to bankroll *The Agony and the Ecstasy, Those Magnificent Men in Their Flying Machines,"* and, last but far from least, *The Sound of Music.*

Lehman's first-draft screenplay proved to be, substantially, the finished version. "Dick had told me, 'We've got to smoke Willy out. You've got to write a first draft, very fast,'" said Lehman. "I told him 'I can't write a screenplay fast.' And he said to me, 'You've got to write it so that we can find out whether Willy is really serious about making this picture!'"

Finished in September 1963, Lehman delivered the script to Wyler. "After he'd gotten it, he called me up right away. He said 'Ernie, I'm embarrassed. I've never read such a wonderful first draft. I can't think of a single suggestion to make! There's nothing I can improve!' After I'd hung up, I called Dick. I said, 'Dick, we are in trouble. Willy's not going to make this picture. There's no such thing as Willy not being able to make suggestions!'"

Whatever doubts Lehman had, they would be proven correct the following week. Richard Zanuck had promptly sent the script to Rome, to his father Darryl, whose reaction was enthusiastic (with, naturally, the customary list of suggestions for changes). Meanwhile, Wyler had come forth to offer a few notes of his own. But Lehman remained suspicious.

Quite rightly so. The following week, he was invited to a weekend party at Wyler's house in Malibu. The director was entertaining Rex Harrison and his wife, Rachel Roberts, and it was Wyler's suggestion that Lehman might help talk Harrison into playing the part of Captain von Trapp.

Lehman agreed. That afternoon, he noted that his host and another guest, Mike Frankovich, the head of Columbia Pictures, were in an intense conference in a far corner of the living room. "The only way I can describe that scene is that they were in a huddle,'" said Lehman. And while Lehman went swimming with Harrison, to talk about the actor's possibly playing Captain von Trapp, the Wyler–Frankovich conversation continued. Lehman finally left the beach and returned to the house. In the living room, there were piles of scripts. "Everybody in town had been submitting scripts to Willy; they were everywhere I looked, face up—I could see all the titles. And then I came upon one script lying face down, so that you couldn't read the title. I flipped it over. It read: The Collector—a Columbia Picture. I turned it back so it was where I'd found it."

In the movie business, everyone specializes in knowing everything everyone else is doing. Lehman knew, from reading the daily "trades," that The Collector was in pre-production at Columbia. Later it would be made in England, starring Terence Stamp and Samantha Eggar. Like a well-trained operative, Lehman put the facts together and came up with the solution. "When I got back home, I called Zanuck, and I said, 'Dick, Willy is going to direct The Collector. Be ready."

When Wyler's agent called the following week, Zanuck was ready. The agent, Paul Kohner, requested that Wyler be given the right to do The Collector before he went to work on The Sound of Music. Would Zanuck kindly postpone the Fox project until The Collector was finished? No, Zanuck would not.

"You can tell your client we are not going to postpone our picture thirty seconds!" he told Kohner. "Let him go make *The Collector!*'"

Which Wyler proceeded to do.

Why had they waited so long for Wyler to jump ship? "I guess it was very perverse of me," said Lehman. "I was willing to endure what I had to endure in order to get one of the best directors in the world. It's kind of like figuring out who your executioner would be. As it turned out, I guess I was pretty stupid, because, looking back on it, Willy wouldn't have been the best director for the picture. . . .'"

"I think Willy got scared," was Richard Zanuck's opinion. "We all ranted and raved about how awful it was, what he'd pulled on us, but deep down inside, I was a bit relieved."

After the dust had settled and the shouting had died down, one immutable truth remained. It was October of 1963, and this project, which the Fox management was counting on being a success, had been in pre-production for ten months. If it were ever to be filmed, a new director was imperative.

Luckily, there was one who would be available.

The Sand Pebbles, the film project on which Robert Wise had been doing pre-production, had been delayed by the onset of the monsoon season in the Far East. Wise was sitting out the logistical problems those storms presented to his proposed shooting schedule. Learning of the director's problems, Lehman devised a quick end-run of his own. He called Wise's agent, Phil Gersh, and suggested sending a copy of the newly completed screenplay for Wise to read. Gersh demurred; hadn't Bob already indicated he wasn't interested? Wasn't Wyler supposed to be directing the picture?

"I told him: 'Phil, please, don't ask any questions, just give Bob my script,'" remembered Lehman. Gersh agreed, and the script went to Wise.

"Then my phone rang," said Lehman. "It was Dick Zanuck, who said, 'Come on down.' I went to his office. He said, 'I've got a surprise for you. What would you say if I told you we could get Bob Wise to direct this picture?'

"I said, 'Great!' He looked at me and smiled and said, 'You son of a bitch, you slipped him the script, didn't you?' And I said, 'Me? Never!'"

In fact, Wise had hesitated before making a commitment. He was sufficiently impressed with the screenplay to call on Saul Chaplin, his associate producer on *West Side Story* and an authority on filmed musical comedy. Would Chaplin enjoy working on this project? He needed his opinion.

"Saul," said Wise, "If you say yes, I'll say yes."

Both men shortly agreed on that monumental yes, but Chaplin also had his doubts initially. "It was a heavy responsibility," he remembered, years later. "I had seen the show in New York and hadn't liked it. It had that first-rate Rodgers and Hammerstein score, but the story was a bit too sweet for me. Then I read it. Before I began reading, I composed polite ways of expressing my objections. 'It's a helluva job, Ernie, but it's still too saccharine,' or 'Bob, it's an improvement over the play, but it's still not for you.'

"Then I read it. I was never so happy reading a script in my life. It was wonderful. Ernie had retained the elements that made the show such an enormous hit, but by changes and additions, he had improved it enormously. The characters were more clearly defined, it was more charming, and he had invented a truly exciting and suspenseful finish. Also, it read as if it had been written originally for the screen, instead of being an adaptation of a stage play," he recalled.

With both Wise and Chaplin agreeing to work on the project, after Lehman's intensive ten months' work on the script, it seemed finally as if the film version of *The Sound of Music* could be headed for the screen. A very wide screen, too; the Panavision filming in that magnificent Austrian landscape would in time bail out the shaky Twentieth Century-Fox empire.

Still, in 1964, such a happy ending was very much touch and go. In the cynical talk at the Beverly Hills dinner parties, and the gin rummy tables at Hillcrest, and on the greens at Bel-Air and Lakeside, people were down on the musical about a nun, and a bunch of singing kids, all of them ending up fleeing the Nazis across the Alps. Who needed that?

Who among those oh-so-shrewd naysayers could have imagined that Wise, Chaplin, Lehman, and Zanuck were about to create a classic? One which could be shown all over the world for decades to come, while throwing off an endless waterfall of golden profits far beyond any accountant's wildest imagination?

Three decades later, the same Saul Chaplin would sit in his Beverly Hills living room and remark, "Whenever those profit checks arrive, year after year, I look at the numbers and believe me, I'm always amazed!"

Verdant and Over Budget

T he casting began. A difficult process, because there would be a large cast of characters to fill.

Beginning, of course, with Maria. Which actress would be the new, sparkling, charming lead? Not Mary Martin. Years before, she'd decided she wasn't interested in re-creating her stage triumph. She'd brought the show to life, she'd played Maria for two years, and now she was on to other projects. And she and Dick Halliday had earned so much in profits from their ownership of *The Sound of Music* that she had taken the advice of her lawyer and her accountant—let them remain anonymous—to stop paying tax to the IRS and to sell her ownership for a final capital gain.

When one considers how much profit she'd have accrued over the years from her share of ownership in the film version, plus earnings from soundtrack albums, and so on, the mind boggles.

It would be Jack Warner, who'd dispatched Swifty Lazar to try to purchase the rights to *The Sound of Music*, in a back-door effort to keep the project dormant while his production of *My Fair Lady* went into the theatres, who proved to be, inadvertently perhaps, the matchmaker to provide Wise, Lehman, Zanuck, et al., with their perfect leading lady.

In a monumentally wrong call, Warner had decided to find himself a major star for *My Fair Lady*. No matter that Julie Andrews had captivated New York audiences as the Eliza Doolittle of the original Lerner and Loewe production. Sure, she was talented, but she wasn't a big enough film star, Warner figured. So he passed on her as the lead, and to play opposite her Broadway leading man, Rex Harrison, he hired Audrey Hepburn instead. No matter that Hepburn wasn't a good singer, and that she'd have to be dubbed by Marni Nixon. Warner had his star insurance. Which left Julie Andrews in limbo.

Until Walt Disney decided she'd be the perfect lead opposite Dick Van Dyke in a musical version of *Mary Poppins*.

"We'd been tipped off how great she was in *Poppins*," remembered Lehman. "So Bob and Saul and I went over to Disney and saw some footage from their picture. The minute we saw her, we all knew she was perfect for Maria von Trapp. 'Let's get her before somebody else does!' said Bob."

But Andrews wasn't sure she wanted to do the part. She was now in the midst of playing the lead in *The Americanization of Emily*, the film Wyler had thought of directing but eventually turned down. She was enjoying a non-musical role; perhaps she'd continue doing such parts.

But the negotiations continued.

"Everyone from Audrey Hepburn to Anne Bancroft was mentioned for the part," said Chaplin. "The leading contender to play Captain von Trapp was Bing Crosby. He was the studio's suggestion, which we never really took seriously because we never considered him right for the part.

"Then there were the seven children," he remembered. "A conservative guess would be that about two hundred children were interviewed for those seven parts."

Before the casting was completed, Wise, Chaplin, and a production crew flew to Salzburg to scout locations. Following the notes which had been amassed by Lehman and Wyler on their previous trip, they looked at sites. In Lehman's descriptions for Maria's opening scenes among the Alps, he'd noted the site as *verdant*. So a running gag among Wise's crew was "Let's go find Ernie's *verdant*."

But the mountains they wished to scout were covered in snow. Where up there should Maria, whoever she might be played by, sing her opening song? The local guide, hired as a production man, led the Americans to a large field which was knee-deep in snow, surrounded by tall trees, also cloaked in white. An opening song, to be shot high up in this frozen locale? Absolutely! "He assured us that at the time we planned to shoot, the field would be a lovely green," said Chaplin. "The verdant one Ernie had described for us in his script. I couldn't imagine how that was possible, but it turned out to be true."

While the crew was roaming the streets of old Salzburg, scouting other locations such as the venerable Nonnberg Abbey, where Maria Rainer was a postulant, there came news from far-off Hollywood. No less an authority than the all-powerful gossip columnist, Louella Parsons, had provided her readers with a scoop: Julie Andrews had been signed by Fox to play Maria!

"We were overjoyed and furious," remembered Chaplin. "Why did we have to find out about it in Parsons' column? It was a case of everyone at the studio assuming that someone else was going to let us know. In the meantime, we had wasted hours discussing other actresses who could play the part."

Now came the problem of casting Captain Georg von Trapp. Eventually, the choice would be the Broadway leading man Christopher Plummer. A fine classical actor, Plummer had hesitated at first. The role did not appeal to him; it provided him with no challenge. Years later, he said "I wanted to give the Captain a little edge, a little humor. His character didn't have much substance. He came off as a fearful square. I wanted him to be equal to Maria."

He finally agreed to take on the role, but not before he'd been assured he and Lehman could meet to discuss the character he would portray. Then Plummer discovered his singing would be dubbed by another voice. He promptly decided such a process was demeaning. Let somebody else play Captain Von Trapp!

"He said it robbed him of his masculinity," said Lehman. "I was on vacation, but I got a frantic call to come back immediately; I had to try to get Plummer back for the project. After a lot of phone calls, Chris agreed to come over to my office, and we sat down for a few days, and we began to go over his scenes, one by one."

Lehman had made himself a note regarding Von Trapp's screen character. "Captain and Elsa," it said. "More familiar with each other—they joke with each other—charming, intimate, and evasive—light, witty and amusing. Captain is comfortable with Elsa."

With that as a starting point, Lehman and Plummer would work together for the ensuing week, making changes in the Captain's character. "I've never worked with an actor who is so intelligent about how his scenes would work," Lehman commented later. "This guy was insisting that I be a good writer. So he came off better than before. And he *helped* me!"

William Luce, the author of Plummer's enormously successful one-man show of the late 1990s, *Barrymore* (in which he played the great actor John Barrymore), echoed Lehman's experience. "Plummer is a classically trained 'pianist,'" Luce observed. "I've seen how he intuitively feels in the dialogue the dynamics of music. While working on *Barrymore*, he would say, 'There's one syllable too many in this line.' Only a poet or a musician would say that."

So with the revisions he and Lehman had agreed upon in the script, Plummer was willing to play Captain Von Trapp. But there was still the problem of his singing. Why should he agree to have his voice dubbed? It was finally agreed that Plummer would be permitted to sing his own songs. "We agreed with his agent to have him do so," said Lehman. "Then we figured we'd show him the rushes of himself, to prove that his voice wasn't absolutely right. And when we'd finished with this process, guess what? Plummer's voice was finally replaced by a dubbing, the way we'd wanted to do it in the first place."

Before the film was considered ready for production, however, there were changes made in Rodgers and Hammerstein's score. "My Favorite Things," which had been sung onstage by the Abbess to Maria, would now be filmed as a sequence between Maria and the children. And "The Lonely Goatherd" would be used as the basis for a delightful puppet-show sequence.

Then came the problem of two songs in the score which Rodgers and Hammerstein had written for Max and Elsa, "How Can Love Survive?" and "No Way to Stop It." In Lehman's adaptation, Max had a far more aggressive role, and Elsa certainly as much, if not more so, in her near-romance with the Captain. Thus, their somewhat cynical attitudes toward life, and the joys of being surrounded by the upper class, and the advantages of the status quo, as expressed in Hammerstein's original lyrics, did not jibe well with their altered characters.

And the duet between the Captain and Maria, "An Ordinary Couple," so gentle and quiet, now seemed far too muted for their romantic involvement. Certainly the two characters played by Julie Andrews and Christopher Plummer were far from being ordinary!

Chaplin and Wise flew to New York to consult with Rodgers on the changes they contemplated for the film. Might he consider writing a ballad for the two leads, to replace "An Ordinary Couple"? Rodgers was in total agreement. The song should obviously be replaced; in fact, he and Hammerstein had discussed such a change, but the lyricist, alas, had been too ill to do the work.

The second suggestion offered by Wise and Chaplin was for Maria, a solo number beginning when she departed from the abbey to go to the Captain's mansion. Might it be a soliloquy, one in which Maria expressed her feelings as she travels toward her new life?

"I described what I hoped the song might be about," said Chaplin. "She leaves the abbey and is fearful of facing the outside world alone, yet it is God's will—she must obey. She believes everything in life has a purpose, so perhaps her fears are groundless. Gradually, as she moves on through her journey, she convinces herself that it will all turn out fine. By the time she reaches the villa, she is looking forward to this new challenge."

Rodgers proceeded to go to his piano and commenced writing both the melody and the lyrics for two new numbers. Soon he had completed a new song for Maria and the Captain, "Something Good." Both Wise and Chaplin received it with enthusiasm; it was obviously right for the film.

Rodgers had also written a soliloquy for Maria; its title was "I Have Confidence." This wasn't exactly what Chaplin had suggested; it seemed too brief. There ensued a series of communications back and forth. Rodgers rewrote his original number; but once again, it didn't seem quite sufficient. Chaplin felt it needed an inner progression, one in which the audience could see how Maria would go from being unsure to growing in self-reliance, and finally displaying high-spirited optimism.

After several more tries, Rodgers completed his version. Once again, it wasn't quite what Wise and Chaplin had contemplated.

Rodgers finally suggested to Chaplin, since he was so clear on what was needed, that he try to rewrite the song himself. Reluctantly, Chaplin agreed to put together a version which would be based completely on Rodgers' music, in an arrangement to make the proper progression. "I was determined not to write it myself," said Chaplin, "because I am no Richard Rodgers!"

Chaplin promptly went to work with Lehman to put together lyrics and set them to Rodgers' melody for "I Have Confidence." Chaplin cleverly included the verse to "The Sound of Music" which wasn't yet being used in the film. The second section of the soliloquy was pure Rodgers, and then it was followed by a third section, a reprise of Rodgers' music with additional lyrics. That would be the final version of "I Have Confidence."

Throughout this delicate process, Julie Andrews would continue to question Chaplin: What was happening with her new soliloquy?

"I invented all sorts of excuses," confessed Chaplin. "I didn't want her to know we were asking her to sing a song which was not as written by Rodgers. And, in any case, before she heard it I had to get Rodgers' permission to use it in the picture." He brought in Marni Nixon, swore her to secrecy, and had her record the number. The recording went off to the composer in New York. A day later there came Rodgers' telegram reply. He preferred his version of "I Have Confidence," but since the revised version seemed to be the choice of the filmmakers, he would give it his official okay.

The soliloquy went into the film. "Postscript: . . ." added Chaplin. "Julie didn't know how her number had come about until about two years later, after the picture was released, when I felt it was safe to tell her."

Years later, he remembered, "Working with Julie Andrews reminded me of working with Judy Garland. They both learned music instantly, as if by magic. They both made songs sound better than you imagined they could. Both made suggestions about how a song should be sung, and if their ideas were rejected, they accepted the rejection gracefully. They had great objectivity about their own work, and knew when they had done well. And they were very bright and fun to be with."

The Sound of Music began shooting in Hollywood, at the Fox studio, on March 23, 1964—at last.

The first sequences were interiors, done on the Fox sound stages. "Marc Breaux and I left for Salzburg a week before the rest of the company," said Chaplin. Breaux and his wife Dee Dee had been assigned to choreograph the film. "We'd pre-recorded two numbers, "Do-Re-Mi," and "I Have Confidence," which we'd planned to shoot on the streets and environs of Salzburg. We put both tracks on a portable tape recorder, and took them out to test the numbers on the actual locations, to see whether or not we had gotten them right for time. If the length of the music had to be changed, then the studio could adjust the music tracks before the rest of the company left for Salzburg."

That Chaplin and Breaux were not killed was a miracle. The first time they went out to test their timings, they hadn't counted on the traffic flow during daytime hours. "We would both stand at the top of the street where the action was to start and wait for the traffic light to turn red. The moment it did, I turned on the tape, loud, and Marc would go down the street, dancing. Unfortunately, the traffic lights had no regard for the length of our playbacks. Often, they'd go green before our music had run out. Then it became a matter of dodging the traffic to stay alive! The onlookers thought we were crazy."

Finally, the cast and crew arrived in Salzburg, and went to work to film the Von Trapp story, right where it had happened. That production manager who'd previously helped scout locations had known what he was about, and that snowy site he'd chosen for Julie Andrews' opening scene was high, impressive, and quite verdant. Breathtakingly so.

But when it came to weather, no production manager could have foreseen what would ensue. It was to be a very wet summer. "It isn't just that it rained," said Chaplin. "It often rained aggravatingly. We could come down to breakfast at 7 A.M., the weather sparkling, nothing but blue skies up above. . . . We would get into our cars and head for our location, happily jabbering away. By the time we reached our destination, we would be in the middle of a torrential downpour! We would sit around on location all day, waiting for the sun to reappear. A few times, it did, too late to start shooting. But the sunny days compensated for the waiting."

Later, there would be an ironic aspect to that wet summer Wise and his crew struggled through. When the film was out and playing in theatres, Fox would receive all sorts of mail from moviegoers who were confused by their experience. They'd loved seeing *The Sound of Music*; they'd been enormously impressed by the beauty of medieval Salzburg, and they'd gone to visit that city while on holiday. But somehow they must have picked the wrong time to go—possibly?—"because it rained quite a bit while we were there!"

These and other such unforeseen delays meant that when the cast and crew finally returned to Hollywood the film was well over its original budget. One of the Fox executives confronted Chaplin with this problem. Did he realize how much more the film was costing? Of course Chaplin did; as associate producer, such matters were a daily headache.

"But have you seen how beautiful the film is?" he asked.

"Yes, but what's important now is: Do you think you could talk to Wise about shooting faster, so we can make up for some lost time?" asked the studio executive.

"Without even blinking, I replied, 'I'll try.'" said Chaplin.

"Although I said it, I hadn't the slightest intention of even mentioning the conversation to Bob, and I never have. He knew better than I how far behind we were. My talking to him about it would have accomplished nothing. Bob's films were always so masterfully created," added Chaplin, "that we stayed out of his way. The film finally did finish, considerably over budget, but history has since proved it to be a sound investment indeed."

Which may be one of the great understatements of our time.

Post-production work began in the fall. There were weeks of dubbing, looping and editing, all meticulously carried out under Wise's supervision. He'd begun his career years back at RKO, working for the legendary Val Lewton as an editor. In the film world, he was considered a master of his craft.

Meanwhile, Irwin Kostal, who'd been hired as music director, went to work to do the film score.

Finally, in February, there would be a "sneak" preview.

Wise had always been an advocate for such an event. For the finishing touches to the film, he felt audience input was vital. He'd written Zanuck a memo extolling the value of such a process. "We spend years, much effort, and millions of dollars getting a picture on film, and then, so often, we don't spend the additional time and effort to give it the proper acid test before a nonprofessional audience."

That first preview would take place in middle America, far away in Minneapolis, in circumstances which would be less an acid test than an endurance contest.

At the Mann Theatre, on February 1, 1965, there was typical Minnesota weather. It was about thirty degrees below zero. But outside, an audience was patiently standing in line, waiting to be permitted into the theatre.

Their reaction was universally enthusiastic. According to Zanuck, the response was incredible: "They even gave us a standing ovation at the intermission!"

When the audience reaction cards had been inspected, the comments were a steady stream of *Excellent*. There were three cards which merely indicated good. "Suddenly, we were focusing on those three cards, trying to figure out what we did wrong!" commented Zanuck.

The second preview, in Tulsa, Oklahoma, was very different. The theatre managers opened the box office late; the Oklahomans had been standing in line in freezing weather. When the people finally got inside the theatre, they were in an aggressive mood.

Thus, the opening sequence of the film, as the camera moves in silence across the impressive Alpine landscape, met with an angry reaction. "The audience assumed there was something wrong with the sound system, I guess," remembered Chaplin. "They started cat-calling, then they booed and yelled, all through the opening. It was pandemonium . . . and finally, they quieted down when, on the screen, Julie had begun her number."

When the film ended, there were cheers and applause.

But the future was still iffy.

Would *The Sound of Music* be the big hit picture which Twentieth Century-Fox so desperately needed? "I remember, when that preview was over," said Chaplin, "Mike Kaplan was talking about the reaction, and he said, 'Make no

Richard Rodgers and Julie Andrews smile for the photographers at the premiere showing of *The Sound of Music* in New York. (Courtesy of Photofest)

mistake about it: This is much more than a musical hit. This is going to be a *classic.'* " He correctly echoed Hammerstein's prediction about the stage version six years earlier.

But then, it was his job as a press agent for Fox to be an optimist, right? So who could believe *him?*

Triumph Again

The film of *The Sound of Music*, on which the future existence of Twentieth Century-Fox films was dependent, opened in Manhattan at the Rivoli Theatre, on March 2, 1965.

While the invited premiere audience of New Yorkers sat through the first unreeling of the film, on which so much time and effort had been lavished, Robert Wise sneaked out of the theatre and went to the lobby, where he met with Jonas Rosenfeld, Fox's head of publicity.

Rosenfeld had obtained an advance copy of Bosley Crowther's *New York Times* review of the following morning. Crowther was a major power in film criticism; from his office typewriter on West 43rd Street, there came daily the most important verdicts on films, domestic and foreign.

Inside, the Rivoli opening-night audience could be heard through the lobby doors as they applauded and enjoyed the film. Standing in the lobby, the two men read:

> . . . The great big color movie Mr. Wise has made from the play . . . comes close to being a careful duplication of the show as it was done on the stage, even down to its operetta pattern, which predates the cinema age. . . . Julie Andrews provides the most apparent and fetching innovation in the film. . . . Her role is always in peril of collapsing under the weight of romantic nonsense and sentiment.

Then came the true bashing.

> The septet of blonde and beaming youngsters who have to act like so many Shirley Temples and Freddy Bartholomews when they were young, do as well as could be expected with their assortedly artificial roles . . . but the adults are fairly horrendous, especially Christopher Plummer. . . . The movie is staged by Mr. Wise in a cosy-cum-corny fashion that even theatre people know is old hat. . . . *The Sound of Music* repeats, in style—and in theme. . . .

And so on. The stunned Wise and Rosenfeld must have wondered if they were in the right theatre.

The following morning, Judith Crist, of the *Herald-Tribune*, took careful aim at *The Sound of Music* and fired. The title of her review was an eye-catcher: "If You Have Diabetes, Stay Away from This Movie."

On went the bashing. "Everything is so icky-sticky purely ever-lovin' that even Constant Andrews Admirers will get a wittle woozy long before intermission time," Crist moaned. "There is nothing like a super-sized screen to convert seven darling little kids in no time at all into all that W. C. Fields indicated that darling little kids are—which is pure loathsome. The movie is for the five to seven set, and their mommies, who think their kids aren't up to the stinging sophistication and biting wit of *Mary Poppins*."

If that weren't sufficient, Crist, who was also the resident film critic on the NBC *Today* show, would repeat her opinion to a far vaster, national audience.

Which would induce the restored grand panjandrum of Fox, Darryl Zanuck, to send an angry memo to one of his executives, in which he blazed back at Crist with both guns. "She has built her reputation with a knife and the evil skill of an abortionist!" he declared. "She uses the tactics of a concentration camp butcher!"

However, when his underling responded by suggesting enthusiastically that they spearhead an attempt to remove Crist from her NBC position, Zanuck controlled his rage. "While I would thoroughly enjoy the pleasure of inserting the toe of my ski boot in Miss Crist's derriere," he replied, "I prefer to leave the job to moviegoers, who, in due time, will take good care of her."

For once, Zanuck had controlled his temper; his decision to do so would prove remarkably tactful. Crist remembered, years later, "My review was also reprinted in the *Paris Herald*, and when it appeared, I got hate mail from all over the world!"

The shock of those bad reviews was tough to handle. Lehman and Wise commiserated with themselves, while the New York critics continued their barrage. In *The New Yorker*, Brendan Gill wrote, ". . . A huge, tasteless blow-up of the celebrated musical. Even the handful of authentic location shots have a hokey studio sheen. I felt myself slowly drowning in a pit of sticky-sweet whipped cream, not of the first freshness."

And in *McCall's*, Pauline Kael also fired a salvo. "*The Sound of Music* is the sugar-coated lie that people seem to want to eat . . . and this is the attitude that makes a critic feel that maybe it's all hopeless. . . . Why not just send the director, Robert Wise, a wire: 'You win. I give up.'"

As they had with Judith Crist, the ever-growing phalanx of faithful fans would retaliate; they deluged the *McCall's* editorial office with angry letters protesting Kael's scorn. So vehement was the *McCall's* readers' rebellion that it impelled the editors to take action. Since Kael seemed so obviously out of touch with their readers' tastes, they went looking for her replacement, someone less acerbically disturbing to their paying customers, and she was let go. (A remarkable statement about the position of criticism in that magazine's pages.)

Pauline Kael went on to *The New Yorker*, while *The Sound of Music* went on to its California openings. There, remarkably, the film met with almost universal approval. Years later, Wise would comment, "The East Coast intellectual papers and magazines destroyed us, but the local papers and the trades out here gave us great reviews."

Many years back, a shrewd writer named Hopkins, who was employed at MGM, ad-libbed a phrase: He said of a certain producer known for his lack of talent that "his criticisms had all the impact of a mouse peeing on a blotter." So it was with the criticisms of *The Sound of Music*.

Consider what had happened in London, after the stage show opened in 1961. Hadn't those acerbic critics taken aim and vented their spleen upon the show? Remember Bernard Levin's assessment: "A marsh of treacle, bathed in a dim religious light"? Or Harold Hobson, insisting "It is a mistake to treat the von Trapps as heroes"? And what of W. A. Darlington, with his line about "Austrian sugar icing an inch thick"? Those tirades had been printed, and now, four years later, satisfied British theatregoers were packing the seats at the Palace Theatre for eight performances a week. By now, the show was on its way to becoming the longest-running musical ever to play London.

And it would be a show that would continue to pack in the audience even *after* the Fox movie version of *The Sound of Music* opened as a two-a-day attraction, three short blocks away. Even though common theatrical knowledge dictated that the presence of Julie Andrews in the film would destroy the audience's appetite for live performances of the show. Not bloody likely! London would be treated to the remarkable phenomenon of the play *and* the film version of the play, running in tandem, week after week, to full houses.

One loyal *Sound of Music* fan, Mrs. Myra Franklin, came religiously to see the film at a Monday matinee, once a week, in the same seat, for the entire run of the film! Obviously she agreed with that shrewd fellow Hopkins at MGM with respect to Bernard Levin's critique.

Bashing *The Sound of Music* was not only the fashionable territory of scornful critics and sophisticated naysayers, but professional cynics in all quarters. Was it not Christopher Plummer himself who was famous in show business for his suggestion that the film in which he had starred be retitled *The Sound of Mucus*? And in that same interview, did he not suggest that "practically anyone could write a musical about nuns and children, and have it become a success"?

"How interesting," replied Russel Crouse, when he was apprised of Plummer's observation. "I wonder why nobody ever did it?"

From California, in 1965, it was *Daily Variety*'s savvy critic who delivered the most cogent assessment of the film: ". . . bears the mark of assured lengthy runs . . . and should be one of the season's most successful entries."

The Sound of Music quickly went out to play in 131 American theatres, as a "road-show" attraction. The road-show was a time-honored Hollywood marketing ploy, one which dates back to the early silent days. Films with the size and status of *Birth of a Nation*, *Ben-Hur*, and *King of Kings* were played in large theatres on a two-a-day schedule, with impressive hoopla, and tickets were sold on a reserved-seat basis.

The summer of 1965, Twentieth Century-Fox needed an infusion of capital desperately and took a gamble. The company also had its other two blockbusters—*The Agony and the Ecstasy*, from Italy, and *Those Magnificent Men in Their Flying Machines*, from England—as possible road-show attractions to play in large theatres where the projection system could accommodate a 70mm-wide print accompanied by a stereophonic soundtrack. The studio sent all three attractions out to the public. The gamble paid off, better than the wildest of any Las Vegas winning streaks.

Audiences loved them—especially *The Sound of Music*, and paid no attention to its bad reviews. They loved the Rodgers and Hammerstein score, and the Lindsay and Crouse libretto which Lehman had so lovingly adapted, and which Wise had so skillfully directed. They loved Julie Andrews, they loved the Alps, they loved the children. Within a matter of four short road-show weeks, the film became number-one in gross receipts at the American box office. For the next four and a half years, it would continue to retain that position, and then become *Variety*'s all-time box office champion in rentals derived from the U.S. and Canadian market.

And, in the words of another classic Hammerstein character, Cap'n Andy of *Show Boat*: "That's only the beginning, folks, only the beginning!"

Years later, Saul Chaplin said, "None of us anticipated what a wildfire hit the film would be, particularly after it received such mixed reviews from the critics. Now it just throws off those remarkable profit checks." Beamed Chaplin: "Go figure."

At Academy Award time, *The Sound of Music* was nominated in ten categories. The film was nominated for Best Picture, Robert Wise for Best Director, and Julie Andrews for Best Actress.

The results of the voting would be, putting it mildly, confusing. After the fanfares, the oohs and ahs at the spectacular gowns, the introductions, and the oh-gosh-I-want-to-thank-all-those-who-helped-me-make-this-happen acceptance speeches, *The Sound of Music* won for Best Editing, Best Sound, and Best Scoring of a Musical.

Irwin Kostal won the latter. Saul Chaplin reported that Kostal approached him, Oscar in hand, and said, "We should be sharing this! I don't know why you didn't hand your name in with mine!" Chaplin demurred; for years he'd decided if he received any producer credit, he'd forgo that music credit, "even though my contribution might have merited it," he added modestly.

Julie Andrews had already won a Best Actress Oscar previously, for *Mary Poppins*, and on this occasion, she lost to Julie Christie, who'd played the lead in *Darling*. When the Best Director award came up, the winner was Robert

Wise. Andrews came up from the audience to accept on Wise's behalf. The director was in Taiwan, wrestling with the formidable difficulties involved in completing *The Sand Pebbles*. As Andrews stood on the stage, she received an enormous accolade from the audience. Was there, perhaps, some disagreement over her loss this year?

Then, finally, came the Best Picture award. . . .

The Sound of Music!

Who can make sense of the ins and outs of Academy Award voters? And how to explain the conspicuous absence from the Best Screenplay award of Ernie Lehman's carefully crafted adaptation?

In effect, the voters were saying that the winning edifice had been built without a blueprint. Wise, who certainly knew better, wrote to Lehman from Taiwan. (Lehman, by that time, was wrestling with his own formidable difficulties, making the Warner Bros. film of Edward Albee's *Who's Afraid of Virginia Woolf?* starring Elizabeth Taylor and Richard Burton.) "All I can say," wrote Wise, "is *you was robbed.* I guess that's one of the prices that the writer—and some of the others connected with making the picture—pays for taking an established Broadway show and transposing it to the screen."

Lehman responded, "I value your letter very much. The enormous success of the picture all over the world and my own realization . . . that I guessed right in believing that the play would become a very rewarding and popular film . . . that I actually did have an important role in getting it from stage to screen . . . make it very difficult for me to have any unhappy feelings about anything connected with this picture. . . . When you stop to consider what we achieved . . . this miracle that comes only to a very few, once in a lifetime . . . well, out with the champagne!"

Thirty-odd years later, Lehman reflected on the writer's lot: "Funny, every few weeks, I get called by some TV producer or documentary outfit . . . and they're putting together some retrospective, on Bob Wise, or Burt Lancaster, or any of the stars or directors I've worked with. And they want some sort of a firsthand comment from me. But you know something? They never seem to do a documentary about a writer." He smiled. "At least, not one I've heard about."

The film's worldwide success—by the time this history is being written, the gross has mounted to, according to *Variety*, $293,600,000 worldwide)—is even more spectacular when one considers that at the time of its production, American film musicals had fallen upon hard times in European and Asian markets. Why? Consider the problem of dubbing American films. An ordinary thriller, or a spectacle, or a love story, presents no problems when it comes to reaching international audiences. Go into a studio with actors, dub a film into foreign languages, or add subtitles, and presto! the audience in South America, or the Far East, or Middle Europe, can enjoy it. But when it comes to musicals, the problems are tremendous.

"The songs in most musicals were left in English, and there would be subtitles added at the bottom of the screen," explained Saul Chaplin. "But having to read those subtitles during the songs annoyed foreign audiences, and detracted from their enjoyment of the film. Can you blame them for preferring Sly Stallone?"

Since *The Sound of Music* was such a big draw domestically, Fox executives shrewdly decided that both the songs and the dialogue should be dubbed into various languages. Chaplin was sent to Paris, Barcelona, Rome, and Berlin with the assignment to supervise the dubbing of the songs and to reproduce the energy and the spirit of the original soundtrack. Which turned out to be a very complex task.

First, there needed to be translations of the Hammerstein lyrics. Sounds simple. Perhaps, until you come to a song like "Do-Re-Mi," for one example. The scale, as Chaplin pointed out—do, re, mi—exists in all languages, so it can be retained. But then the Hammerstein lyrics begin with "Doe, a deer, a female deer." "While 'doe' means female deer in English," sighed Chaplin, "it doesn't in any other language. So, not only did a substitute have to be found in each of the four other languages for every note of the scale, but the translations had to be in sync with what Julie and the children were singing."

Perhaps the meticulous work done in translating Hammerstein's lyrics helped make the film version of *The Sound of Music* the remarkable and lasting triumph that it was all over the world. Years after its production, Ernest Lehman expressed some wonder at this overwhelming success, which crosses boundary lines and languages everywhere. He shrugged: "Who sits down and says, 'Now we're going to make a classic'?" Then, recalling how he first reacted to the Mary Martin production on Broadway and, over that intermission bowl of Howard Johnson's chowder, believed it might make a successful film, he said: "When I see the picture today, I have a lot of respect for it. People love this picture. . . . Bob Wise shot it beautifully. Every frame works! And the story has universality. I think in some way it taps into every audience's emotional response."

Everywhere, that is, except for two countries: Germany and Austria, where the movie's returns are not as hefty. "The Austrians never understood why we were making another film about the Von Trapps, since the Germans had already done so," said Chaplin. "But the primary reason was that the last third of our picture dealt with their Nazi past. Neither the Austrians nor the Germans liked to be reminded of that period. In fact, Fox's German manager took it upon himself to delete the last third of the film, which completely eliminated all the Nazis!"

What could be the result of that minor putsch?

"The Fox studio people in L.A. learned about that very quickly," grinned Chaplin. "Fired the manager, and had the film restored to its original length."

One postscript to this saga: The enormous success of *The Sound of Music* prompted other studios to follow the age-old Hollywood tradition: Always try copying a hit. Large, expensive musicals once again became the order of the day. Out of the studios came *Fiddler on the Roof, Man of La Mancha, Doctor Dolittle,* and so on. Millions of dollars went into their production, and into the theatres they came, singing and dancing. And what became of all those expensive blockbuster musicals?

They all died.

Robert Wise's next musical venture would be one of those very expensive wide-screen productions. It seemed like a natural: Julie Andrews portraying the legendary British musical comedy performer Gertrude Lawrence. Lavish production numbers set to wonderful music by Noël Coward, Cole Porter, Kurt Weill, with their sparkling lyrics. Enthusiastically underwritten by Twentieth Century-Fox—with Saul Chaplin as Wise's ever-reliable co-producer.

Did lightning strike twice?

Hardly. You just might see that dazzling movie, *Star!,* every once in a while on television, or rent it from your videotape library, if they carry it at all.

Meanwhile, Rodgers and Hammerstein's finale continues to be a grand one.

Which brings us full circle. The show-business magic cannot be lost on us: Just as the great team's first risk-taking show, *Oklahoma!,* had brought the Theatre Guild back from the brink of financial disaster, their final, unrevolutionary one saved a major Hollywood studio from ruin. The movie continues to play to large and adoring audiences everywhere, year after year—but then. . .

So does the Broadway show.

Revival

It's forty years and counting now since the night at the New Haven Shubert when the curtain rose for the first time to reveal those nuns at the Nonnberg Abbey, as they sang their beautiful opening "Preludium." Forty theatrical seasons of steady weekly grosses, pouring in from packed houses of ticketholders, here and abroad, who've sat enthralled through the drama of the Von Trapps and come up the aisles humming "Edelweiss," or chanting "Doe, a deer . . . ," who've brought home the sheet music or the LP, or the CD, to play over and over, whose children have danced around the room singing "My Favorite Things." Generations who know Maria's story from having seen the movie—not once, but often—who've snatched up the videotape as soon as it surfaced at the mall, and who've brought it home to sit before the TV, with their family, absorbed by the romance of the nun and the naval captain, and whose offspring have empathized with those brave Von Trapp children, as they wave and sing, "So Long, Farewell."

While paying not the slightest attention to anyone who might suggest that they've already seen this videotape so many times that they know it all by heart!

For what does it matter how often you've seen *The Sound of Music?* If you loved it the first time, it's a lifetime romance, not only for you but for your kids, and probably their offspring, as well.

A phenomenon, indeed, considering the bad notices the show met with. As we shall see, the show continues to be denigrated critically. Balance that with Oscar Hammerstein, at the second performance, predicting: "Make no mistake about it, this is a hit!"—the words of a master.

Summer stock? Touring companies? High school and college theatres? Been there, and continues to do that, that, and that. In fact, *The Sound of Music* and *Oklahoma!* are the two most popular musicals in the Rodgers and Hammerstein catalogue. Over the years, since 1960, more than 17,500 stock and amateur productions of *The Sound of Music* have been licensed. So where do we go from here?

Back to Broadway, of course—in a major revival produced in 1998 by Hallmark Entertainment.

With a new leading lady to play Maria, ravishing Rebecca Luker, a tall blonde—who was one of the leads in the 1997 revival of *Show Boat*—and directed by Susan H. Shulman, who also directed Luker on Broadway in the 1991 musical success, *The Secret Garden*—and also in a revival of Rodgers and Hart's *The Boys from Syracuse,* (in an "Encores" series of concert-style presentations at Manhattan's City Center).

Chatting about her remounting of Rodgers and Hammerstein's last show, Shulman was lavish in her praise of Luker's talent: "During her audition," she recalled, "Rebecca brought such a freshness to the music . . . little hairs stood up on the back of my neck. You don't expect songs that you are so familiar with to take you by surprise that way."

Add Luker to the category of long-time *Sound of Music* fans. "My mother dragged me to the movie when I was nine years old," she proudly related, "and two years later, I sang 'My Favorite Things' in a talent show, and won first prize!"

Never underestimate the power of an advertising man's mind. Some brilliant agency thinker, perhaps picking up on his own offsprings' zeal, has created TV spots for the revival in which we see a mother and daughter; the mother is reminiscing with her about having seen the show as a child, and the response from the daughter is "Do I get my *own* ticket?"

Don't bet she won't.

Of course, director Shulman is also an enthusiast. "As I've been telling people that I'm doing this show—people that you know must be part of the New York intelligentsia and whom you might think would be snobbish about it and ask me, 'What are you doing *that* for?'—no, indeed, I get: 'Oh, I'm so excited, that's my favorite show! I'm in theatre because of it. It was my first musical!'

Or they say: 'I saw the movie and that made me want to become involved in musical theatre!' People I never dreamt would have that response."

She noted that during one recent summer prior to the revival, a screening of *The Sound of Music* was run in Bryant Park, near Times Square, admission-free. Huge crowds turned out for it. "The response to the movie was as if they were at some rock concert!" said Shulman. "They were applauding, and yelling, and screaming for everything that happened up on the screen. And singing the score, as well!

"Somebody recently gave me an article about Caroline Kennedy's fortieth birthday," she added. "The whole gist of the story was that *The Sound of Music* is her favorite musical, and for her birthday, Julie Andrews herself came to the party and sang to her."

So how does Shulman approach the revisiting of this classic musical work, this icon?

She is well aware of the changes since 1959 in audience attitude concerning the underlying Trapp Family story. The Mary Martin production had occurred in the days when there was a subtle de-Nazification in the theatre. Listen to Theodore Bikel: "As the show came closer to Broadway from Boston, the Nazi uniforms got lighter and lighter. And by the time we arrived at the Lunt-Fontanne Theatre, there wasn't an armband or a swastika on anyone."

Certainly not, back then. In those days, with Mary Martin heading the cast, director Vincent Donehue and the creative minds he was working with were concentrating on the creation of a typical star-driven New York entertainment, not a polemic. Even though Hammerstein, Rodgers, Lindsay, and Crouse were all avowed anti-Nazis, they were all creating, first and foremost, a theatre piece.

But this time, in 1998, the show was being staged in an era when Swiss bank accounts were being cracked open to reveal gold and money, hidden for half a century from desperate Jewish refugees, and when art treasures stolen by the Nazis all over Europe were being reclaimed from museums by the descendants of their rightful owners. After three decades of profound dramatizations of the Holocaust, audiences seem to be interested as much in truth as in entertainment. The 1955 stage play *The Diary of Anne Frank*, revised for a restaging during the same year, underscored the bestial cruelty of the Nazi regime. And yet another concurrent revival, the Kander and Ebb musical *Cabaret*, was being staged to inject a harsher-than-ever reality into its portrait of the decadence of 1930s Berlin.

This is the time, then, to re-examine *The Sound of Music*, is it not?

"Absolutely," affirmed Shulman. "If you do the show today, you must be historically accurate . . . or else it becomes frivolous. And this is not a frivolous story. The courage of the Von Trapps, in the light of the ugly events taking place in their beloved Salzburg, is truly profound.

"It must have been such a dreadful shock," she observed. "Right up until the Nazi takeover, the Anschluss, in Salzburg the Mayor lied to the people. He told them the Nazis weren't coming. The next day, the Nazis moved in; the people watched their city being taken over . . . and the Mayor said he was sorry."

The day the Nazi forces took over, Nazi flags were draped everywhere—as they will be, she explained, on the set of the revival in the second act. "So when Captain Von Trapp refuses to fly that flag, it's no small gesture. He was a wealthy man, a man of no small position. He could easily have collaborated with the Nazis, but no, he chose to leave, taking his family with him. . . . It was an extremely courageous act.

"I'm in no way rewriting this show," Shulman pointed out. "You could say I've simply been digging into it."

To begin with, she and her scenic designer, Heidi Ettinger, traveled to Salzburg, taking with them a list (provided by Julie Andrews) of sights that were must-sees. "That scenery is so spectacular," she declared. "And when the weather is good, everyone immediately goes outdoors. The time we spent immersing ourselves in that remarkable city was most helpful to our eventual concept. Everywhere you look, if you're in the Salzburg below, there are those magnificent Alps all around you. They can seem beautiful and inviting, and then they can also seem ominous and scary." As Maria says in the script, "I thought these mountains were my friends, and now they are my enemies." "That's the feeling I'm trying to impart," said Shulman. "That ominous feeling of a world sitting on a precipice, on something so potentially dangerous."

Which inevitably brings us to the question of what the director believes is the reason that *The Sound of Music* has had such a lasting impact on its audiences, wherever it has played?

Said Shulman: "I think that's quite simple to explain. At its heart, it's a great love story. A May–December romance. If you believe that great musicals are always great love stories, as I do, that's got to be it. . . . And this story comes with an amazingly good score that's very accessible. People of every age can remember those songs. It's an inspirational family show. And I mean that in the most positive sense."

Sixty years to the day after Hitler's forces marched into Salzburg, on the night of March 12, *The Sound of Music* opened at the Martin Beck Theatre, on West 45th Street.

"It's a perfect theatre for the show," said Shulman. "Because the theatre itself looks exactly like Nonnberg Abbey. When we walked in there, I thought, 'How could any house be more perfect?' Once you're inside, it has a very Gothic character to it."

In March of 1999, a star, Richard Chamberlain, joined the cast of this remounting—playing Captain Von Trapp, of course—and it was announced that he would go on the production's national tour.

Quite a revival.

And a box-office hit, naturally. On the weekend following the Thursday-night opening of the revival, the box office at the Martin Beck sold more than half a million dollars' worth of tickets.

Shall we, then, pick up our theme once again, of the critics vs. the audience? Here are the inevitable New York reviews, and some other comments, on *The Sound of Music*, circa 1998:

BEN BRANTLEY, THE NEW YORK TIMES

This latest version of Rodgers and Hammerstein's final collaboration is the first to be mounted on Broadway since 1959. But despite the refreshing presence of its star, Rebecca Luker, and a perfectly respectable production, it remains the same old cup of treacle. Whether performed in a church basement, or a show palace, *The Sound of Music* will always on some level, work; on another, it will always nauseate. . . .

The director does underscore the threat of Nazism in the show . . . but this mostly registers as just shorthand for indicating evil against the forces of light. . . .This is not the imagery of politics, but of fairy tales. . . .

But face it, *The Sound of Music* isn't really for grown-ups. . . . Indeed, as a fable-like adventure story about reclaiming a lost father and gaining a fun-loving mother, it seems to strike deep responsive chords in the very young. . . .

I can personally confirm this, having seen the movie at least half a dozen times when I was 10, and I know every lyric by heart . . . [I] can't say I rediscovered that inner child watching this version; frankly, it seemed endless. On the other hand, the little girl two seats down from me had a look of religious rapture on her face. . . .

CLIVE BARNES, THE NEW YORK POST

The Sound of Music is not for Do Re Me.

It's almost as bad as confessing you don't like peanut butter and jelly. . . .

However, *The Sound of Music*, which last night was given a spic-and-span and spanking new production, is never going to be one of my favorite things . . . any more than those damned "Bright copper kettles" they sing about.

I try to love it the way many people love it. But it doesn't help me. The mind is willing, but the heart is weak. . . . So it's something of a necessary guess, but I imagine that if you love *The Sound of Music*, this is *The Sound of Music* you will almost certainly love. If you don't love *The Sound of Music*, well, the issue is probably irrelevant, isn't it?

THE NEW YORK POST

THE POST ASKS, DID YOU LIKE "THE SOUND OF MUSIC"? (preview performance)

I liked it more than anything I've ever seen on Broadway! [Diane Russo, East Brunswick, New Jersey]

Donald Lyons, The Wall Street Journal
The Sound of Music is splendid entertainment. Back for the first time since its initial run, the new production echoes less the play than the widely beloved 1965 movie, which starred Julie Andrews and opened up the story spectacularly. This is, under Susan H. Shulman's fresh and clear direction, a *Sound of Music* lit throughout by a warm and infectious generosity of spirit.

David Patrick Stearns, USA Today
The Sound of Music occupies such an exalted place in our affections that it's less a Broadway musical than a modern folk tale we all know by heart. So how could the slick new Broadway revival not be a success? Surprise! It's doomed from the get-go. . . . Returning to Rodgers and Hammerstein's original—even with added songs written for the film—is like trading a Mercedes for a bicycle (2½ stars out of four).

Jeffrey Lyons, NBC-TV
The Sound of Music is back, and for a little while, all seems right with the world.

Dennis Cunningham, CBS-TV
It's a show of many charms, sweet, lovely and melodic. Rebecca Luker is a low-wattage Maria. . . . It's all very harmless and mostly lightweight stuff with some fetching tunes . . . and oh my, is it cute. . . . Still, for many, it's a much beloved musical, so though I wouldn't actually urge anyone to rush off to see this revival, neither would I try to stand in anyone's way. . . .

Jacques Le Sourd, Gannett Newspapers
The Captain is a stiff. Maria is a bore. But the music sounds pretty good, and some of the kids are cute. (The others are ripe for strangling.) . . . . Don't bother with this anemic stage version, which is only technically "live" at $75 a ticket. Just rent the 1965 movie with Julie Andrews, or wait for the annual network broadcast. That, at least, is free.

Joan Hamburg, WOR-Radio
Get tickets! We came out happy as larks. So if you want to feel good, at a time when we are besieged by smut everywhere . . . see something that rings as true as it ever did, and come out singing.

Vincent Canby, The New York Times
Was it not Oscar Hammerstein's grandfather who remarked, years back, "No way can you force an audience to go to something they don't want to"? . . . The news this morning: *The Sound of Music* still isn't about to disappear, certainly not when it is done with the skill evident in the revival. . . .

From the Advertisement for the Martin Beck Theatre
It was really, really good. The kids and the music are terrific!
[Eliza Lewine, age 9]

I loved it! The show was incredible! Maria and all were good!
[Danielle Raso, age 11]

They love this show everywhere.

Asia? They also perform *The Sound of Music* in Beijing, where it has been translated into Chinese.

The Middle East? "You know, the biggest laugh I've had in some time," said Anna Crouse, "is over some producer, who shall be nameless, who put the show on in Israel. And I blew my top, because the cuts he'd made in the script were simply appalling. I protested! I thought: Money isn't that important that we have to ruin this show. So the Rodgers & Hammerstein Organization got to him, and he responded, 'Well, in the first place, it's too long; nobody in Israel wants to stay in the theatre after 10 P.M. and nobody in Israel wants to know about nuns and Nazis. 'So I asked, 'Tell me, what's left?'"

. . . And on and on, all over the globe.

Even as the phenomenon continues, our tale ends here.

Let it suffice to explain the appeal of *The Sound of Music*, and, for that matter, *Oklahoma!*, the two greatest hits of the immortal collaboration of Richard Rodgers and Oscar Hammerstein—be they on Broadway, or on the wide screen, or in a theatre of your choosing—let it suffice for us simply to quote the title Hammerstein wrote for a song in their final show:

"No Way to Stop It"!

Sources & Credits

PUBLISHED SOURCES

Dance to the Piper by Agnes de Mille, Da Capo, 1980.
The Dramatists Guild Quarterly, Summer, 1997.
Getting to Know Him by Hugh Fordin, Ungar, 1986.
The Golden Age of Movie Musicals by Saul Chaplin, University of Oklahoma Press, 1994.
"Interview with Mrs. Dorothy Rodgers," *The New York Times*, April 22, 1990.
Lyrics by Oscar Hammerstein II, Hal Leonard, 1985.
Lyrics by Lorenz Hart, Knopf, 1986.
Mister Abbott by George Abbott, Random House, 1963.
Musical Stages by Richard Rodgers, Random House, 1949.
My Heart Belongs by Mary Martin, William Morrow, 1976.
People Will Talk by John Kobal, Knopf, 1986.
"The Saga of the Ernest Lehman Screenplay," unpublished manuscript
    by Michael Mattesino, 1994.
The Street Where I Live by Alan Jay Lerner, W.W. Norton, 1978.
Take Them Up Tenderly by Margaret Case Harriman, Knopf, 1944.
Twenty Best American Plays, 1918-1958, edited by John Gassner, Crown, 1961.
Theatre in America by Mary C. Henderson, Abrams, 1989.
Theo: The Autobiography of Theodore Bikel, Harper Collins, 1994.
They're Playing Our Song by Max Wilk, Da Capo, 1997
Underfoot in Show Business by Helene Hanff, Moyer Bell, 1989.
A Wayward Quest by Theresa Helburn, Little Brown, 1960.

ORAL HISTORIES

Philip Barry, Jr., Waterford, Conn.
Theodore Bikel, New York
Jay Blackton, Los Angeles
George Church, Fort Myers, Florida
Saul Chaplin, Los Angeles
Anna Crouse, New York
Bambi Linn de Jesus, Massachusetts
Agnes de Mille, New York
Alfred Drake, New York
Leslie Epstein, Brookline, Mass.
Frank Goodman, New York
Hayes Gordon, Australia
William Hammerstein, Connecticut
Edmund Hartmann, Santa Fe, New Mexico
Ethel Heyn, Westport, Conn.

Leland Hayward, New York
Celeste Holm, New York
George Irving, New York
Ernest Lehman, Los Angeles
Miranda Levy, Santa Fe, New Mexico
Lauri Peters, New York
Marc Platt, Florida
Harold Prince, New York
Vivian Smith Shiers, New Jersey
Paul Shiers, New Jersey
Elaine Scott Steinbeck, New York
Miles White, New York
Robert Wise, New York
Kate Friedlich Witkin, New York
Mary Hunter Wolfe, New Haven, Conn.

CREDITS

SOURCES & CREDITS

Index

196

I
N
D
E
X

About the Author

MAX WILK has conducted a not-so-private affair with American show business for more than seven decades.

It began with silent movies (yes, he's that old!), Broadway musical comedies, vaudeville (until Vitaphone buried that art form), and then the all-talking, all-singing and all-dancing movies which followed. When radio took over in the 1930s, he was a dedicated fan, and when television killed radio in the 1940s, he was there to move into that exciting new business as a writer and producer.

Along the way, somehow he's found time to write radio and TV scripts, revue sketches, screenplays, and magazine articles. Novels, yes, and nonfiction, and he's even committed the ultimate madness, Broadway plays and two musicals!

If you are under forty, you will be delighted to know him as the author of the book of the Beatles' *Yellow Submarine*.

While you go to the beach in the summer, Wilk goes to the Eugene O'Neill Playwrights Conference, at Waterford, Connecticut, and works there as a dramaturge (don't ask what that word means) with aspiring playwrights.

But enough biography. The important thing about his books, of which this is the 24th, is that they are filled with facts, truth, anecdotes, and pure entertainment, proof of Wilk's lifelong love affair with our American show business. *Overture and Finale* is not—underline *not*—his finale.

And now, the house lights are going down, the overture is about to begun. Turn back to page 8, and join the rest of the audience. Enjoy!